THE OAK ISLAND ENCYCLOPEDIA: VOLUME II

Other books by the same author:

Legends of the Nahanni Valley (2018)

Mysteries of Canada: Volume I (2019)

The Oak Island Encyclopedia (2019)

Mysteries of Canada: Volume II (2020)

The Oak Island Encyclopedia:

Volume II

BY
HAMMERSON PETERS

Table of Contents

———◆———

Map of Oak Island...

Introduction...

Glossary...

The Oak Island Family...

Part I: Special Episodes...

    The Top 25 Moments You Never Saw.....................

Part II: The Curse of Oak Island: Season 7.............................

    S7E1: The Torch is Passed...........................

    S7E2: Core Values...................................

1   S7E3: The Eye of the Swamp..........................

    S7E4: The Lucky Thirteen............................

S7E5: Tunnel Visions...................................

S7E6: Closing In..

S7E7: Things That Go Bump-Out.................

S7E8: Triptych..

S7E9: An Eye for an Eye.............................

S7E10: Gary Strikes Again..........................

S7E11: The Eye of the Storm......................

S7E12: Fortified..

S7E13: Bromancing the Stones...................

S7E14: Burnt Offerings..............................

S7E15: Surely Templar...............................

S7E16: Water Logged.................................

S7E17: To Boulderly Go.............................

S7E18: The Turning Point..........................

S7E19: Lords of the Ring...........................

S7E20: Springing the Trap.....................................

S7E21: A Leaf of Faith..

S7E22: Marks X the Spot.......................................

S7E23: Timeline..

Part III: Theories..

The Knights Baronet Theory...............................

The Viking Theory...

The Queen Scotia Theory....................................

Index...

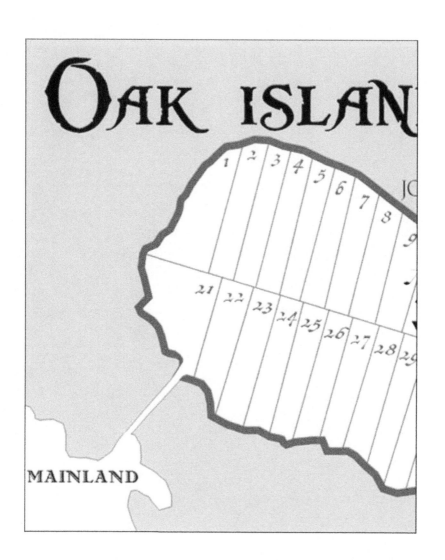

MAINLAND

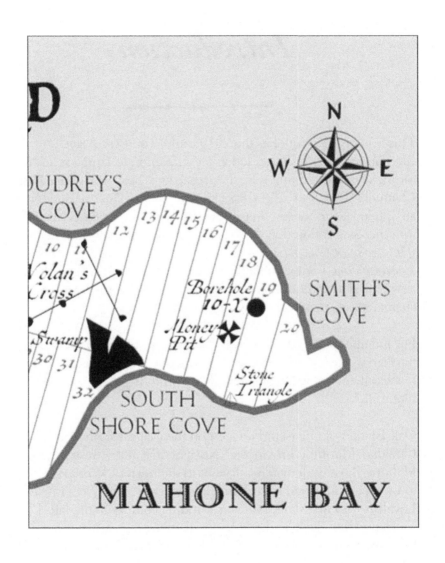

Introduction

———————

This book is the sequel to the 2019 tome *The Oak Island Encyclopedia*, and is intended as a companion to (and a reference for those interested in a refresher regarding) Season 7 of the History Channel's TV series *The Curse of Oak Island*. Due to its nature as an appendage to these other bodies of work, this book is written with the assumption that the reader is either generally familiar with *The Curse of Oak Island*, or has access to a copy of *The Oak Island Encyclopedia*. For example, discoveries made in previous seasons are alluded to without their accompanying backstories, and major characters are mentioned without much preamble.

For the uninitiated- those new to the mystery of Oak Island who, through whatever circumstance, acquired a copy of this book, and possess the tenacity necessary to persist with it- a little context is required.

Oak Island is a tiny island located on the eastern shores of the Canadian Maritime province of Nova Scotia, at the western end of Mahone Bay, immediately adjacent to the town of Western Shore, to which it is attached by an artificial causeway. The New English Loyalists who first settled the surrounding country in the late 1700s whispered that the island was haunted, citing the yarns of local fishermen who claimed that weird lights flickered there from time to time in the dead of night.

According to legend, in 1795, three local boys named Daniel McGinnis, John Smith, and Anthony Vaughan discovered a circular depression in a clearing in the forest on the eastern end of Oak Island. A large oak tree stood at the edge of this depression, one of its limbs stretching out across the clearing. From the centre of this sturdy branch, artificially stunted in days long past by the blade of a carpenter's saw, depended a rusted and rotting block and tackle.

The boys, having grown up on tales of Blackbeard and Captain Kidd, suspected they had stumbled upon a long-forgotten cache of buried pirate loot. They proceeded to excavate the depression and unearthed a circular layer of flagstones just below the surface. Beneath the stones, they found a circular shaft with clay walls, its descent broken by equidistant platforms of oak logs spaced ten feet apart from one another, atop some of which lay thin layers of charcoal, pebbles, or a mysterious blue clay.

Over the next two centuries, a succession of treasure hunters attempted to reach the bottom of this shaft, dubbed the 'Money Pit', and extract the treasure which presumably lay at its bottom, risking financial ruin, social condemnation, and their very lives in the process. Due to an ingenious underground flood trap, triggered when early treasure hunters excavated the Money Pit to a depth of 90 feet, Oak Island retained her mysterious prize throughout the 1800s. 20th Century Oak Island treasure hunters found their own endeavors stymied by the mistakes of their predecessors, which left the Money Pit area a precarious mess of underground tunnels, shafts, timbers, and water. Over time, the precise location of the original Money Pit was forgotten, and treasure hunters began searching for alternative solutions to the Oak Island mystery, sinking shafts on other parts of the island, excavating nearby Smith's Cove, and exploring the swamp which lies at the island's centre.

The current Oak Island treasure hunt is conducted by a syndicate called Oak Island Tours Inc., the efforts of which have been documented throughout Seasons 1-7 of the TV series *The Curse of Oak Island*.

This book is divided into three sections: **Special Episodes**; *The Curse of Oak Island*: **Season 7**; and **Theories**.

The **'Special Episodes'** section, the shortest section in this book, includes a synopsis for one of the four special History Channel episodes which preceded the airing of Season 7 of *The Curse of Oak Island*, namely the episode entitled "The Top 25 Moments You Never Saw". Although three other special episodes (entitled "The Top 25 Theories", "The Top 25 Finds", and "The Top 25 Moments", respectively) were also aired prior to the commencement of Season 7, the subjects of these episodes were all covered thoroughly in *The Oak Island Encyclopedia*, and any synopses of them included in this book would only constitute unnecessary repetition.

The section entitled *The Curse of Oak Island: Season 7* contains plot summaries and analyses for every episode in the show's Season 7. The plot summaries are organized in a chronological fashion; the events which they detail appear in the same order in which they were introduced in the show. The analyses, on the other hand, are broken into subdivisions, each one pertaining to a particular discovery made or development which took place in the episode.

Readers who would prefer plot summaries organized in the same manner as the analyses in this book, in which the information pertaining to particular discoveries and developments are lumped together irrespective of the timeframe in which they were introduced, may benefit from YouTube videos which this author put together on every episode in Season 7, in that fashion. These videos can be found at YouTube.com/HammersonPeters , in the playlist entitled "The Curse of Oak Island: Season 7 Reviews".

The third and final section of this book, entitled **Theories**, describes three intriguing hypotheses regarding the nature of the Oak Island treasure and that of its depositors which this author neglected to include in *The Oak Island Encyclopedia*.

At the back of this book, you'll find an Index directing you to information on just about every discovery, event, character, and theory referred to throughout Season 7 of *The Curse of Oak Island*.

Introduction

When the show mentions something in one of its infamous flashback sequences which you'd like to brush up on, just flip to the back of the book, look up the subject in question, and flip to the relevant pages indicated by the Index.

This book is chiefly intended as a reference, and does not necessarily have to be read from cover to cover. Accordingly, please feel free to read this book in any order you choose, and to jump around from section to section and chapter to chapter if you feel so inclined. However you intend to use this book, I hope that you enjoy it. Happy reading!

Glossary

Treasure Hunting Syndicates

Onslow Company: A treasure-hunting syndicate which searched for treasure on Oak Island from 1804-1805.

Truro Company: A treasure-hunting syndicate which searched for treasure on Oak Island from 1849-1851.

The Oak Island Association: A treasure-hunting syndicate which searched for treasure on Oak Island from 1861-1863.

The Halifax Company: A treasure-hunting syndicate which searched for treasure on Oak Island from 1866-1867.

The Oak Island Treasure Company: A treasure-hunting syndicate which searched for treasure on Oak Island from 1893-1900.

The Old Gold Salvage and Wrecking Company: A one-man treasure-hunting syndicate, run by American engineer Harry Bowdoin, which searched for treasure on Oak Island from 1909-1911.

Chappells Limited: A treasure hunting syndicate, run by William Chappell and his son, Mel, which searched for treasure on Oak Island from 1931-1932.

Gilbert Hedden: A New Jerseyite businessman who searched for treasure on Oak Island from 1935-1938.

Glossary

Erwin Hamilton: A New York-based engineering professor who searched for treasure on Oak Island from 1938-1943.

George Green: A Texan petroleum engineer who searched for treasure on Oak Island in 1955.

Robert Restall: A Canadian stuntman and tradesman who searched for Oak Island treasure from 1959-1965, assisted by his eldest son, Bobby. During his Oak Island tenure, Restall lived on the island with his wife, Mildred, his eldest son, Bobby, and his youngest son, Ricky. Robert and Bobby died on Oak Island on August 17, 1965, falling into a flooded shaft after being overcome by toxic gas.

Robert Dunfield: A Californian geologist who searched for treasure on Oak Island from 1965-1966. Dunfield's operation included the digging of a massive trench in the Money Pit area which destroyed a number of Oak Island landmarks.

Triton Alliance: A treasure-hunting syndicate headed by Dan Blankenship and David Tobias, which searched for treasure on Oak Island from 1966-2005.

Oak Island Tours Inc.: The treasure-hunting syndicate currently searching for treasure on Oak Island, headed by Michigan brothers Rick and Marty Lagina and the late Dan Blankenship.

Oak Island Features

The 90-Foot Stone: A large, rectangular, olive-coloured stone slab discovered in the Money Pit at a depth of 90-feet by the Onslow Company in 1804, lying atop a layer of oak logs. The underside of the stone was said to be inscribed with strange markings. Throughout the 19th Century, the stone changed locations several times, eventually ending up in a Halifax bookbindery, where it was employed as an anvil on which to pound leather and paper. The stone disappeared sometime in the early 1930s. In Season 6, Episode 7 of *The Curse of Oak Island*, members of Oak Island

15

Tours Inc. discovered an artifact bearing vague resemblance to the description of the 90-foot stone in the basement of the bookbindery from which the stone disappeared.

Smith's Cove flood tunnel: A supposed booby trap allegedly constructed by the builders of the Money Pit and the depositors of the Oak Island treasure, discovered in 1850 by the Truro Syndicate. This feature is supposed to be an underground tunnel connecting Smith's Cove with the Money Pit, which funnels sea water into the Money Pit at a depth of about 110 feet. This booby trap is believed to have been triggered when members of the Onslow Company excavated the Money Pit to a depth of 90 feet in 1804.

Box drains: Five stone drains which converge like the fingers of a fan on the head of the Smith's Cove flood tunnel, which funnel sea water into the Smith's Cove flood tunnel. This structure was discovered at Smith's Cove in 1850 by members of the Truro Company, but its precise whereabouts have seen been lost to history.

Finger drains: See 'box drains'.

Smith's Cove filter: A large, artificial filter composed of layers of eelgrass, coconut fibre, and beach stones which lay atop the Smith's Cove box drains, apparently for the purpose of preventing the drains from becoming clogged with debris. This feature, first discovered by the Truro Company in 1850, was gradually destroyed by treasure hunters over the years.

Cave-In Pit: A 7-foot-wide, water-filled sinkhole east of the Money Pit, discovered in 1875 by Sophia Sellers, the daughter of Oak Island farmer Anthony Graves, when her plough and ox team broke through, or "caved in", its uppermost ten feet. Many researchers believe that the Cave-In Pit lies on the line of the Smith's Cove flood tunnel, and constitutes and airshaft dug by the flood tunnel builders.

Stone Triangle: An arrangement of sixteen beach stones discovered on Oak Island's South Shore Cove, discovered in 1897 by a member of the Oak Island Treasure Company. The stones formed an equilateral triangle, each of its sides measuring ten feet, with an arc girding its base, and with a line running from a point on that arc four feet from its western vertex to the triangle's northern apex. Treasure hunters suspected that the triangle pointed in the direction of the Money Pit. This feature was destroyed in the 1960s, during Robert Dunfield's operation.

Borehole 10-X: A 230-foot-deep shaft painstakingly constructed by Dan Blankenship in the 1970s, located 180 feet northeast of the Money Pit area, and prescribed by Dan Blankenship through the process of dowsing (a controversial method of subterranean prospecting involving the use of so-called 'divining rods', the apparent efficacy of which has yet to be explained by science). Drilling operations conducted in the area prior to the shaft's construction brought up fragments of low-carbon steel from a depth of 165 feet. An underwater camera operation conducted in the cavern at the shaft's bottom in 1971 revealed the presence of what Blankenship interpreted as a floating severed hand, a wooden chest, tools, two outgoing tunnels, and a headless human corpse. In 1976, a section of the shaft imploded, nearly entombing Dan Blankenship beneath it. In Season 3, Episode 13, professional diver John Chatterton manually explored the cavern at the bottom of the shaft and expressed his belief that it is a natural formation, and that the items of interest indicated by the 1971 remote camera operation can be attributed to natural phenomena.

Nolan's Cross: An arrangement of five conical granite boulders on Oak Island which form a perfect Latin cross. This feature, which has an 867-foot-long stem and a 720-foot-long crossbeam, was discovered by treasure hunter Fred Nolan in 1981.

U-Shaped Structure: A large, u-shaped structure discovered beneath Smith's Cove by Triton Alliance in the summer of 1970. The structure was made of 30-65-foot-long logs which were notched at 4-foot intervals. Each notch was labelled with a Roman numeral and was fitted with a wooden dowel. Oak Island Tours Inc. rediscovered this structure in Season 6, Episode 10. In Season 6, Episode 21, dendrochronologist Dr. Colin Laroque of the University of

Saskatchewan determined that the wood from which the structure is comprised is red spruce which was felled in 1769.

Slipway: A wooden structure discovered beneath Smith's Cove in Season 6, Episode 11. In Season 6, Episode 11, dendrochronologist Dr. Colin Laroque determined that the wood from which the slipway is comprised is red spruce which was felled in 1771.

Common Terms

The Fellowship of the Dig: An informal term, coined by Marty Lagina, denoting the members of Oak Island Tours Inc. currently searching for treasure on Oak Island.

The Oak Island Team: A term denoting the friends and relatives who actively participate in the current Oak Island treasure hunt. Throughout Season 7, members typically include Rick and Marty Lagina, Craig Tester, Dave Blankenship, Dan Henskee, Charles Barkhouse, Alex Lagina, Jack Begley, Gary Drayton, Doug Crowell, Laird Niven, Billy Gerhardt, Steve Guptill, and Terry Matheson. See 'The Fellowship of the Dig'.

War Room: A small, one-room, boardroom-style building in which the Fellowship of the Dig frequently congregates to discuss recent developments, new theories, and plans for the future.

Caisson: A large, strong, water-tight steel tube which forms the walls of modern shafts.

Hammergrab: A piece of heavy equipment used to excavate shafts resembling the claw cranes which are sometimes found in arcades.

Oscillator: A piece of heavy machinery used in the creation of shafts, which grinds toothed caissons into the earth.

***In situ* soil:** Undisturbed soil in its original, natural condition.

Glossary

Bobby dazzler: A term often used by Gary Drayton denoting interesting and attractive discoveries (especially pieces of jewelry and ornamental baubles) made while treasure hunting.

Top-pocket find: An exceptionally valuable treasure-hunting discovery worthy of being placed into the treasure hunter's top pocket (rather than the plastic baggies into which small discoveries are usually placed, which the treasure hunters usually bring with them when metal detecting). Term first introduced by Gary Drayton. See 'Bobby dazzler'.

The Oak Island Family

The Restall Family

†Robert Restall: A stuntman and tradesman who searched for Oak Island treasure from 1959 until 1965, living on the island with his wife, Mildred, and his sons, Bobby and Ricky. Restall lost his life on August 17th, 1965, in the Restall Tragedy.

†Bobby Restall: Robert eldest son, who lived with his family on Oak Island and assisted his father with the Oak Island treasure hunt. Bobby Restall lost his life on August 17th, 1965, in the Restall Tragedy, at the age of 24.

Lee Lamb (nee Restall): Robert and Mildred Restall's eldest child and only daughter, and the author of several books. Lamb has written two books on her family's Oak Island treasure hunt, entitled *Oak Island Obession: The Restall Story* (2006) and *Oak Island Family: The Restall Hunt for Buried Treasure* (2014).

Richard "Ricky" Restall: Robert and Mildred Restall's youngest son, who grew up on Oak Island throughout the early 1960s.

The Blankenship Family

†Dan Blankenship: The so-called "Mayor of Oak Island" and co-founder of Triton Alliance, a Florida building contractor who searched for Oak Island treasure from 1969 until his death on March 17th, 2019, at the age of 95. The builder of Borehole 10-X.

Dave Blankenship: Dan Blankenship's son, a construction steelworker who came to Oak Island in 1975 to assist his father with the Oak Island treasure hunt, and never left.

The Nolan Family

Fred Nolan: A Nova Scotian surveyor and Oak Island landowner who searched for treasure on the island from 1966 until his death on June 4th, 2016, one month and a day before his 89th birthday. Long-time rival of Dan Blankenship, and the discoverer of Nolan's Cross.

Tom Nolan: A construction contractor and the son of Fred Nolan, who inherited his father's Oak Island properties.

The Lagina Family

Rick Lagina: A former postal worker from the Upper Peninsula of Michigan. The elder brother of Marty Lagina, and the co-founder of Oak Island Tours Inc. Often described as the "spiritual leader" of the current Oak Island treasure hunt.

Marty Lagina: A mechanical engineer and successful businessman who earned a fortune in the oil and gas boom of the 1980s. The younger brother of Rick Lagina, the business partner of Craig Tester, and the father of Alex Lagina. Co-founder and financier of Oak Island Tours Inc. Skeptical of the Oak Island legend.

Alex Lagina: The son of Marty Lagina, and a semi-regular participant in the Oak Island treasure hunt.

Peter Fornetti: Rick and Marty Lagina's young nephew, and an occasional participant in the Oak Island treasure hunt.

The Tester Family

Craig Tester: A mechanical engineer and successful businessman. Marty Lagina's business partner in the petroleum industry. Father of Drake Tester, and step-father of Jack Begley.

Jack Begley: The step-son of Craig Tester, and a regular participant in the Oak Island treasure hunt.

†Drake Tester: The son of Craig Tester, and occasional participant in the Oak Island treasure hunt. Drake passed away suddenly and unexpectedly on March 16, 2017, due to complications resultant of an epileptic seizure.

The Oak Island Team

Charles Barkhouse: Oak Island tour guide, historian, and Freemason.

Dan Henskee: An eccentric farmer from upstate New York who has intermittently assisted with the Oak Island treasure hunt since the 1960s.

Gary Drayton: A British-born metal detection expert who honed his treasure-hunting skills on the shores of Florida's 'Treasure Coast'.

Doug Crowell: Oak Island historian and an employee of the Centre of Geographic Sciences in Lawrencetown, Nova Scotia.

The Oak Island Family

Laird Niven: An archaeologist who was hired to supervise the treasure hunting operations of Oak Island Tours Inc. in accordance with a recently-passed Nova Scotian law.

Terry Matheson: A geologist who actively assists in the Oak Island treasure hunt, particularly during drilling operations and excavations.

Tony Sampson: An Australian born diving master and Freemason who is occasionally hired to make investigative dives in the waters off Oak Island's shore and in the island's swamp.

Billy Gerhardt: Heavy equipment operator and regular participant in the Oak Island treasure hunt.

Steve Guptill: Surveyor and regular participant in the Oak Island treasure hunt.

Part I

Special
Episodes

The Top 25 Moments You Never Saw

This special episode serves as a prelude to Season 7, Episode 1 of *The Curse of Oak Island.*

Plot Summary

Host Matty Blake informs us that the subject of this special episode will be old footage (presumably shot from 2014-2018) which never made it into the final cut of *The Curse of Oak Island.* "These are the moments," Blake explains, "that, for some reason- often because of time, or the needs of a story- ended up in our vaults, but not in an actual episode."

25: The Personality Interviews

The first of the '25 moments we never saw' (which the show's producers labelled 'Moment 25', apparently starting at the bottom of their list and working their way to the top), are the 'personality interviews' to which Rick and Marty Lagina and other the main characters of *The Curse of Oak Island* were subjected during the preparatory stages which preceded the filming of Season 1. "What you're seeing," Blake explains, as we're treated to scenes of younger, fresh-faced cast members sitting in front of a camera, "is the very first footage ever shot of Rick, Marty, and members of their team."

In Rick and Marty Lagina's interview, Marty explains that, when he and Rick were growing up, Rick was "always the classic older brother" in that he had a habit of ordering Marty around.

Alex Lagina, in his own interview, states a desire to spend time on Oak Island and "be a part of the actual work". He also suggests that his father, Marty, like himself, is more skeptical of the Oak Island legend than his uncle, Rick.

Jack Begley, in his interview, expresses enthusiasm for the upcoming treasure hunt and his desire to do some dirty, physical, hands-on treasure hunting.

Craig Tester, in his interview, states his belief that the modern techniques which he and the crew will apply in their efforts to unlock the secrets of Oak Island will "greatly enhance [their] ability to find the treasure."

Dave Blankenship, in his interview, explains that he first came to Oak Island in 1972 in order to assist his father, Dan, in the Oak Island treasure hunt. He also discloses that he suffered a stroke during a work accident in 1986, when he was 36 years old, which destroyed his mental-verbal filter. "If I think it, it comes out my mouth," he says. "There's no in-between."

Lastly, Dan Blankenship, in his interview, explains that he first became involved in the Oak Island treasure hunt in 1965.

24: The Spanish Object

'Moment 24' is a scene in which metal detection expert Gary

Drayton discovers a mysterious metal object on Oak Island's Lot 11, at the edge of the Oak Island swamp.

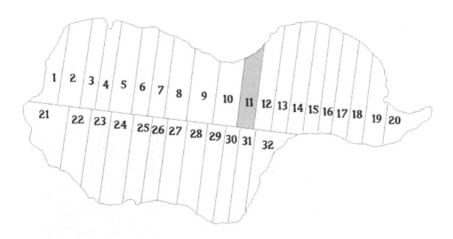

Drayton identifies the object as the broken head of an old Spanish tool or weapon. When complete and mounted on a wooden shaft, the object would resemble a garden hoe with two curved, pointed prongs in place of the flat head.

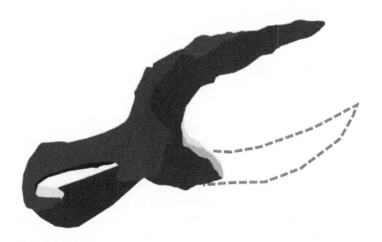

Blake suggests that this artifact is another piece of evidence supporting the theory that members of the Spanish Empire were behind the Oak Island mystery.

23: Mysteries of the Museum

'Moment 23' is a scene cut from Season 1 in which Charles Barkhouse gives Alex Lagina, Jack Begley, and Peter Fornetti a guided tour of the artifacts on display at the Oak Island Visitor Centre, all of which were discovered by previous treasure hunters on the island.

First, Charles shows the boys the 17th Century Mexican-Spanish scissors, which he explains Dan Blankenship discovered in 1967 below Smith's Cove. Next, Barkhouse shows the young treasure hunters some of the links of wrought iron chain discovered at a depth of 165 feet in Borehole 10-X. He finishes his tour by showing the boys a replica of the 90-foot stone, complete with the engraving alleged to have been carved onto its surface (i.e. the Kempton symbols; a simple substitution cypher encoding the message: "FORTY FEET BELOW TWO MILLION POUNDS ARE BURIED."

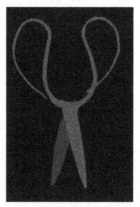

22: Stuck Together

'Moment 22' is a scene apparently cut from Season 3. In this snippet, Rick Lagina and Dave Blankenship set up a pump and begin to drain a section of the Oak Island swamp. Once the pumping operation is underway, the treasure hunters attempt to leave the area in their truck with the intention of returning when the drainage is complete. However, the treasure hunters are unable to drive away on account of the swampy ground on which they are parked. After spinning their tires hopelessly deeper into the muck, Rick and Dave decide to walk back home, Rick blaming Dave for their misfortune.

21: The Stone Compass

'Moment 21' is a scene cut from Season 2 in which Rick and Marty Lagina laboriously haul a large ovoid rock up the Smith's Cove beach, which Blake explains is a component of a "megalithic structure" the brothers intended to build which "would help them find their way while working on the island; a stone compass." The brothers collect three more large stones and bury all four of them upright in the fashion of the Bronze Age menhirs, or standing stones, of Northwestern Europe, arranging them so that each one points towards one of the four cardinal directions. "This should last a thousand years," laughs Marty, the mastermind behind the project, once the final stone is embedded in the earth.

20: Jack and Dave Go Shopping

In 'Moment 20', Dave Blankenship and Jack Begley drive from Oak Island to the nearby town of Chester, Nova Scotia, for supplies. While Dave drives, Jack bombards the veteran treasure hunter with questions regarding Oak Island. "Do you ever shut up with these damned questions?" Dave explodes after the fourth query.

The treasure hunters drive to Chester's Home Hardware store and pick up some metal mesh, engaging in some friendly small talk with the cashier on their way out.

19: The Rochefoucauld Archive

'Moment 19' is a scene deleted from Season 5, Episode 9, in which Sonia Matossian, the stewardess of the Chateau de la Rochefoucauld, takes Rick Lagina, Alex Lagina, and Peter Fornetti to the French castle's archive. Matossian pulls a box from the archive's shelf and withdraws an original 18th Century document.

She explains that this document contains an inventory of the diamonds and gems which the French Queen Marie Antoinette carried with her during the royal flight to Varennes during the French Revolution, these jewels being the focus of a particular Oak Island theory. Unfortunately, none of the document's text is read aloud.

18: Going for a Dip

'Moment 18' is a deleted scene from Season 3, Episode 9, cut from Rick and Marty Lagina's visit with diver Harvey Morash, who would later attempt to dive to the bottom of Borehole 10-X. In preparation for a practice dive, the Lagina brothers slide a length of caisson with the same diameter as that of the narrowest section of Borehole 10-X down a dock ramp with the intention of rolling it into the ocean. "Poseidon!" exclaims Marty, as the brothers push the caisson over the dock, "I commit this object to the sea!" That accomplished, the brothers, at Rick's suggestion, empty their pockets and run off the dock into the water for an impromptu swim.

"Big, heavy pipe," says Marty of the incident in a later interview. "We muscled it down, we pushed it in the water. At least there was some sense of accomplishment, and I think Oak Island robs you of that so often that you've got to go with little victories."

17: Dan's Reunion

'Moment 17' is a deleted scene in which Dan Blankenship, accompanied by Dave Blankenship and Rick Lagina, drives to the Mahone Bay Nursing Home to meet with the elderly Gerald Dorey, a labourer and skilled dowser who once assisted the Triton Alliance team with their Oak Island treasure hunt. Dorey explains that, many years prior, Dan Blankenship handed him a pair of dowsing rods and asked him to walk over certain sections of Oak Island (when a dowser's 'divining rods' cross, ostensibly on their own, without any special force applied by the dowser, proponents of this mysterious and unorthodox technique believe the dowser has located an underground anomaly). Incredibly, Dorey's blind, independent dowsing operation indicated the presence of fifteen underground tunnels at exactly the same spots at which Dan's own dowsing operation indicated the presence of subterranean anomalies.

"But you didn't know what he had found, did you?" asks Rick Lagina of the veteran dowser.

"No," Dorey replies.

Dan Blankenship then asks his old friend if he remembers what they saw that night, in the summer of 1971, when they lowered a waterproof video camera into the chamber at the bottom of Borehole 10-X (10-X being a shaft which Blankenship sank in 1969/70, its location prescribed by his and Dorey's dowsing operations). For years, Blankenship has claimed that the camera, the live feed from which he and his crew watched from a screen on the surface, picked up a severed human hand floating in the water, as well as a pick, a chest and a headless human corpse lying at the bottom of the chamber.

"Yeah," Dorey replies. "It looked like someone's hand. That's what it looked like. It had four fingers and a thumb on it... That's what I saw." Dorey's memory, which accords with Dan Blankenship's own recollection of the incident, supports the latter's theory that a human corpse- perhaps a sacrificial victim left to die underground by the treasure's original depositors in the hope that his spirit would guard the treasure- lies at the bottom of Borehole 10-X.

Rick Lagina then asks Dorey where he would look if he had one shot at solving the Oak Island mystery. "There's one place I would look," Dorey replies. "In 10-X."

At the end of this segment, Matty Blake informs us that Gerald Dorey passed away in 2016, prior to Blankenship's own passing in 2019.

16: An Oak Island Hero

'Moment 16' is a deleted scene from Season 2 in which Dan Blankenship, Dave Blankenship, and Rick Lagina welcome Ed White Jr. to Oak Island. Matty Blake explains that White, then 16-years-old, was visiting Oak Island with his father on August 17, 1965, when Robert and Bobby Restall, Karl Graeser, and Cyril Hiltz drowned in a shaft near Smith's Cove, having been rendered unconscious by hydrogen sulfide gas.

During this event, often referred to today as the 'Restall Tragedy', two more men, Leonard Kaizer and Andrew Demont, fell into the same shaft in which the aforementioned four lost their lives. Fortunately, Kaizer and Demont were saved by Ed's father, Ed White Senior. A fireman by trade, Ed Sr. recognized that the six men who fell into the shaft must have succumbed to some sort of toxic gas. Tying a rag around his mouth and nose and a rope beneath his arms, he asked some bystanders to lower him into the shaft. White managed to haul Kaizer and Demont from the pit, which was quickly filling with subterranean water, before nearly passing out himself on account of the gas.

"We were vacationing," says Ed White Sr. of the incident. "We were heading up to Cape Breton, and my mother had read about Oak Island in the *Reader's Digest*, and she wanted to stop at Oak Island. And we had no idea what was going on here at the time...

"When we walked up the beach, we weren't sure what was happening. We didn't know that there was anybody in the pit. All we could hear was this sound. We just ran up to the pit, looked down, and saw Andrew there.

"Immediately, my father saw there was an emergency here, and he gave orders, said 'Get me some rope. I need some rope.' And my mother came up to my dad, and she said, 'Edward, you have a wife and three children.' And he said, 'Audrey, I know what I'm doing. We're not going away. I'm not going to let this man die.'

"After that, it was all business. My dad was a fireman. He was a rescue expert. It was very, very emotional for my mother. She was almost hysterical. I guess it kind of rubbed off on me from my dad. It was just, 'We're going to get this guy out of here,' so I followed his lead. It was the urgency of the moment, and so the fear factor, though it should have been there, wasn't, because it was just all about business.

"We pulled Andrew up, and he was unconscious, of course. My dad stayed in the shaft for maybe another 30 seconds. I felt a tug, and so I started pulling on the rope, and so my dad hollered out, 'Give me some rope!' And that was the first time he had to take a breath. And he said as soon as he took a breath, he could just feel burning in his lungs. And so he knew he only had a little bit of time to get out of there.

"There were eight or ten people gathered around the top of the shaft, but given the fact that there were already four dead people down there, and there was poison gas, nobody else was going to go down there."

Following Ed Jr.'s account, Rick Lagina and Dave Blankenship praise Ed Sr. for his courage.

15: The Restall Visit

'Moment 15' is a scene cut from Season 5, Episode 4, in which siblings Lee Lamb and Richard Restall- the children of Oak Island treasure Robert Restall, who perished with his son, Bobby, during the aforementioned 'Restall Tragedy'- sit at a seaside bench on Oak Island and reminisce, looking through old photographs of their family taken during the Restall family's Oak Island tenure in the 1960s.

"Looking at the pictures," says Richard Restall in a later interview, "sort of took me back to what it was like living on the island... Being on the island was one of the better things that ever happened to me.

When I arrived as a 9-year-old boy, it was like leaving the city and arriving in some paradise. It was just full of life, colour, nature, and I thought it was really neat. Growing up in an unusual and not very mainstream way, I was the luckiest kid in the world. I think I discovered parts of myself that other people don't get to find, until they're perhaps older, or perhaps they never find."

14: Dan's Ancient Shoes

'Moment 14' is a cutting-room scene from Season 4 in which Charles Barkhouse shows Rick Lagina an antique leather shoe which Dan Blankenship discovered at Smith's Cove, about five feet below the mysterious slipway he unearthed and eight or nine feet below the surface of the beach.

In a later scene, Rick and Charles bring the shoe to Dan Blankenship's house on Oak Island. "Initially, when I found that," Blankenship says of the artifact, "it was in the ground about six, seven feet down. And also, there was another, smaller shoe. I think I still have it downstairs."

The elderly treasure hunter proceeds to take Rick and Charles to the archive in his basement, where he produces another leather shoe much smaller than the artifact shown earlier. The treasure hunters suggest that the shoe must have belonged to a child or a woman.

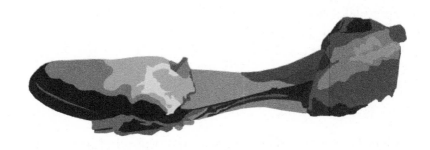

13: Saying 'Goodbye' to Fred Nolan

In 'Moment 13', Rick Lagina, Dave Blankenship, and Charles Barkhouse drive back to Oak Island from the funeral of the late Oak Island treasure hunter Fred Nolan, Dan Blankenship's contemporary and long-time rival (Nolan passed away on June 4, 2016, at the age of 88). During the drive, the treasure hunters agree that Nolan's most enduring legacy is the tenacity with which he pursued the Oak Island mystery despite the adversity he faced.

12: The Thermal Drone

'Moment 12' is a scene cut from Season 4 in which Craig Tester has John Frost of Aerhyve Aerial Technologies fly a drone equipped with infrared cameras over the Oak Island swamp. Later, in a War Room meeting (the 'War Room' being a small, one-room, boardroom-style building on Oak Island in which the treasure hunters occasionally congregate in order to discuss new developments, theories, and plans for the future), Frost informs the Oak Island crew that the topographical map he was able to produce through the use of his drone indicates that Oak Island may have once consisted of two separate islands which were separated at the point at which the swamp now lies. This notion that Oak Island once consisted of two separate islands features in a number of different Oak Island theories, including that of the late Oak Island treasure hunter Fred Nolan.

11: The Rod in the Stone

'Moment 11' is a scene cut from Season 6, Episode 1, following Gary Drayton and Jack Begley's discovery of a drilled stone with an iron spike embedded in it on Oak Island's Lot 2, and following Laird Niven's subsequent investigation of the object. In this scene, Rick Lagina shows the stone to his brother, Marty, and informs him that Niven believes the stone to be evidence of a failed quarrying operation. Presumably, Niven believes that men had drilled holes into the stone and hammered an iron spike into it in an effort to split it in two, hoping to incorporate the fractured pieces into the foundation of a cabin. This theory conflicts with Gary Drayton's initial speculation, voiced earlier in the episode, that the spike and holes in the stone constitute the remains of a ring bolt through which a chain or rope could be threaded for the purpose of hauling heavy objects.

With Niven's permission, the Lagina brothers attempt to extract the metal spike from the stone. They return to the site with a sledgehammer, whereupon Marty bets his brother that he will be unable to liberate the spike from its lithic prison with ten hammer blows or less, the stakes being a $100 donation to the local orphanage. Rick proceeds to deliver ten blows to the stone and loses the bet. Rick continues to pound on the stone for some time before relinquishing the sledgehammer to his younger brother, who similarly finds himself unable to crack the stone with ten hammer blows. The brother continue to chip away at the granite boulder until the top section of the spike finally breaks loose. Pleased with their success, Marty agrees to match his brother's loss and also donate $100 to the orphanage.

Matty Blake then informs us that subsequent tests determined that the spike was forged sometime prior to 1840.

10: Ross Valory's Journey

'Moment 10' constitutes a series of scenes cut from Season 3, in which rockstar Ross Valory, the bassist from the band 'Journey', and his road manager, Pasquale Vartolo, toured Oak Island with the Lagina brothers.

Although Matty Blake failed to mention it, these sequences are not truly deleted scenes, as many of them featured in Season 1, Episode 3, of *The Curse of Oak Island's* appendant series, *Drilling Down*, which succeeded Season 3, Episode 11 of *The Curse of Oak Island*. In that episode, Valory stated that his brother has an uncanny knack for dousing, the controversial process by which Dan Blankenship first discovered Borehole 10-X, and agreed to ask him to apply his skills on Oak Island.

9: FDR: Treasure Hunter

'Moment 9' is a scene cut from Season 1, in which Marty Lagina reads a letter typewritten by U.S. President Franklin Delano Roosevelt on White House stationery to Oak Island treasure hunter Erwin Hamilton, dated August 31, 1938.

The letter reads:

"Dear Mr. Hamilton,

"Your note came while I was on my cruise in the Pacific. I wish

much I could have gone up the coast this summer and visited Oak Island and see the work you are doing- for I shall always be interested in that romantic spot. I hope that you will let me know how you have been getting on with modern methods- ours were, I fear, somewhat antiquated when we were there more than a quarter of a century ago.

"Very sincerely yours,

"Franklin D. Roosevelt"

8: Making-A-Wish

'Moment 8' is a scene cut from Season 4, in which Evan Berry, a high school senior from McPherson, Kansas, suffering from a rare and dangerous blood disease, visited Oak Island under the auspices of the 'Make-A-Wish Foundation'.

After taking Berry on a tour of the island, the Oak Island crew sits down with him in the War Room to discuss Oak Island theories. Equipped with a stack of loose leaf paper containing 200 questions, Berry proceeds to pick the treasure hunters' brains. At the end of the meeting, Rick Lagina thanks Berry for coming to the island and declares that he is now a member of the 'Oak Island family'.

7: The Bones Live Again

'Moment 7' is a fascinating scene inexplicably cut from Season 5 in which forensic scientist Valerie Blackmore of Guelph, Ontario's, Wyndham Forensic Group, during a War Room meeting, discloses the results of the tests conducted on the fragments of human bone discovered in Borehole H8. Both of these bones were carbon dated from the late 1600s to the early 1700s, and determined to have come from two different individuals of European and Middle Eastern extraction, respectively. In this deleted scene, Blackmore informs the treasure hunters that the bone determined to have come from a person of Middle Eastern extraction is also the bone of a female.

While discussing this most interesting and unexpected development, Marty Lagina casually remarks that, several days prior, Rick Lagina had been talking about female pirates. "Maybe we've got a new Anne Bonny here," he says, referring to an 18th Century female Irish pirate who prowled the Caribbean with her partner-in-crime, Captain John "Calico Jack" Rackham, from 1718-1720.

6: 10-X Enhanced

'Moment 6' is a scene cut from Season 6 in which video enhancement specialist Frank Schiefelbein, the CEO of Barnett & Associates, presents the Oak Island team with the 1971 footage of the chamber at the bottom of Borehole 10-X (mentioned in 'Moment 17'), which he enhanced for clarity using Prohawk technology (a technology which featured in Season 3, Episode 2, and Season 5, Episode 1).

This enhanced footage shows a clearer image of what Dan Blankenship believes to be a post to which a sacrificial human victim was chained, as well as what Dan identifies as an iron pin driven into the chamber wall.

5: The Mystery of Samuel Ball

'Moment 5' is a scene cut from Season 4, Episode 7, during Charles Barkhouse and Randall Sullivan's visit to the headquarters of the South Shore Genealogical Society in Lunenburg, Nova Scotia. In this scene, Society president Stephen Ernst reads Barkhouse and Sullivan an excerpt from the first edition of Mather Byles DesBrisay's 1895 book *History of the County of Lunenburg* particularly relevant to Oak Island. This excerpt reads:

"One of the earliest residents was Samuel Ball, a coloured man who came from South Carolina, where he had been enslaved to a master whose name he adopted."

Ernst then invites the treasure hunters to peruse the volume at their leisure. While doing so, Barkhouse and Sullivan come across a passage indicating that the Money Pit was discovered by Daniel McGinnis, John Smith, and Samuel Ball. In the second edition of Des Brisay's book, the only edition with which Sullivan had hitherto been familiar, Anthony Vaughan replaces Samuel Ball as one of the Money Pit's three co-discoverers.

The next day, during a meeting in the War Room, Sullivan reveals his discovery to the Oak Island team and expresses his belief that Samuel Ball played a more important role in the Money Pit's discovery than the popular legend indicates.

At the end of this segment, Matty Blake cryptically reveals that "later research contradicted Randall Sullivan's early findings."

4: The Return of Samuel Ball's Family

'Moment 4' constitutes cutting room footage in which brothers Anthony and Ivan Boyd, the direct descendants of former Oak Island landowner Samuel Ball, visited Oak Island. Upon their arrival, Rick Lagina ushers the Ball descendants into the War Room, where they and the crew discuss the possibility that Samuel Ball discovered some sort of treasure on his Oak Island property, which he used to purchase additional land on the island and the mainland.

After the War Room meeting, Rick Lagina, Jack Begley, and Charles Barkhouse take the Boyd brothers on a tour of Oak Island. The last stop on the tour is the foundation of Samuel Ball's old Oak Island home. At Rick's suggestion, Tony and Ivan Boyd spend some time alone at the Ball foundation, during which Ivan bursts into tears, overcome by emotion. "My family and I have a great sense of pride on what Samuel Ball was able to accomplish," Anthony explains in a later interview. "Being born into slavery and fighting his way for freedom, and persevering through the harsh conditions of Oak Island."

In the same interview, Ivan concludes, "What's most remarkable about Samuel Ball to me was his tenacity, his 'never ever give up' attitude."

3: The Dean Brothers Visit

'Moment 3' is a deleted scene in which brothers Andrew and Matt Dean visit with the Oak Island crew in the War Room. Matty Blake reveals that Matt Dean has been diagnosed with the deadly neurodegenerative disease ALS, and that his brother, Andrew, decided to visit Oak Island with him- an activity which had been on both of their bucket lists.

In the War Room, the Dean brothers ask the Oak Island crew members a number of questions pertaining to their treasure hunt. First, the brothers ask whether the crew believes that Oak Island once consisted of two separate islands. Rick Lagina replies to that question in the affirmative.

After the War Room meeting, Rick Lagina and Charles Barkhouse take the Dean brothers on a tour of Oak Island in which they visit both the swamp and the Money Pit. The scene ends with a brief memorial to Matt Dean, indicating that he passed away in 2019 at the age of 40.

2: Dan's 95th Birthday Party

'Moment 2' is a scene cut from Season 6, in which the Oak Island crew attends Dan Blankenship's 95th (and final) birthday party in his Oak Island home. During the celebration, Rick Lagina extends his congratulations towards the veteran treasure hunter.

"For surviving so long?" Blankenship quips.

"No!" Rick replies. "For being able to do what you wanted to do for your entire life, and you continue to do it. That's pretty amazing."

When asked to deliver a speech, the taciturn Blankenship addresses his guests with the words, "I'm very surprised."

1: Marty's Musical Moment

"All right," says Matty Blake in his introduction to the top moment we never saw, "the time has arrived for our #1 never-before-seen moment, and I've got to say, this one's a real treat. It happened at the end of a long day, when Rick and Marty sat down to discuss some new discoveries in the swamp." Specifically, this discovery was the plank which Tony Sampson unearthed from the Oak Island swamp in Season 4, Episode 3.

After being asked to elaborate on the discovery, Marty raises a steaming cup of coffee to his lips and begins to sing an adulterated rendition of *The Ballad of Gilligan's Isle*, the theme song of the old sitcom 'Gilligan's Island'.

The lyrics of Marty's song are as follows:

"Come sit right back, and you'll hear a tale,

"The tale of a fateful trip

"That started from this tiny port

"Aboard this fateful ship.

"The mate was a mighty sailin' man,

"And the skipper brave and sure-"

"Brave and true, isn't it?" Rick interrupts.

Marty continues to sing, ignoring his brother:

"Five passengers set sail that day

"For a three hour tour. A three hour tour."

"Isn't it 'brave and true'?" Rick asks again.

"No," Marty replies brusquely, before resuming the ballad:

"The weather started getting rough.

"The tiny ship was tossed.

"If not for the courage of the fearless crew,

"The Minnow would be lost-"

"Brave and true, not brave and sure," mutters Rick Lagina, looking to a member of the camera crew for affirmation.

Marty continues:

"The ship set ground on the shore of this

"Enchanted desert isle-"

"Uncharted desert isle," Rick corrects.

"I'll give you that one," Marty concedes, before continuing:

"With Dave Blankenship,

"And Dan, his dad,

"The used-to-be millionaire and his brother.

"Dan Henskee, the professor- we've got a professor. I mean, he makes a metal detector out of a canoe paddle.

"And Jack Begleeeey,

"Here on Oak Island!"

Part II

The Curse of Oak Island:

Season 7

Season 7, Episode 1

The Torch is Passed

Plot Summary

The Curse of Oak Island's 2-hour-long Season 7 premiere begins with Rick Lagina, Alex Lagina, and Craig Tester driving to Oak Island for another season of treasure hunting. During the drive, the narrator explains that legendary Oak Island treasure hunter Dan Blankenship passed away in his home on March 17, 2019, at the age of 95, having dedicated over fifty years of his life to the search for Oak Island's elusive treasure. The treasure hunters mourn Dan's passing before heading to the War Room to meet with the rest of the crew.

In the War Room, the Fellowship of the Dig calls up Marty Lagina and Jack Begley via Skype. First, the team observes a moment of silence in honour of Dan Blankenship. Rick laments that he and the crew were unable to "give Dan his breakthrough", or unearth an artifact or piece of treasure which might justify Dan's lifelong quest to solve the Oak Island mystery, and suggests that they ought to try make that breakthrough this year.

Next, surveyor Steve Guptill shows the crew the results of
the seismic survey carried out in the Oak Island swamp by Eagle
Canada in Season 6, Episodes 21 and 22. We learn that the survey
indicates the presence of a 200-foot-long anomaly in the swamp, the
shape of which, Marty remarks, bears some resemblance to the side
profile of a sailing ship. Marty's observation accords with the theory,
once held by the late treasure hunter Fred Nolan, that an old ship
lies at the bottom of the Oak Island swamp, having been buried by
the mysterious builders of the Money Pit and the Smith's Cove
flood tunnel. According to this theory, the eastern and western ends
of Oak Island were, at one point, actually separate islands, joined
together in a massive earthworks project by the original builders.
This exotic hypothesis is supported by some intriguing evidence,
including a potential scupper and piece of spar which Nolan
discovered in the swamp in the 1980s; an iron spike discovered in
the swamp, which one expert identified as a nail used in late
17th Century Spanish galleons; and the wooden plank unearthed
from the southwestern corner of the swamp in Season 4, Episode 3,
which was carbon dated from 1680-1735. The treasure hunters
agree that they ought to investigate this new anomaly, which Gary
Drayton speculates might be the remains of a Spanish galleon.

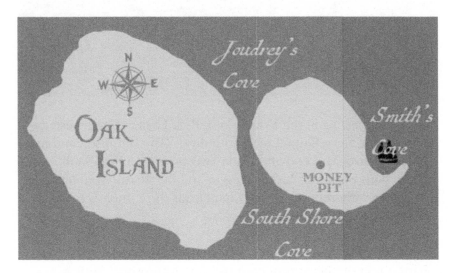

Next, the treasure hunters discuss their plans for the Money Pit this
season. Craig Tester suggests that they drill some more holes in an
effort to pinpoint the locations at which they will later conduct a

larger excavation. Doug Crowell expresses interest in Borehole S6, which yielded large, old, axe-hewn oaken timbers and a link of hand-wrought iron chain in Season 6, Episode 17.

Lastly, talk turns to the U-shaped structure and the slipway discovered at Smith's Cove the previous season, the wood from which dendrochronologist Dr. Colin Laroque determined was felled in the 1760s and '70s. Craig Tester suggests that the crew conduct a rigorous search for artifacts at the end of the slipway, where it seems likely a ship would have been moored several decades prior to the discovery of the Money Pit. In order to do this, the crew will need to extend the cofferdam fifty feet seaward.

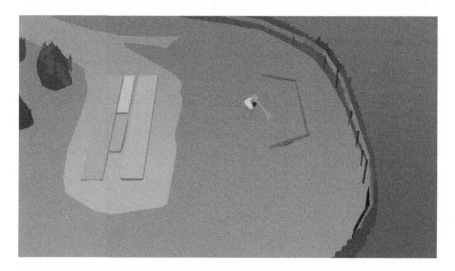

After their meeting in the War Room, Rick Lagina, Craig Tester, and surveyor Steve Guptill meet with diver Tony Sampson and his assistants Krista McLeod and Dana Sweeny at the Oak Island swamp. Sampson dons his diving gear and the treasure hunters pile into a dingy, whereupon Steve Guptill leads the company to the northernmost section of the anomaly.

About fifteen metres northwest of the anomaly, Sampson discovers a hard object on the swamp floor using an iron probe. Shortly thereafter, he discovers two similar objects closer to the edge of the swamp, each of them located directly on the line between the first object and the point on the shoreline to which it is most proximate.

Sampson suggests that the pattern evokes the cobblestones of an ancient roadway. He dives on the objects, which indeed prove to be rocks with flat surfaces. He then marks the rocks' locations with inflatable buoys, allowing Guptill to plot their coordinates.

Later, Gary Drayton and Charles Barkhouse conduct a metal detecting operation on Isaac's Point, at the easternmost end of the island. This is not the first time such an operation has been carried out at Isaac's Point. Back in Season 5, Episode 1, Gary Drayton and Peter Fornetti unearthed the rusted head of an old woodcutter's axe and an 18th Century copper coin of either French or English origin at that particular section of the island. In the following episode, Drayton, Fornetti, and Jack Begley discovered a musket ball and a neatly-cut quarter of a copper coin which Drayton suspected might be a Spanish maravedis. Later, in Season 5, Episode 4, the trio discovered a cowboy-style cap gun at Isaac's Point which belonged to Richard Restall, who grew up on the island with his family in the 1960s.

On this latest excursion, Drayton and Barkhouse uncover a modern 12-gauge shotgun shell. Shortly thereafter, they discover an old silver dandy button bearing a starburst design, which Drayton dates from 1650 to 1750. This date range corresponds with many of the fascinating discoveries made in Season 5, including the human bones discovered in the Money Pit and the late 17th Century British coins found on Lot 16.

Later that day, Drayton and Barkhouse meet with other members of the team in the Oak Island Research Centre. There, they show their fellow treasure hunters the button they discovered at Isaac's Point, which they subsequently examine under a microscope. Archaeologist Laird Niven observes that the button's starburst design appears to be hand-carved rather than molded. Niven opines that the object is slightly younger than Drayton's estimate, dating it from the 1720s to the 1770s- a range which accords more closely with that of the various wooden structures discovered at Smith's Cove. The archaeologist then expresses his hope that a maker's mark revealing the artifact's date, the identity of its crafter, and the city in which it was made will be revealed when the button is professionally cleaned.

The next day, Rick Lagina accompanies his brother, Marty, to Oak Island. The brothers head to the War Room, where Steve Guptill updates Marty on the swamp anomaly indicated by the seismic survey. He also shows the crew a diagram which indicates that the potential roadway discovered by Tony Sampson appears to be about twelve feet wide and runs perpendicular to the anomaly, the southern edge of its midsection lying about two metres north of the anomaly's northernmost tip. Historian Doug Crowell then opines

that the stones discovered by Sampson might actually constitute a
wharf rather than a cobbled path, suggesting that it may have been
built for the purpose of transporting treasure from the supposed
ship to the shore. Despite his historic aversion to the swamp, Marty
Lagina agrees that the seismic data and Sampson's discovery justify a
future drilling operation in the anomaly area.

Later, the Lagina brothers and Craig Tester meet with Fred Nolan's
son, Tom, and Brennan McMahon of Choice Drilling at the Oak
Island swamp. The five men watch as Brennan's crew members
transport their equipment to Oak Island and begins to erect a
floating drilling platform in the swamp.

Later that afternoon, the Oak Island crew meets in the Research
Centre with conservator Kelly Bourassa, who has come to clean the
silver button discovered at Isaac's Point. After seeing the button,
Bourassa explains that he intends to clean the object with a
toothbrush, and with a glass fibre brush if necessary.

Gary Drayton and Alex Lagina then embark on yet another metal
detecting operation. Although the show states that the pair have
returned to Isaac's Point, the men appear to be scouring the woods
that front Smith's
Cove. There, not
far from what is
later revealed to be
the Cave-In Pit, the
two come across
what appears to be
the frame of a
Victorian lady's
hand-mirror.

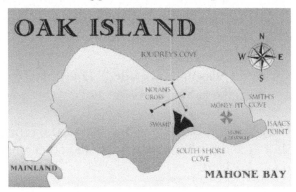

Later, while actually searching on the beach at Isaac's Point, Gary
Drayton and Alex Lagina find a hand-forged iron spike. Alex
observes that the spike is not pitted, which Gary suggests is an
indication that it is made of old wrought iron with a high carbon
content. Drayton further suggests that the spike came from a
galleon, and speculates that it might be much older than the 1700s.

This is not the first iron spike to be uncovered on Oak Island:

- Back in Season 4, Episode 7, Gary Drayton discovered a large iron nail at the northern end of the Oak Island swamp. Although the artifact strongly resembled a railroad spike, antiquities expert Dr. Lori Verderame identified the item as an iron barrote nail of the type commonly used in the construction of Spanish galleon decks, and dated it from 1575-1600.
- Later, in Season 5, Episode 1, Drayton discovered a hand-forged rose head nail in the spoils from Borehole C1.
- In Season 5, Episode 5, Drayton discovered an 18th Century wharf nail on the Boulderless Beach not too far from Isaac's Point.
- In Season 5, Episode 10, Drayton discovered a wrought-iron spike coated with limestone or concrete in the same batch of spoils from Borehole H8 which yielded fragments of human bone.
- In Season 6, Episode 3, Drayton discovered a strange-looking spike-like object on the beach of Oak Island's Lot 26. Although variously identified as a medieval crossbow bolt and an Imperial Roman *pilum*, the artifact was eventually determined to be an old crib spike- a nail-like tool used in the creation of wharves, derricks, platforms, and cribbing.
- In Season 6, Episode 8, Drayton discovered an 18th Century spike at Smith's Cove, along with a gold-plated coin.

Gary Drayton claims that this latest spike is unique in that it is shorter and thicker than most of the other spikes he has uncovered on Oak Island.

Later, Rick Lagina and Laird Niven meet with Kelly Bourassa in the Oak Island Research Centre. There, Bourassa shows the men the freshly-cleaned button from Isaac's Point. The conservator informs them that the starburst design on the button's face appears to be stamped, that the button's back is affixed with a raised foot, and that the silver laminate on the artifact's surface appears to be covering a mold seam- a feature unique to objects cast in a mold. Upon consulting Ivor Noel Hume's 1970 book *A Guide to the Artifacts of Colonial America*, Bourassa dated the artifact from 1720-1770, consistent with Niven's earlier diagnosis. When prompted by Rick Lagina, he states that it is possible that the button was worn by a military officer.

Later that day, members of the Oak Island team meet at Smith's Cove with Mike Jardine of Irving Equipment Ltd. The treasure hunters explain that they would like to add a fifty-foot extension, which they refer to as a "bump-out", to the existing cofferdam which will enable them to excavate more ground in the vicinity of the mysterious slipway.

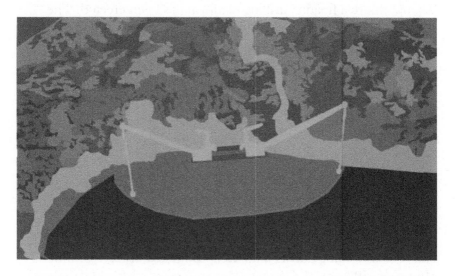

That afternoon, members of the Oak Island team congregate in the Research Centre in order to update each other on the developments of the day. The crew nominates the wrought iron spike discovered by Gary Drayton and Alex Lagina the most interesting find of the day, and suggests that they have it analyzed by Carmen Legge, the blacksmith who identified the Smith's Cove crib spike discovered in Season 6, Episode 3, and who analyzed the iron hinge discovered in Season 6, Episode 16.

Later, Rick Lagina and Gary Drayton travel to the Ross Farm Museum in the town of New Ross, Nova Scotia. There, they meet with blacksmithing expert Carmen Legge, to whom they show the iron spike discovered at Isaac's Point. Legge identifies the artifact as a hand point chisel- a tool used to carve stone- and dates it from the 14th to the late 18th Century. Rick remarks that the artifact's connection to masonry evokes the theory that members of some Freemasonic fraternity are behind the Oak Island mystery. Carmen Legge then suggests that the artifact may have been used to etch characters onto some of the many inscribed stones on Oak Island, including, perhaps the legendary 90-foot stone.

After Rick and Gary share Carmen Legge's analysis of the iron spike with the team at the Mug & Anchor Pub in the town of Mahone Bay, Nova Scotia, the Fellowship of the Dig meets at the Oak Island swamp, where a floating drilling platform has been erected. The platform is towed into position and the drilling rig is started up. The episode ends as the drill descends into the swamp.

Analysis

The Silver Button

In this episode, Gary Drayton and Alex Lagina discovered a badly corroded silver laminate button at Isaac's Point, on the easternmost end of Oak Island. Conservator Kelly Bourassa, using Ivor Noel Hume's 1970 book *A Guide to the Artifacts of Colonial America* as a reference, dated the artifact from 1720-1770 and suggested that it was possibly worn by a military officer.

Back in Season 5, a number of fascinating discoveries were made which seemed to indicate a European presence on the island in the late 1600s or early 1700s. The dendrochronological dating of the U-shaped structure and the slipway near the end of Season 6, however, hinted that a significant event took place on the island sometime in the late 1760s or early 1770s. Bourassa's dating of the silver button

is among the first items discovered on the island consistent with this dating. Another artifact congruent with the date range in question is a British copper coin bearing the date 1771, which Gary Drayton discovered on Oak Island's South Shore Cove back in Season 2, Episode 3. Another such artifact is a fragment of Staffordshire slipware which Gary Drayton discovered on Oak Island's Lot 22 in Season 5, Episode 9, which Laird Niven dated from the mid-1700s to the 1770s. It must be mentioned that artifacts of this age are not necessarily out of place on Oak Island; the island was surveyed and subdivided back in 1762, and private citizens owned some of its lots as early as 1765.

The Hand Point Chisel

In this episode, Gary Drayton and Alex Lagina discovered a wrought iron spike at Isaac's Point. Although Drayton initially expected that the artifact was a deck nail from an old Spanish galleon, he conceded that it was shorter and thicker than all the other spikes he had uncovered on the island. Sure enough, blacksmithing expert Carmen Legge identified the artifact as a hand point chisel- a tool used to carve stone- and suggested that it might have been used to create many of the mysterious stone inscriptions found throughout the island, including, perhaps, those said to have been scratched onto the surface of the legendary 90-foot stone.

The Ship Anomaly

In this episode, we learn that the seismic survey carried out in the Oak Island swamp by Eagle Canada in Season 6, Episodes 21 and 22 indicate the presence of a 200-foot-long anomaly beneath the swamp. Members of the Oak Island team remarked that the shape of this anomaly bears some resemblance to a sailing ship, evoking Fred Nolan's theory that a ship lies buried in the swamp.

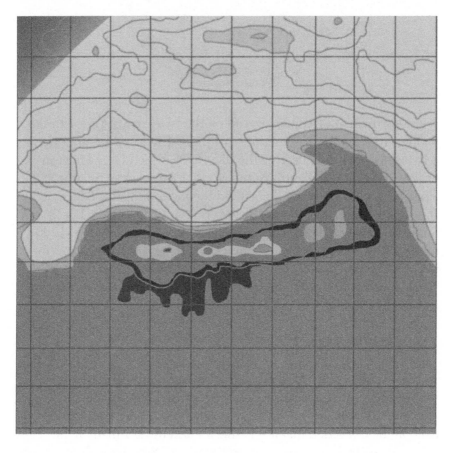

History tells us that we ought to take the exciting implication of the survey results with a grain of salt. Back in Season 6, Eagle Canada conducted seismic surveys in the Mega Bin and Money Pit areas and retrieved data indicating the presence of multiple underground chambers. A subsequent investigation, however, revealed these potential chambers to be nothing more than pockets of sand and

S7E1: The Torch is Passed

loose earth which were less dense than the surrounding rock and till. Perhaps a closer examination of the ship anomaly will yield similar results.

[For the results of the subsequent investigation of the Ship Anomaly, please see 'Exploration Drilling in the Swamp' in the Analysis of Season 7, Episode 2]

Season 7, Episode 2

Core Values

Plot Summary

This episode begins in the Oak Island swamp, where Choice Drilling is busy retrieving core samples of the mysterious 'ship anomaly' indicated by the results of the seismic survey carried out at the end of the previous season. Tom Nolan, the son of Fred Nolan, joins members of the Oak Island team as they inspect a sample

taken from a depth of 13-16 feet below the swamp floor. Disappointingly, the sample appears to contain little aside from mud and organic matter.

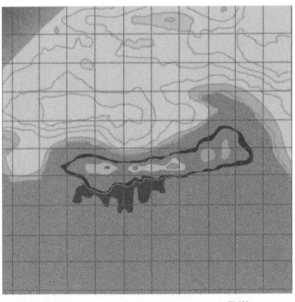

A second sample, taken from 18.5-21.5 feet, is composed of arid, crumbly clay, being perhaps the driest core sample ever collected on Oak Island. Heavy equipment operator Billy Gerhardt remarks that that the clay is similar to some of the material he has seen in core samples taken from the Money Pit area. The narrator then attempts to draw a parallel between this clay and the blue clay said to have been found in the original Money Pit by the Onslow Company in 1804, neglecting to point out that the latter was described as having a puttylike consistency very different from that of the moistureless material found beneath the swamp.

At a depth of 30 feet, the drill bites into something hard. A core sample taken from that depth contains more dry clay similar to the material found at 18.5-21.5 feet. Within the sample is a piece of hard rock, which Marty Lagina refers to as a "caprock". The narrator explains that "caprocks" are sheets of hard rock which overlie weaker material, forming impermeable barriers which prevent the flow of fluids from one side of the rock to the other. Marty's reference implies the theory that this caprock and others

like it prevent the swamp water from leeching deep into the ground below, suggesting that the presence of such rocks might explain the dryness of the core samples the team has unearthed.

When Choice Drilling attempts to drill further into the swamp, the drill seizes up, presumably having encountered a hard rock. The Oak Island crew reluctantly decides to abandon the hole and sink another one later.

The next morning, while Choice Drilling repositions the floating platform upon which their drilling rig stands, Craig Tester, Alex

Lagina, Laird Niven, and Steve Guptill meet at Smith's Cove with Ground Penetrating Radar experts Don Johnston and Steve Watson of Global GPR Services Inc. Tester explains that he would like the GPR experts to search the area for underground voids in the hope that they might locate the legendary Smith's Cove flood tunnel. Equipped with a Noggin 100 GPR sensor- a geophysical tool which uses radio waves to map the underground- Johnston and Watson proceed to scan Smith's Cove's upper beach, where the team believes the convergence point of the flood tunnel's supposed finger drains might be located. The pair quickly discovers a 7-metre-long anomaly which begins 5 metres below the surface and runs roughly parallel to the shoreline.

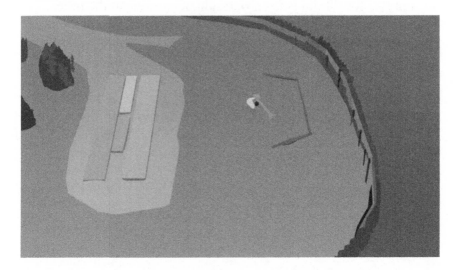

Meanwhile, Rick Lagina Dan Henskee, and Gary Drayton head to Oak Island's Lot 21 to do some metal detecting. Located at the westernmost end of Oak Island, Lot 21 is the area at which Gary and other crew members discovered the glass brooch in Season 6, Episode 1; a French grenadier's hat badge in Season 6, Episode 5; and a lead *cloisonné* in Season 6, Episode 18, the isotopic signature of which proved to be identical to that of the lead cross found at Smith's Cove. On this latest excursion, the trio discover a hefty triangular piece of iron with a large hole through the middle, which Drayton suspects might be the head of a quarry hammer. In a later interview, Rick Lagina remarks that the possibility of the artifact's being a quarry hammer evokes the headstone at the centre of Nolan's Cross, believed by some to have been shaped by man. Shortly thereafter, the three men come across what appears to be yet another quarry hammer head, this one more substantial than the first one.

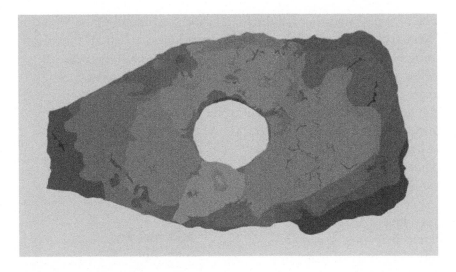

The next day, Rick and Marty Lagina meet with geoscientist Dr. Ian Spooner of Acadia University on the South Shore road and show him some of the core samples taken from beneath the swamp. Dr. Spooner observes that the sediment from the samples contains a high concentration of clay, which he states is a characteristic of marine environments. He also remarks that the samples contain less organic material than he would expect to find in an ancient wetland, and concludes that the swamp floor likely constituted sea bottom at some point in the relatively recent past. Spooner agrees to conduct a more thorough examination of the core sample material in his lab.

Later, Craig Tester, Doug Crowell, and Laird Niven take GPR experts Don Johnston and Steve Watson to the Cave-In Pit, around which they ask them conduct a GPR scan. The narrator explains that some theorists believe that the Cave-In Pit lies directly on the Smith's Cove flood tunnel, constituting an air-shaft constructed by the flood tunnel builders. The Oak Island team members hope that Johnston and Watson might be able to locate the tunnel which the Pit possibly intersects with their sensor. Sure enough, Johnston and Watson discover several anomalies in the vicinity of the Cave-In Pit, one of them 25 metres (82 feet) below the surface and the other 28 metres (91 feet) deep. Tester remarks that those depths roughly correspond with the depth at which the flood tunnel is believed to lie in the area of the Cave-In Pit.

The next day, members of the Oak Island team meet in the War Room with blacksmithing expert Carmen Legge, to whom they show some of the metal artifacts discovered on Oak Island this season. Legge identifies one artifact, the discovery of which was apparently made off-camera, as an 18th Century English ox shoe. He then identifies the triangular pieces of iron, which Drayton suspected might be quarry hammers, as crude swage blocks used for

sharpening rock drills, and opines that their presence on the island is suggestive of "some major mining or tunneling operation". He claims that such artifacts are very rare, and estimates that the ones found on the island may date as far back as the mid-15th Century.

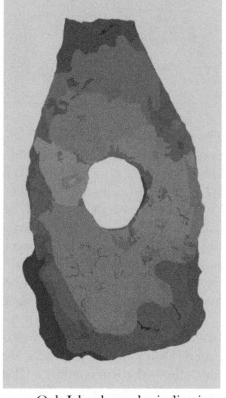

Following Legge's revelation, Marty Lagina deduces that the builders of the Money Pit and the Smith's Cove flood tunnel would not have had much use for the swage blocks, as they dug through glacial till rather than rock, and would therefore probably have done their tunneling with pickaxes rather than rock drills. He suggests that the artifacts' presence on Oak Island may be indicative of tunnel work that took place on the western side of Oak Island, as the bedrock there is composed of hard slate as opposed to the softer anhydrite limestone which characterizes the bedrock on the eastern side of the Island.

Later that day, the Oak Island crew heads to the swamp, where Choice Drilling has finished extracting a number of core samples from depths up to 50 feet. Geologist Terry Matheson, who examined the samples beforehand, informs the team that the cores are absent of wood or any other evidence which might indicate the presence of a ship, which some crew members hoped the 'ship anomaly' might designate. The cores do, however, contain more of the same dry clay found earlier, through which, Marty Lagina remarks, it would be possible to tunnel.

Later, members of the team meet in the War Room to discuss the inconclusive results of the exploration drilling operation in the swamp. In light of the discovery that the swamp is underlain by a layer of hard, dry clay, Steve Guptill theorizes that the 'ship anomaly' revealed by the seismic survey might denote an underground tunnel rather than a buried ship. Talk then turns to the many steps the team will need to make in order to acquire a digging permit which will enable them to test this theory. "First, we have to decide what our target is, and how deep we're going to go," says Marty Lagina in a later interview, "and then we [have] to figure out how and what's permissible." Rick Lagina concludes the meeting by suggesting that the team attempt, in a scientific matter, to determine, once and for all, whether or not the swamp is manmade. The team concurs with Rick's suggestion.

Analysis

Exploration Drilling in the Swamp

In this episode, the Oak Island team took core samples of the so-called "ship anomaly" in the Oak Island swamp, the presence of which was indicated by the seismic survey carried out at the end of Season 6. Although the samples did not contain any wood or other evidence indicating that a ship might lie buried beneath the swamp, as some crew members had hoped, they did contain curiously dry clay, along with fragments of natural caprock which presumably prevents the swamp water from leeching deep into the ground below.

Dr. Spooner's First Swamp Theory

In this episode, geoscientist Dr. Ian Spooner of Acadia University inspected some of the core samples taken from beneath the Oak Island swamp. Spooner argued that the samples' high concentrations of clay, coupled with their dearth of organic material, appear to indicate that the swamp is a young wetland, and that the area which it comprises lay beneath the sea sometime in the relatively recent past. This hypothesis is consistent with the theory that Oak Island is an artificial conjunction of two separate islands, the strait between which now constitutes the Oak Island swamp.

Dr. Spooner's intriguing theory appears to conflict with the handful of oak stumps which have been discovered in the swamp over the years, including the stump discovered at the Mercy Point area in Season 2, Episode 1, which was carbon dated from 1450-1640, as well as the stump which Tony Sampson discovered in Season 4, Episode 3, which appeared to be rooted to the swamp floor. Back in Season 2, Episode 4, tree expert Joe Peters analyzed one of the stumps pulled from the bottom of the swamp and determined that it could not possibly have grown to its current size while submerged in brackish water. Discounting the possibility that they were thrown into the swamp by former treasure hunters, Island residents, or the mysterious men behind the Oak Island mystery, the presence of oak stumps in the Oak Island swamp hints at the possibility that the swamp area once comprised dry ground in which oak trees were able to take root- a notion which appears to conflict with the idea that the swamp area was covered by seawater in the not-so-distant past.

[For follow-ups to Dr. Spooner's first swamp theory, see: 'Dr. Spooner's Analysis' in Season 7, Episode 3; 'Dr. Spooner's Second Analysis of the Swamp' in Season 7, Episode 9; and 'Dr. Spooner's Third Analysis of the Swamp' in Season 7, Episode 23]

Cave-In Pit Anomaly

In this episode, GPR experts Don Johnston and Steve Watson conducted a Ground Penetrating Radar scan of the Cave-In Pit with the aim of locating the flood tunnel which the Pit is believed to intersect. The pair discovered two anomalies, one of them 25 metres (82 feet) deep and the other 28 metres (91 feet) deep. Craig Tester pointed out that those depths roughly correspond with the depth at which the flood tunnel is believed to lie in that area.

[For the results of the subsequent investigation of the Cave-In Pit anomaly, see 'The Composition of the Smith's Cove Flood Tunnel' in Season 7, Episode 5]

[For Eagle Canada's independent discovery of an anomaly near the Cave-In Pit, see 'The Cave-In Pit Anomaly' in Season 7, Episode 16]

Swage Blocks

In this episode, Gary Drayton, Rick Lagina, and Dan Henskee discovered two hefty triangular pieces of iron with large holes through the middle on Oak Island's Lot 21. Although Drayton initially suspected that the artifacts might be the heads of quarry hammers, blacksmithing expert Carmen Legge later identified the items as swage blocks which would have been used for sharpening rock drills, and dated them from 1450-1750. Legge opined that presence of these objects on the island appears to be indicative of "some major mining or tunnel operation" which took place in the distant past, evoking the theory that the original Money Pit builders tunneled beneath Oak Island's bedrock.

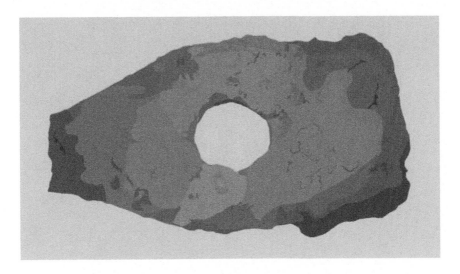

Marty Lagina expanded on Legge's theory by proposing that the rock drills which the swages sharpened would have been employed most effectively in tunneling operations on the western end of Oak Island, the bedrock of which is composed of hard slate. Unfortunately, aside from the swages, there is currently little evidence to support the notion that any such operation was ever carried out on the western part of Oak Island.

David Hanson's Theory

One facet of the theory that tunnels run beneath Oak Island is the argument put forth by the late Oak Island theorist David Hanson, which holds that 16th Century English explorer and privateer Sir Martin Frobisher discovered iron pyrite, or fool's gold, on Oak Island by chance in 1575. In a misguided effort to encourage the Queen to finance future voyages, the Englishmen sailed back to Britain with the erroneous news that they had discovered gold in the North Atlantic.

With the approval of Queen Elizabeth I, English mining engineer Thomas Bushell and a crew of Cornish miners sailed to Oak Island, where they spent two years sinking shafts and digging tunnels beneath the island, extracting iron pyrite ore form the earth. When the Britons returned to England with their worthless haul, the Queen considered the fraud so humiliating that she erased all records of the incident.

Hanson believed that a crew of Englishmen later returned to Oak Island and interred treasures of great value within Bushell's mine shafts. Specifically, Hanson believed that these treasures consisted of the original handwritten plays and sonnets of William Shakespeare- which, he argued, were actually penned by English noblemen Edward de Vere- the corpse of de Vere himself, and the lost treasure of the Plantagenet dynasty, lost by King Richard III of England during the 1485 Battle of Bosworth Field.

Season 7, Episode 3

The Eye of the Swamp

Plot Summary

The Oak Island crew meets in the War Room with geoscientist Dr. Ian Spooner, who collected some of the core samples taken from the swamp anomaly in the previous episode and brought them to his lab for further analysis. Dr. Spooner, who has since performed that analysis, informs the team that sedimentation present in the core samples appears to indicate that the swamp is relatively young-specifically three to four hundred years old. When prompted by Rick Lagina, he concedes the possibility that the swamp might be artificial. He goes on to speculate that, prior to the swamp's formation, the triangular area which comprises the swamp today may have supported terrestrial vegetation. This notion accords with

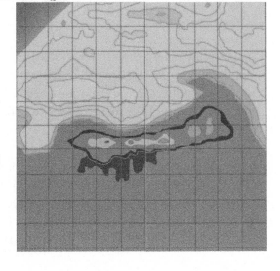

the implication of the various stumps discovered in the swamp over the years, and appears to challenge the theory that the triangular area constituted sea floor at the time of the swamp's creation. When questioned by Dave Blankenship, Spooner states that Oak Island may indeed have comprised two separate islands at some point in the distant past, as some theorists believe, but implies that these islands would have amalgamated into the larger Oak Island long before the swamp's formation.

We then learn that Dr. Spooner and his team, in a previous operation which was not featured on the show, collected additional core samples from the swamp and probed its floor with an iron rod. Using a map, Dr. Spooner points out a small oval-shaped body of water devoid of vegetation at the northernmost tip of the swamp and states that he and his team discovered a circle of stones there which appeared to skirt the feature's perimeter. The geoscientist says that the stone pattern, coupled with the area's lack of vegetation, seems unusual to him, and advises the team to investigate the anomaly.

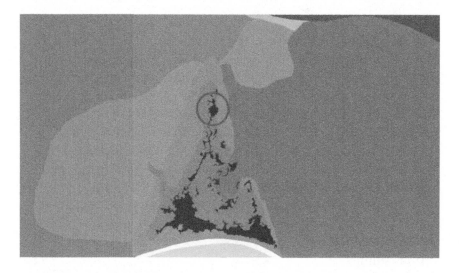

The next day, Marty Lagina, Alex Lagina, Gary Drayton, and Steve Guptill meet at the swamp, where they intend to investigate the anomaly identified by Dr. Spooner. After Drayton dons a wetsuit and a snorkel, the four men pile into a dingy and row out to the feature. When they reach the area in question, Drayton gets out of the dingy and, using a probe, quickly discovers a stone on the feature's perimeter. He then applies his pin-pointer metal detector to the stone and gets a hit indicating the presence of iron. Drayton goes on to discover several more stones nearby, all but the largest of which similarly appear to nuzzle iron. As Drayton probes and scans, Steve Guptill plots the coordinates of the rocks with a GPS receiver.

When Marty Lagina dubs the mysterious formation "the Eye of the Swamp", the narrator attempts to connect the feature with the "all-seeing eye"- a Freemasonic symbol which treasure hunters and theorists have previously associated with the triangular swamp itself; the mysterious stone triangle which once lay on Oak Island's South Shore Cove; and a marking on a rock in a water well in the nearby town of New Ross, Nova Scotia, discovered in Season 4, Episode 2.

Later, the Fellowship of the Dig congregates in the War Room, where Marty Lagina, Alex Lagina, Gary Drayton, and Steve Guptill inform the team of the discoveries they made at the Eye of the Swamp. Guptill shows the team a map depicting the rocks that they discovered in the area, one of which is highlighted in red. Guptill explains that the red-highlighted rock is the largest rock that Drayton discovered, which the metal detecting expert described as being cone-shaped and having a single flat side, similar to the boulders which comprise Nolan's Cross. This stone also happens to be the only one in the area around which Drayton failed to find any evidence of iron. The team agrees that they ought to drain the swamp and investigate the rocks.

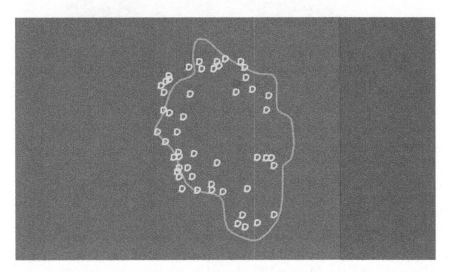

The next day, several members of the Oak Island team meet at the swamp with Shawn Wilson of Wilson Excavation Ltd. We learn that Wilson has been tasked with excavating three areas of interest in the swamp, namely the 'Ship Anomaly' indicated by the data of the seismic survey carried out at the end of the previous season; the pattern of stones which Tony Sampson discovered in the Season 7 premiere, which have collectively been dubbed the "Paved Wharf"; and the Eye of the Swamp. Wilson explains to the team that he intends to excavate the areas of interest by using 16'x16' trench cages, or dig boxes- square caissons which will isolate the areas of interest from the surrounding swamp.

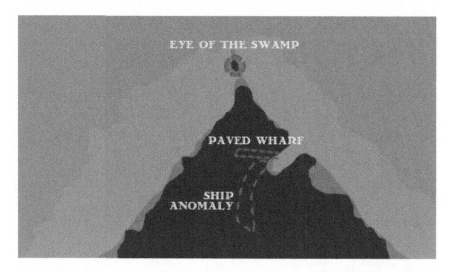

That afternoon, Alex Lagina, Peter Fornetti, and Charles Barkhouse drive to St. Mary's University in Halifax, Nova Scotia. There, they meet with Dr. Christa Brosseau, to whom they show the iron swages which Gary Drayton discovered on Oak Island's Lot 21 the previous episode. Dr. Brosseau uses a file to strip away some of the rust which coats the artifacts and extracts samples of the metal beneath. Then, with the help of research instrument technician Dr. Xiang Yang, she examines the samples under an electron microscope and finds them absent of manganese- a characteristic which, she claims, indicates that the artifacts were likely made prior to 1840. Charles Barkhouse remarks that only two companies searched for treasure on Oak Island prior to 1840- the Onslow Company and the Money Pit's three legendary discoverers. "Other than that," he says, "[the swage could only have belonged to members of] a recovery operation or a deposit operation..." Peter Fornetti then asks whether the Onslow Company or the Money Pit co-discoverers are known to have worked on Lot 21, where the

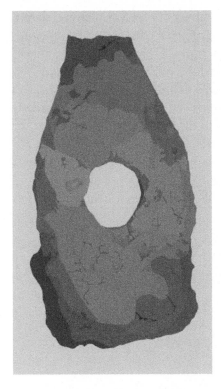

swage blocks were found. Barkhouse replies that both of these treasure hunting groups are believed to have concentrated their activities at the opposite end of the island, where the Money Pit lies, the implication being that the swages probably belonged to pre-1795 depositors or recoverers.

The next day, Rick Lagina, Doug Crowell, Terry Matheson, and Paul Troutman meet with Brennan McMahon of Choice Drilling at Smith's Cove. Matheson explains that Craig Tester drew up a plan to have Choice Drilling drill five holes on Smith's Cove's Upper Beach, in the area at which the team hopes the convergence point of the Smith's Cove box drains might be located. As the contractors begin sinking the first of the holes, Steve Guptill explains to some crew members that the flood tunnel is believed to lie somewhere between 90-120 feet below the surface, the wide depth range being attributable to the many topographical changes which the area between the Money Pit and Smith's Cove has undergone in the past 150 year. In a later interview, Rick Lagina augments the potential depth of the flood tunnel from 50-130 feet below the surface.

Brennan McMahon and Terry Matheson examine a 69.5-73.5-foot-deep core sample from the first hole and find that it contains moist but solid earth. A second three-foot-long core sample, taken at a depth of 91 feet, contains soft clay mixed with small stones. Matheson describes the material as "amorphous", or formless, and states that this is the first time such material has appeared in a core sample on Oak Island. He suggests that the material's shapeless nature might be attributable an explosion which took place in its vicinity. A third sample, taken at a depth of 99 feet, contains charred earth that smells of gunpowder, a fragment of what Terry Matheson believes to be the paper wrapping of a stick of dynamite, and a piece of twisted metal tubing inside which the suspected dynamite may have been set. Paul Troutman remarks that dynamite is known to have been used in the area by members of the Oak Island Treasure Company back in 1897, in an effort to destroy the Smith's Cove flood tunnel. The crew members agree that the material they discovered in the 99-foot-deep core sample undoubtedly constitutes evidence of the Oak Island Treasure Company's operation, and decide to search for the flood tunnel between this new site and the Money Pit area.

Analysis

Dr. Spooner's Analysis

In this episode, Dr. Ian Spooner presented his analysis of the core samples collected from beneath the Ship Anomaly in the Oak Island swamp in the previous episode. Dr. Spooner concluded that the sedimentation of the core samples appears to indicate that the swamp is only three to four hundred years old, and that the area which comprises it likely supported terrestrial vegetation immediately prior to its transformation into a wetland.

This theory conflicts with the notion that Oak Island consisted of two separate islands prior to the swamp's formation.

[See: 'Dr. Spooner's First Swamp Theory' in Season 7, Episode 1; 'Dr. Spooner's Second Analysis of the Swamp' in Season 7, Episode 9; and 'Dr. Spooner's Third Analysis of the Swamp' in Season 7, Episode 23]

The Eye of the Swamp

In this episode, we learned that Dr. Ian Spooner and his team collected core samples and probed for anomalies in the swamp in a previous operation which was not presented on the show. In a small oval pond curiously devoid of vegetation, located at the northernmost tip of the swamp, Spooner and his crew discovered a number of stones on the swamp floor which appeared to encircle the area.

Marty Lagina, Alex Lagina, Gary Drayton, and Steve Guptill investigated these rocks and found that most of them appeared to contain or lie on top of some sort of iron object, which the men were unable to locate. The only rock which appeared to be devoid of iron was the largest rock in the area. Conical, boulder-like, and bearing a flat side, this rock strongly resembles those which comprise Nolan's Cross.

The Oak Island team plans to investigate this anomaly, dubbed the "Eye of the Swamp", and its strange circle of stones by draining the swamp and having Shawn Wilson of Wilson Excavation Ltd. excavate the area in question through the use of a 16'x 16' trench cage- a caisson-like device which will isolate the area from the surrounding swamp.

Upper Beach Core Sample

In this episode, the Oak Island team sank a hole on the Upper Beach of Smith's Cove, at a location at which they hoped the convergence point of the Smith's Cove box drains might lie. At a depth of 91 feet, the drill encountered soft clay mixed with small stones. Geologist Terry Matheson described the material as "amorphous", and suggested that its formless nature might be attributable to an explosion which took place in its vicinity. At a depth of 99 feet, the drill brought up charred earth that smelled of gunpowder, a fragment of what appeared to be the paper wrapping of a stick of dynamite, and a piece of twisted metal tube- perhaps the remains of the setting for the supposed dynamite. The crew agreed that they had almost certainly uncovered evidence of the dynamiting operation carried out by the Oak Island Treasure Company back in 1897.

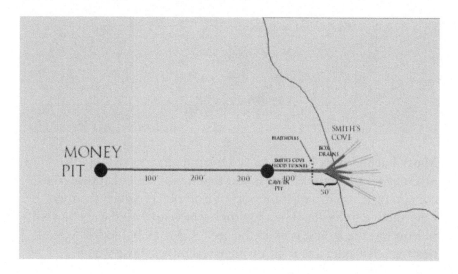

Although it is likely coincidental, the combination of clay and small stones found at a depth of 91 feet, coupled with the piece of metal tubing discovered at 99 feet, evokes a discovery made by Triton Alliance back in 1970. That summer, Dan Blankenship and David Tobias hired a contracting company called Becker Drilling to punch holes in the Money Pit area. Below the Hedden Shaft, at a depth of 160-190 feet, Becker Drilling encountered a chamber filled with blue clay in which were suspended equidistant layers of pebbles. At the bottom of this chamber was some sort of brass object which the drill chewed into.

The Oak Island Treasure Company's Dynamiting Operation

In this episode, the Fellowship of the Dig discovered charred earth, a fragment of what appeared to be the paper wrapping of a stick of dynamite, and a piece of metal tube, all of which they suspected was likely evidence of the dynamiting operation carried out by the Oak Island Treasure Company back in 1897. That spring, the Oak Island Treasure Company had attempted to destroy the Smith's Cove flood tunnel, hoping that by doing so, they would be able to excavate the Money Pit without having to contend with floodwater. They drilled five blastholes in a line running from north to south about 50 feet from the shoreline and loaded them with dynamite charges. Although the two 90-foot-deep blastholes on either end were dry, the middle one filled with seawater upon reaching the 80-foot level, apparently having hit the flood tunnel. When the charges were detonated, a massive jet of water exploded more than 100 feet into the air before subsiding. At the same time, the water in both the Money Pit and the Cave-In Pit, in the words of treasure hunter Frederick Blair, "boiled and foamed for a considerable time, and after the disturbance subsided, the oil in the dynamite showed on the water in both these pits." This development verified that the Money Pit and the Cave-In Pit were both fed by the same water source, namely seawater from Smith's Cove, which apparently travelled underground by way of the Smith's Cove flood tunnel.

Season 7, Episode 4

The Lucky Thirteen

Plot Summary

The episode begins at Smith's Cove Upper Beach. There, Paul Troutman informs us that Choice Drilling has punched a second hole ten feet northwest of the hole drilled at the end of the previous episode, in which was discovered evidence of the dynamiting operation carried out by the Oak Island Treasure Company back in 1897. In a core sample taken from a depth of 50-53 feet in this new hole, which is dubbed OITC-6, Paul Troutman and Terry Matheson discover two pieces of wood separated by two feet of moist earth. The wood pieces appear to be fragments of hand-cut beams, leading Troutman to speculate that they might constitute the

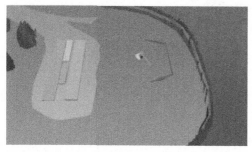 remains of some sort of underground tunnel. Matheson expands on Troutman's theory by suggesting that the undisturbed quality of the earth above the wood, coupled with the fact that there are no documented tunnels in the area, may indicate that the wood is part of the Smith's Cove flood tunnel. The treasure hunters call over Rick Lagina and inform him of the development.

The Fellowship of the Dig then meets in the War Room, where Paul Troutman presents the recently discovered wood pieces to his fellow treasure hunters. Gary Drayton remarks that the wood bears some resemblance to that which comprises the slipway unearthed at Smith's Cove the previous season. Steve Guptill then shows the crew a diagram depicting where OITC-6 lies in relation to other landmarks on Oak Island. Specifically, a line drawn from the drillhole to the centre of the U-shaped  structure intersects one of the walls discovered at Smith's Cove, which has been entitled "Wall 2"; and another wall closer to the U-shaped structure, which Billy Gerhardt discovered the previous season. When the line is extended westward, it runs through the Money Pit area. The team members conclude their meeting by agreeing to carbon date the wood discovered in OITC-6.

Later, Alex Lagina, Peter Fornetti, Charles Barkhouse, and Terry Matheson meet at Smith's Cove's Upper Beach, where Choice Drilling is busy sinking another hole. A core sample taken from 51-54 feet yields nothing but undisturbed till.

While the drilling operation continues at Smith's Cove, Rick Lagina and Craig Tester meet with Tom Nolan, son of the late Oak Island treasure hunter Fred Nolan (who now owns his father's old properties on Oak Island), in the War Room. There, they explain that they have identified three locations they would like to excavate in the Oak Island swamp, namely the Ship Anomaly, the Paved Wharf, and the so-called 'Eye of the Swamp'. As talk turns to the swamp, Nolan informs his two companions that the swamp bottom has risen substantially over the past thirty years due to an accumulation of organic material. "What you're walking on today isn't what we were walking on back then," he says, referring to the surveying operation his father conducted on the island in the 1960s, before recommending that the crew remove the top layer of the swamp before proceeding with any of their planned excavations.

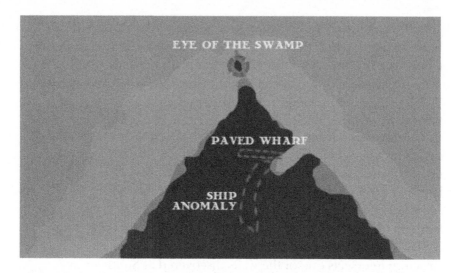

Later, Rick and Marty Lagina and Steve Guptill meet with Jack Nichols of Dam-it-Dams, the contractor who constructed a successful inflatable cofferdam around Smith's Cove back in Season 4, Episode 12. They inform Nichols that they would like him to dam off a section of the swamp so that they might be able excavate the three aforementioned areas of interest without having to contend with water. After touring the area in question, Nichols declares the task feasible and accepts the job.

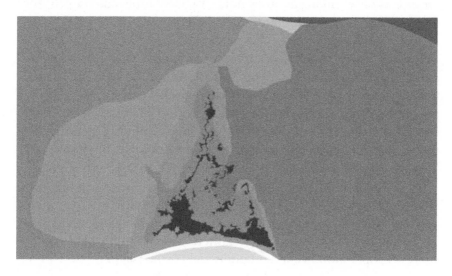

Meanwhile, Charles Barkhouse and Gary Drayton conduct a metal detecting operation on Oak Island's Lot 21, where Drayton discovered the iron swage blocks in Season 7, Episode 2. The pair quickly discover a British copper halfpenny bearing the image of a young Queen Victoria- a feature indicating that the coin was

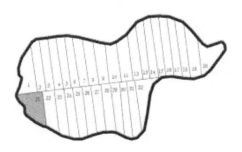

probably struck in the 1840s or late 1830s. Shortly thereafter, west of the old McGinnis family cabin and not far from the shore, they unearth a decorative brooch bearing a fern-like design. The two men call up Rick Lagina and Doug Crowell to inform them of the find. When prompted by Rick, Drayton tentatively dates the artifact from 1500-1700. Crowell then ventures the opinion that the brooch might actually be a military cap badge similar to that which was found on the same Lot back in Season 6, Episode 5, prompting the narrator to remind us of the theory that the Money Pit was constructed by members of the Duc d'Anville Expedition of 1746.

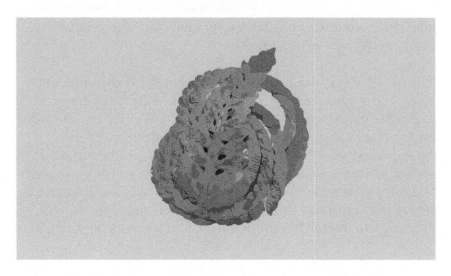

Later, Alex Lagina and Laird Niven drive to Acadia University in Wolfville, Nova Scotia, where they present the brooch-like object recently discovered on Lot 21 to conservator Kelly Bourassa.

Bourassa proceeds to clean the object with a wooden skewer, a glass fibre brush, and a toothbrush, revealing a unique design consisting of twin coils of rope surmounted by a fern-like leaf. Bourassa suggests that the object, which indeed appears to be a brooch, has a Maritime flavour to it, but tells the two men that, despite the thorough cleaning he administered, he is still unsure of its age or maker. He also tells Alex and Laird that he has never seen another artifact like it.

Following Alex and Laird's return, the Fellowship of the Dig congregates at the Mug & Anchor Pub in Mahone Bay, where Alex presents the Oak Island team with the leaf brooch. Marty Lagina observes that the leaf on the brooch appears to have thirteen veins, evoking a tree-like symbol on the Evans stone and the tree on the Appeal to Heaven flag– symbols also associated with the number 13, which were introduced in the Season 6 finale. On Laird Niven's suggestion, the crew agrees that they  ought to continue to scour Lot 21, on which the brooch was found, in an archaeological manner.

The next day, the Oak Island team meets in the War Room, where Craig Tester presents the results of the carbon dating of the wood fragments discovered in Drillhole OITC-6. Tester tells the crew that the wood appears to date from 1735-1784- a date range which corresponds perfectly with the dendrochronological dating of the various structures found beneath Smith's Cove throughout Season 6. All of the crew members, including an especially enthusiastic Jack Begley, agree that the carbon dating is very encouraging, and that they ought to thoroughly investigate the area surrounding OITC-6.

Season 7, Episode 5

Tunnel Visions

Plot Summary

This episode begins just north of the Cave-In Pit, at one of the anomalies discovered during the ground penetrating radar scan conducted in Season 7, Episode 2. We learn through Terry Matheson's conversation with Doug Crowell that Choice Drilling is in the process of sinking a hole, dubbed "Cave-In Pit 2", in this location. While core samples are retrieved from the hole, the narrator reminds us that the Oak Island Treasure Company, back in 1897, discovered the junction of the Smith's Cove flood tunnel and the Money Pit at a depth of 111 feet.

Matheson, Crowell, Jack Begley, and Paul Troutman examine a core sample from Cave-In Pit 2, taken from a depth of 99-109 feet. The sample contains four feet of sand which stands out from the surrounding till, which the treasure hunters- including an especially enthusiastic Doug Crowell- speculate might be remnants of the Smith's Cove flood tunnel. The four men call over Rick and Marty Lagina, Craig Tester, and Dave Blankenship and inform them of the potential discovery. Rick observes that the core sample contains no wood, unlike the sample discovered on Smith's Cove's Upper Beach in the previous episode. Marty responds by remarking that, if he had been tasked with constructing a flood tunnel that was to last a thousand years, he might have packed it with sand rather than support it with cribbing. The treasure hunters agree to sink another hole west of Cave-In Pit 2, on a line connecting the U-shaped

structure with the Money Pit area, in order to determine whether or not the sand continues in that direction.

Later, Gary Drayton, Jack Begley, and Peter Fornetti go metal detecting on Oak Island's Lot 27, first owned by Daniel McGinnis. After passing over some unknown metallic object which Drayton dismisses as "modern junk", the metal detecting expert discovers a rusted iron chisel. When prompted by Jack Begley, Drayton speculates that the object might be as old as the swage blocks which he discovered on Lot 21 in Season 7, Episode 2, and that it might have been used for tunneling through rock.

That afternoon, the Oak Island crew returns to the Cave-In Pit area, where a hole 5 feet west of the so-called "Cave-In Pit 2" is being drilled. A core sample taken from a depth of 99-109 feet contains some sand mixed with clay, but nothing resembling the four feet of pure sand found in "Cave-In Pit 2". In light of this setback, the crew decides to abandon the drilling operation and later conduct a seismic scan in the area.

The next day, members of the Oak Island team meet with Alex Gauthier and Scott Graychick of Eagle Canada. During their subsequent conversation, we learn that Eagle Canada has been tasked with conducting a massive seismic survey of the entire eastern end of Oak Island.

That afternoon, Craig Tester, Alex Lagina, and Laird Niven meet with GPR experts Steve Watson and Don Johnston at the foundations of the old McGinnis family cabin. We learn that the Oak Island team has decided to conduct an archaeological investigation of the foundations, and that the first step in this process is to perform a Ground Penetrating Radar scan of the area. "We're going to have you guys come in and do your work," Niven explains to the GPR experts, "and identify anomalies that could be significant, and based on that data, we're going to write a new permit application for some subsurface testing- some excavation."

Later, the Fellowship of the Dig meets in the War Room with naval historian Chipp Reid, who has come to share his theory regarding the nature of the structures discovered at Smith's Cove. Reid shows the boys a diagram depicting a 'water battery', which he describes as "an artillery position that's constructed as close to the shoreline as possible" (although it is not mentioned in this episode, this diagram is from a map of Cartagena, Colombia, drawn by English engineer John Thomas the Elder in 1741). He claims that the particular water battery depicted in the diagram was common from roughly 1600-1850. He then points out structures on the diagram which closely resemble the U-shaped structure, the L-shaped structure, and the slipway, respectively, implying that the mysterious workings at Smith's Cove constitute the remains of a water battery. Reid then suggests that, if the structures discovered at Smith's Cove indeed comprise a water battery, and if the structures indeed date to the mid-18th Century (as the dendrochronological dating carried out in Season 6, Episode 21 indicate), then the battery was probably constructed by members of the French military. The narrator proceeds to lecture us on the history of the Fortress of Louisbourg, an enormous French fortress constructed on Cape Breton Island from 1713-1740. Reid concludes his presentation by theorizing that the French military used Oak Island as a water battery in the early 1700s, and a company of French soldiers hid the treasury of Louisbourg on the island prior to the First Siege of Louisbourg in 1745.

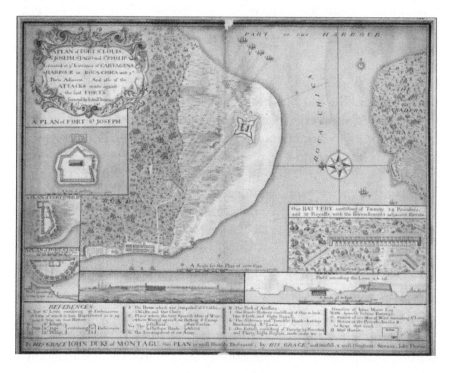

Following Reid's presentation, Craig Tester, Alex Lagina, and Laird Niven meet at the foundations of the McGinnis family cabin. There, Steve Watson and Don Johnston, who have already carried out their GPR scan of the foundations and surrounding area, point out some of the anomalies they came across. The strongest of these is a four-foot-wide anomaly located four feet below the surface. The treasure hunters agree that they ought to excavate these anomalies, for which they will need to acquire a permit from the provincial government.

Later, the Lagina brothers and Doug Crowell drive to Oak Island's
Southern Shore. During the drive, Crowell explains that, according
to Dan Henskee, Triton Alliance went through the papers of former
Oak Island treasure hunter Mel Chappell and learned an interesting
piece of Oak Island history. Back in 1863, the Oak Island
Association dug a 120-foot deep shaft, called 'Shaft 9', about 100
feet southeast of the Money Pit. In order to prevent this tunnel from
flooding, the Association men constructed a sluiceway which
directed any water which might collect in the tunnel towards the
South Shore Cove. That accomplished, the Association built
another 108-foot-deep tunnel from Shaft 9 towards the Money Pit.
Unfortunately, the Oak Island Association went under before the
workers were able to complete this tunnel. Doug Crowell hopes
that, if the Fellowship of the Dig manages to locate the sluiceway
beneath the South Shore Cove, they may be able to trace it back to
Shaft 9 and the tunnel connected to it, which extends in the
direction of the Money Pit.

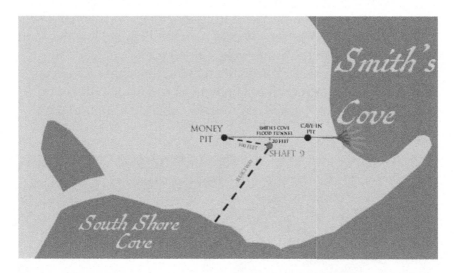

Doug Crowell directs the Lagina brothers to the site at which the
mouth of the sluiceway is believed to lie, whereupon Marty Lagina
begins excavating the area with a backhoe. At first, Marty unearths
nothing besides a rusted length of pipe. When he reaches a depth of
about ten feet, water begins flooding into the hole. The younger
Lagina brother proceeds to dig in the direction of the water source
and discovers a wooden tunnel which appears to be the mouth of

the sluiceway. The treasure hunters watch with pleasure and surprise as water gushes from the opening, marveling that the sluiceway still works after 156 years. They agree that they ought to follow the sluiceway to Shaft 9, and hopefully to the Money Pit beyond.

Analysis

The Composition of the Smith's Cove Flood Tunnel

In this episode, the Oak Island team drilled into one of the anomalies near the Cave-In Pit discovered during a GPR scan carried out in Season 7, Episode 2. Although nothing of interest appeared at the depth of interested indicated by the GPR scan (either 82 feet or 91 feet, depending on which anomaly was investigated), a core sample taken from 99-109 feet contained four feet of pure sand. Some members of the crew believed that this sand might be remains of the Smith's Cove flood tunnel. Indeed, Marty Lagina, who is an engineer by trade, remarked that if he had been tasked with constructing a flood tunnel that was to last a thousand years, he might have packed it with sand rather than support it with cribbing.

S7E5: Tunnel Visions

The notion that the Smith's Cove flood tunnel might have been packed with sand is a new idea that has not previously been suggested on the show. This notion appears to conflict with the generally accepted purpose of the coconut-eelgrass filter discovered at Smith's Cove by the Truro Company in 1850, namely that the filter was designed to prevent the Smith's Cove flood tunnel from becoming clogged with sand and debris. It also runs contrary to the idea that the tunnel is supported by wooden cribbing, as suggested by members of the Oak Island team following the discovery of hand-cut beams in OITC-6 the previous episode. Perhaps most importantly, however, it conflicts with a discovery made by the Oak Island Treasure Company, which was mentioned in this episode. In the spring of 1897, the men of the Oak Island Treasure Company cleared out the Money Pit to a depth of 111 feet. There, they got a good look at the entrance of the Smith's Cove flood tunnel before floodwater overcame their pumps. According to the workers, the flood tunnel was 4 feet high, 2.5 feet wide, and constructed from rock.

Whatever the case, a second hole sunk five feet west of the sand anomaly, on a line connecting the U-shaped structure with the Money Pit area, yielded nothing of interest, prompting the crew to abandon their drilling operation.

Upcoming Seismic Survey of the Eastern Drumlin

In this episode, we learned that the seismic exploration company Eagle Canada has been tasked with conducting an enormous seismic scan of the entire eastern end of Oak Island. This operation will be the third seismic scan conducted on Oak Island. Throughout Season 6, Eagle Canada carried out seismic scans in the Money Pit area, the Swamp, and a place northwest of the swamp dubbed the 'Mega Bin' area. Although these scans revealed several tantalizing anomalies, further investigation of these anomalies failed to yield anything of interest.

[For the results of this seismic survey, see 'The Cave-In Pit Anomaly' in Season 7, Episode 16; and 'The Teardrop' in Season 7, Episode 21]

Chipp Reid's Theory

In this episode, naval historian Chipp Reid presented his own theory regarding the nature of the mysterious workings discovered at Smith's Cove the previous season. Using a map of Cartagena, Colombia, drawn by English engineer John Thomas the Elder in 1741, he demonstrated that some of the structures discovered at Smith's Cove- including the U-Shaped structure, the L-shaped structure, and the slipway- bear remarkable resemblance to components of a 'water battery', or a beachside artillery station. He went on to suggest that the battery was constructed by members of the French military, who had a major presence in Nova Scotia throughout much of the 17th and 18th Centuries. He also suggested that the battery was constructed in the early 1700s, and expressed partiality towards the theory that the Oak Island treasure consists of the treasury of the Fortress of Louisbourg, buried by members of the French military prior to the First Siege of Louisbourg in 1745.

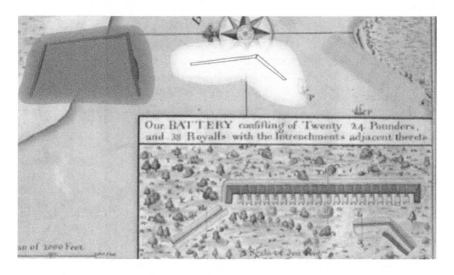

One major problem with Reid's theory, of which the naval historian is doubtless aware, is the dendrochronological dating of the various Smith's Cove structures carried out in Season 6, Episode 21. Specifically, wood from the slipway was dated to 1771, and wood from the U-shaped structure was dated to 1769. If the dendrochronological dating is accurate, then it is unlikely that the French had a hand in the structures' construction. The French lost peninsular Nova Scotia to the British during Queen Anne's War (1702-1713), the North American theatre of the War of Spanish Succession, only retaining the large island that lies north of the peninsula, known today as Cape Breton Island. Although the French made several attempts to retake peninsular Nova Scotia, including the disastrous Duc d'Anville Expedition of 1746, they never succeeded in their endeavors. The French lost their Nova Scotian holdings to the British for good in 1758, following the second Siege of Louisbourg. By 1769, when the trees of which the U-shaped structure is comprised were felled, all of Nova Scotia was firmly in British hands.

[For evidence supporting Reid's theory, see 'Dendrochronological Dating of the Wharf' in Season 7, Episode 12']

Shaft 9 and the Sluiceway

Near the end of this episode, we learn about a lost Oak Island landmark discovered years prior by Dan Henskee and members of Triton Alliance, who made the discovery while looking through the papers of former Oak Island treasure hunter Mel Chappell. Back in 1863, the Oak Island Association dug a 120-foot deep shaft, called 'Shaft 9', about 100 feet southeast of the Money Pit and 20 feet south of the Smith's Cove flood tunnel. In order to prevent this tunnel from flooding, the Association men constructed a sluiceway which directed any water which might collect in the tunnel towards the South Shore Cove (it must be mentioned that, in his 1958 book *The Oak Island Mystery*, Oak Island lawyer R.V. Harris stated that this tunnel connecting Shaft 9 with the South Shore Cove was intended to intercept the supposed South Shore Cove flood tunnel). That accomplished, the Association built another 108-foot-deep tunnel from Shaft 9 towards the Money Pit. Although the narrator informed us in this episode that the workers were unable to complete this tunnel, R.V. Harris, in his book, stated that this tunnel "entered the [Money] Pit at a point 100 feet down and there they found the hard bottom of the Pit on the west side."

Whatever the case, Doug Crowell, in this episode, directed Rick and Marty Lagina to a place on the South Shore Cove where the mouth of the Shaft 9 sluiceway was believed to be located. Marty Lagina excavated this area with a backhoe and unearthed a wooden tunnel from which water gushed forth. The crewmembers then agreed that they ought to follow this tunnel to Shaft 9, and to the Money Pit beyond.

[For the discovery of Shaft 9, see the end of Season 5, Episode 6]

[For the subsequent search for Shaft 2, see 'Shaft 2' in Season 7, Episode 7; and the end of the Plot Summary of Episode 8]

Season 7, Episode 6

Closing In

Plot Summary

Rick Lagina, Dan Henskee, and other members of the Oak Island team head to the South Shore Cove, where the terminus of an old searcher tunnel (called the Shaft 9 sluiceway) was discovered at the end of the previous episode. Doug Crowell, Billy Gerhardt, and contractor Scott Barlow, using shovels and a backhoe, uncover enough of the structure to determine the sluiceway's orientation. The crew members then decide to dig a hole 25 feet along the supposed line of the sluiceway in order to verify that they have correctly estimated the structure's subterranean route.

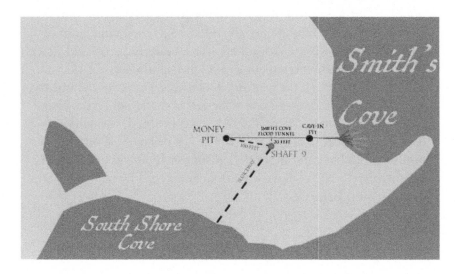

Later, Rick and Marty Lagina, Craig Tester, and Steve Guptill head
to the Cave-In Pit, where they meet with Alex Gauthier and other
members of Eagle Canada. We learn that the seismic exploration
company has laid crisscrossing lines of geophones and dynamite
charges across Smith's Cove and the Cave-In Pit area, and will be
detonating around 1,000 (out of a total of 18,000) charges in the
Cave-In Pit area that evening. The seismic crew proceeds with the
operation as the sun sets.

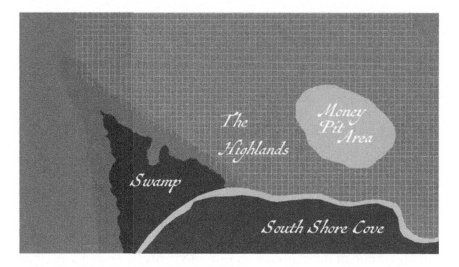

The next morning, the Eagle Canada crew begins laying out
geophones in the section of island between the swamp and the
Money Pit area, which the narrator refers to as the "Highlands".
While the jughounds go about their work, Gary Drayton and Peter
Fornetti do some metal detecting on Oak Island's Lot 32, not far
from the swamp. First, the pair uncovers what Drayton identifies as
an 18th Century decking spike at the edge of the beach. After that,
the treasure hunters unearth a curved, hand-forged, wrought-iron
rod which Drayton likens to the crib spikes discovered on Oak
Island's Lot 26 back in Season 6, Episode 3. The treasure hunters
agree that they ought to have the artifact analyzed by blacksmithing
expert Carmen Legge.

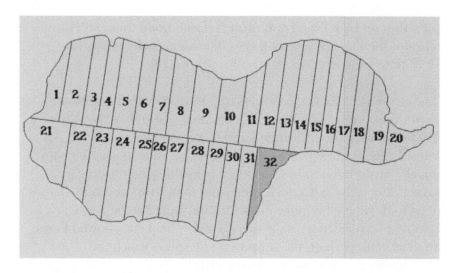

Meanwhile, Billy Gerhardt, Scott Barlow, and other members of the Oak Island team dig a hole about 25 feet uphill from the terminus of the Shaft 9 sluiceway in the hopes of intersecting the searcher tunnel. Gerhardt digs the hole as deep as his backhoe will allow and finally uncovers the very top of the sluiceway.

Later, various members of the Oak Island team meet in the War Room with Canadian journalist and writer D'Arcy O'Connor, author of the excellent book *The Secret Treasure of Oak Island: The Amazing Story of a Centuries-Old Treasure Hunt*, and his daughter, Miranda. O'Connor presents his theory that the Oak Island treasure constitutes the contents of a Spanish treasure galleon bound for Spain, which foundered off the island's coast during a storm. When prompted by Marty Lagina, the writer states that, throughout the course of his research, he read about approximately 200 Spanish treasure galleons which disappeared on the route from Havana, Cuba, to Europe. "They carried large crews," O'Connor continues, "as well as engineers who'd been opening up the new silver mines in Bolivia and other places. So they had intelligent people aboard, and so I came up with a theory that maybe one of these ships got caught in a storm as they were following the Gulf Stream and was driven all the way north to a little island in Nova Scotia- maybe Oak Island." Rather than attempt to sail their precious cargo through waters patrolled by the French and English- their colonial rivals- the Spaniards decided to bury the contents of their ship on Oak Island and protect it with flood tunnels. The narrator then recites several pieces of evidence which bolsters O'Connor's theory.

The next day, Alex Lagina and Gary Drayton drive to the Ross Farm Museum in New Ross, Nova Scotia, where they show blacksmithing expert Carmen Legge some of their recent Lot 32 finds. Legge verifies that the decking spike is indeed what Drayton initially suspected it to be. Alex then concludes the meeting by saying, "So, we've got a deck spike, and then a mystery item that we need to do a little bit more work on," implying that he and Gary, in a scene which failed to make this episode's final cut, showed Legge another item- perhaps the supposed crib spike- which the blacksmithing expert was unable to identify (perhaps this 'mystery item' is the tool, supposed by Gary Drayton to be the head of a Spanish weapon, discovered on Lot 11, alluded to in 'Moment 24' of the special episode 'The Top 25 Moments You Never Saw').

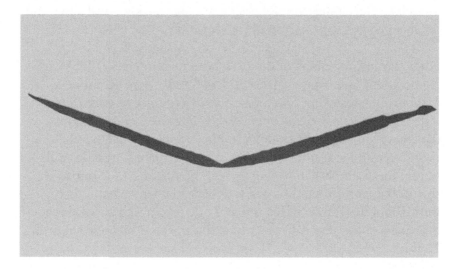

Later, Gary Drayton meets with Charles Barkhouse, Billy Gerhardt, and Scott Barlow at the Money Pit area, at a location at which the treasure hunters believe Shaft 9 once lay. Gerhardt begins excavating the area with a backhoe, and Drayton proceeds to sift through the spoils he removes with a metal detector. About six feet below the surface, Gerhardt discovers cribbing from what must be Shaft 9. That accomplished, the contractor- assisted by shovel-wielding Rick

Lagina and Scott Barlow, who have since joined the operation-proceeds to uncover all four corners of the 6'x12' shaft. Shortly thereafter, the team discovers the beginning of the sluiceway connecting Shaft 9 with the South Shore cove, whereupon water seeps in to fill the hole they dug. The treasure hunters, all of whom appear visibly pleased with their discovery, agree that they ought to have Steve Guptill plot the coordinates of Shaft 9 so that they might be able to estimate the location of the original Money Pit.

Later, Rick Lagina, Jack Begley, and Doug Crowell meet with Alex Gauthier of Eagle Canada, whose team has completed the massive seismic scan of the eastern half of Oak Island. The narrator informs us that it will take several weeks for the data from the seismic survey to be analyzed and prepared.

Season 7, Episode 7

Things That Go Bump-Out

———➤—◆—————

Plot Summary

The Fellowship of the Dig meets at Smith's Cove with Mike Jardine of Irving Equipment Ltd., who has come to construct the "bump-out", or extension, to the Smith's Cove cofferdam first discussed in the Season 7 premiere. Jardine and members of his crew begin their operation by removing sections of the metal cofferdam with a crane, allowing seawater to flow back into Smith's Cove.

While the work continues at Smith's Cove, Rick Lagina meets with Doug Crowell and Steve Guptill in the Oak Island Research Centre. Guptill shows the treasure hunters a diagram of his own making which shows the location of the searcher Shaft 9 (discovered the previous episode) in relation to other shafts and landmarks on the Island. As Shaft 9 was said to lie 100 feet southwest of the Money Pit area, the diagram includes a semi-circle with a radius of 100 feet extending northeast of Shaft 9, its circumference representing all the possible locations at which the original Money Pit might have lain.

Doug Crowell then shows Rick a photo taken in 1931, when Chappells Ltd. was hunting for treasure on the Island. In the photo, a depression in the earth is clearly visible at what now appears to be the location of Shaft 9. Crowell points out another depression in the earth, and suggests that it might mark the location of Shaft 2, built by the Onslow Company in 1804. Crowell reminds Rick that Shaft 2 was said to have been built 14 feet southeast of the Money Pit. If

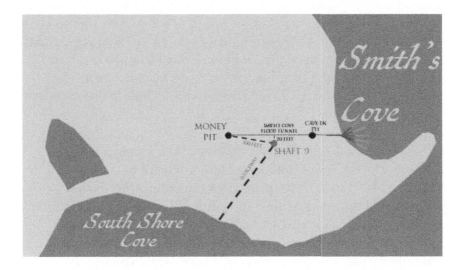

they manage to ascertain the location of Shaft 2, then they will be able to determine the exact location of the original Money Pit; the Money Pit would lie at the northwestern intersection of circles drawn around Shaft 9 and Shaft 2, with radii of 100 and 14 feet, respectively. As Steve Guptill succinctly summarizes, "if we can find [Shaft] 2, we have an X-marks-the-spot." Doug suggests that they attempt to locate Shaft 2 through exploration drilling, and Rick concurs.

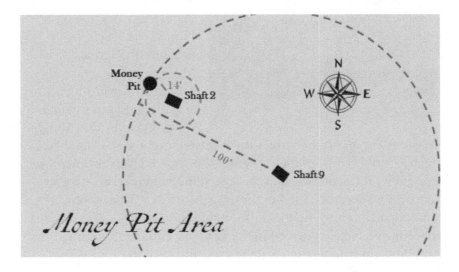

That afternoon, various members of the Oak Island team meet at the Money Pit area, where the search for Shaft 2 is about to commence. Using old aerial photographs of the Money Pit site in conjunction with the GPS coordinates of the newly-discovered Shaft 9, the team has estimated the location of Shaft 2, and has tasked Choice Drilling with retrieving core samples from the area. The Fellowship stands by as Choice Drilling sinks a hole at the prescribed location.

While the drilling operation is underway, Rick Lagina, Peter Fornetti, Doug Crowell, and Billy Gerhardt drive to the Dartmouth Heritage Museum (which the narrator refers to as the "Helen Creighton Heritage Museum") in Dartmouth, Nova Scotia. During the drive, Rick explains that a man named Kevin Rideout approached him at Dan Blankenship's funeral and told him an interesting story. More than forty years ago, while visiting the museum, Rideout was made aware of a rock in the museum's yard which a tour guide claimed was the Money Pit's legendary 90-foot stone. In a later interview, Rick Lagina states his belief that the supposed 90-foot stone found beneath the old Halifax bookbindery in Season 6, Episode 7 was an unfinished replica of the original stone, and expresses his hope that the real 90-foot stone is the artifact which Rideout described.

The treasure hunters arrive at the so-called "Evergreen House", in which the Dartmouth Heritage Museum is housed, and meet with Kevin Rideout and the museum's curator, Terry Eyland. After Rideout recounts the experience which Rick related in the car, Eyland takes the treasure hunters to the museum's backyard. Using his memory as a guide, Rideout estimates that the stone he was showed forty years prior was embedded in the grass in an area overtop of which a rhododendron bush now stands. Eyland then informs the crew that the stone was likely interred in the yard prior to the museum's founding, prompting the narrator to explain that the Evergreen House was purchased by Nova Scotian folklorist Dr. Helen Creighton in 1919. The narrator points out that 1919 is the same year in which the bookbindery of Helen's distant relative, A.O. Creighton, at which the 90-foot stone was last seen, went out of business. In a later interview, Rick Lagina infers that the Creighton family may have transported the 90-foot stone from the Halifax bookbindery to the Dartmouth estate in 1919 when A.O.'s establishment closed.

Without further ado, the treasure hunters walk over to the rhododendron bush in the yard of the Evergreen House, under which Kevin Rideout suspects the stone might be located. Rick Lagina and Peter Fornetti crawl beneath the bush and make an unsuccessful preliminary search for the stone. The treasure hunters suggest that they ought to apply for a permit to excavate the area in an archaeological manner, and Terry Eyland gives them his blessing to do so.

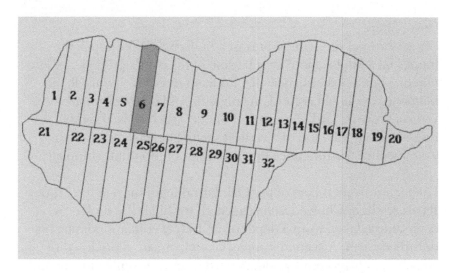

Later, Gary Drayton and Jack Begley do some metal detecting on Oak Island's Lot 6, on the northwestern side of the island, where Drayton discovered an iron chain and an old coin back in Season 4, Episode 6. A shovel-wielding Begley explains that he has a particular interest in Lot 6, attributable in part to the relatively small amount of metal detecting to which the area has been subjected. The treasure hunters head to the beach, where Drayton discovers a modern nail. Shortly thereafter, the metal detecting expert comes across two old square-headed iron pins lying side by side, which Drayton suggests might be the remains of an 18th Century shipwreck. The treasure hunters then find another larger pin closer to the water, which Drayton calls a "crib spike". In a later interview, Drayton outlines his belief that the iron objects he discovered on the shores of Lot 6 are evidence that the beach "was a place where boats came into, and there was activity in the area. Whether this was a place where ships were repaired or a place where treasure was unloaded, we've got the finds to back those theories up now."

The next day, Rick and Marty Lagina, Craig Tester, and Dave Blankenship meet with Mike Jardine at Smith's Cove, where construction of the bump-out is well underway. "We got all the frames in, all in location" says Jardine of his crew's progress, before pointing out a new structure that his team discovered outside the boundary of the old cofferdam consisting of both horizontal and vertical timbers. Jardine remarks that the structure bears some resemblance to the top of a vertical shaft. The team agrees to examine the structure once the cofferdam bump-out is complete.

Later, various members of the Oak Island team meet at the Money Pit area, where Choice Drilling's search for Shaft 2 is underway. A core sample taken from a depth of 12-15 feet contains nothing but disturbed earth. A second sample, taken from an undisclosed depth, contains a few pieces of wood. A third sample, taken from a depth of about 30 feet, contains significant quantities of wood- perhaps cribbing from Shaft 2. The crew members agree that they ought to search for the other walls of the suspected shaft in order to determine the structure's orientation.

The next day, Marty Lagina, Alex Lagina, Charles Barkhouse, and Gary Drayton head to Smith's Cove, where the cofferdam's bump-out has been completed. Mike Jardine takes the treasure hunters to the new wooden structure that he and his crew discovered, the most prominent part of which is a vertical timber sticking out of the ground. Although it is not mentioned in this episode, this vertical timber strongly evokes an object which Rick Lagina spied at Smith's Cove during low tide back in Season 1, Episode 1, which he likened to "an elephant tusk coming out of the water". In that episode, both Dan Henskee and Charles Barkhouse declared that they had never noticed the tusk-like object before.

In the next scene, Rick Lagina, Craig Tester, archaeologist Laird Niven, and heavy equipment operator Billy Gerhardt conduct their own inspection of the new structure discovered at Smith's Cove. Niven gives the crew the green light to excavate the sides of the structure, which Gerhardt proceeds to do with his backhoe. Gerhardt removes a load of material immediately adjacent to the structure, exposing a wall of horizontal logs covered by sheets of what appears to be 19th or 20th Century tar paper. Immediately beside the wall is a pile of rocks, which some of the treasure hunter suspect might be the remains of the legendary finger drains believed to feed the Smith's Cove flood tunnel. This supposition is bolstered by the large

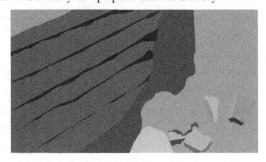

volume of water which quickly rushes in to fill the hole. The treasure hunters agree that they ought to uncover more of the structure so that they might better ascertain its nature.

Analysis

Shaft 2

In the previous episode, the boys discovered Shaft 9- an old searcher shaft which was connected with the original Money Pit by a 100-foot-long tunnel. Rather than attempt to locate this tunnel via exploration drilling, the crew decides in this episode to take a different course of action prescribed by Doug Crowell. In an aerial photograph of the Money Pit area taken in 1931 by a former treasure-hunting syndicate called Chappells Ltd., Crowell noticed two depressions in the earth. One of these appears to be in the same location as the recently-discovered Shaft 9. Crowell theorized that the other depression might be the backfilled remains of Shaft 2, a searcher shaft constructed by the Onslow Company in 1804 fourteen feet southeast of the Money Pit. Crowell observed that, if the crew manages to ascertain the location of Shaft 2, then they will be able to determine the exact location of the original Money Pit; the Money Pit would lie at the northwestern intersection of circles drawn around shaft 9 and Shaft 2, with radii of 100 and 14 feet, respectively.

Using Chappell Ltd.'s aerial photograph of the Money Pit site in conjunction with the GPS coordinates of the newly-discovered Shaft 9, the team estimated the location of Shaft 2 and tasked Choice Drilling with retrieving core samples from the area. A core sample taken from a depth of 12-15 feet contained nothing but disturbed earth. A second sample, taken from an undisclosed depth, contained a few pieces of wood. A third sample, taken from a depth of about 30 feet, contained significant quantities of wood- perhaps cribbing from Shaft 2. The crew members agreed that they ought to search for the other walls of the suspected shaft in order to

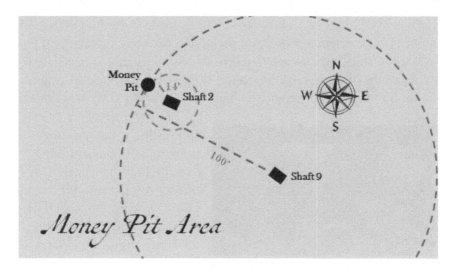

determine the structure's orientation, which will, in turn, enable to them to ascertain the precise location of the original Money Pit.

[To follow the progress of the search for Shaft 2, see the end of the Plot Summary of Season 7, Episode 8]

The Stone at the Dartmouth Heritage Museum

In the middle of this episode, Rick Lagina, Peter Fornetti, Doug Crowell, and Billy Gerhardt drove to the Dartmouth Heritage Museum in Dartmouth, Nova Scotia. There, they met with Terry Eyland, the museum's curator, and a man named Kevin Rideout, whom Rick had met previously at the funeral of Dan Blankenship. During their first meeting, Rideout told Rick that, more than forty years prior, while visiting the Dartmouth Heritage Museum, a tour guide pointed out a rock embedded in the grass in the museum's backyard and told him that it was the Money Pit's legendary 90-foot stone.

In an interview showcased in this episode, Rick Lagina stated his belief that the supposed 90-foot stone found beneath the old

Halifax bookbindery back in Season 6, Episode 7 was an unfinished replica of the original stone, and expressed his hope that the real 90-foot stone is the artifact which Kevin Rideout claimed to have been made aware of during his visit to the Dartmouth Heritage Museum more than forty years ago.

Interestingly, the narrator informs us in this episode that the building which now houses the Dartmouth Heritage Museum, called the Evergreen House, was once the residence of Dr. Mary Helen Creighton, a celebrated Nova Scotian folklorist and a distant relative of A.O. Creighton, owner of the old Halifax bookbindery. Helen Creighton purchased the Evergreen House in 1919, the same year in which the Halifax bookbindery went out of business. Rick Lagina, in this episode, infers that the Creighton family may have transported the 90-foot stone from the Halifax bookbindery to the Dartmouth estate in 1919. It is interesting to note that, in her 1957 book *Bluenose Ghosts*, a collection of Nova Scotian ghost stories, Creighton includes a number of tales set on Oak Island yet fails to mention the 90-foot stone.

In this episode, Terry Eyland takes Kevin Rideout and the visiting treasure hunters to the museum's backyard. Using his memory as a guide, Rideout estimates that the stone he was showed forty years prior was embedded in the grass in an area overtop of which a beautiful rhododendron bush now stands. After an unsuccessful preliminary search for the stone beneath the bush, the treasure hunters suggest that they ought to apply for a permit to excavate the area in an archaeological manner, and Terry Eyland gives them his blessing to do so.

[See 'Follow-Up on the Stone at the Dartmouth Heritage Museum' in Season 7, Episode 13]

The New Structure at Smith's Cove

Throughout this episode, Mike Jardine and the men of Irving Equipment Ltd. constructed the bump-out, or extension, to the Smith's Cove cofferdam, first discussed in the Season 7 premiere. During the process, they discovered a new wooden structure at Smith's Cove which lay outside the original cofferdam. This structure consists of horizontal and vertically-aligned logs, and Mike Jardine suggested that it bore some resemblance to the top of a vertical shaft.

While examining the structure, Marty Lagina made a brief reference to its most prominent section, namely a vertical timber sticking out of the ground. Although it is not mentioned in this episode, this vertical timber strongly evokes an object which Rick Lagina spied at Smith's Cove during low tide back in Season 1, Episode 1, which he likened to "an ancient tusk coming out of the water". In that episode, both Dan Henskee and Charles Barkhouse declared that they had never noticed the tusk-like object before.

Near the end of this episode, Laird Niven gave the crew the green light to excavate the sides of the structure, which Gerhardt proceeded to do with his backhoe. Gerhardt removed a load of material immediately adjacent to the structure, exposing a wall of horizontal logs covered by sheets of what appeared to be 19th or

20th Century tar paper. Immediately beside the wall was a pile of rocks, which some of the treasure hunters suspected might be the remains of the legendary finger drains believed to feed the Smith's Cove flood tunnel. The treasure hunters agreed that they ought to uncover more of the structure so that they might better understand its nature.

[For Laird Niven's final analysis of the structure, see the second paragraph of Season 7, Episode 14]

Season 7, Episode 8

Triptych

Plot Summary

The episode begins at Smith's Cove, where the mysterious tarpapered wooden wall and possible remains of the Smith's Cove flood tunnel were discovered at the end of the previous episode. Various members of Oak Island Tours Inc. puzzle over the structure, which Rick Lagina eventually suggests might be the work of Robert and Bobby Restall, as it bears some resemblance to other structures the Restalls are known to have built. "The only problem I have for this to be Restall work," Rick says, "is [that the structure would have been] underwater [during the days of the Restall treasure hunt]. Now how would they have gotten here?"

Geologist Terry Matheson examines the wooden wall and opines that the cobble-like rocks that lie beside it, which some treasure hunters had suggested might be the remains of the flood tunnel, were stacked by man. Steve Guptill then tells Matheson that the northern end of this structure lies right next to the southern end of the slipway discovered back in Season 6, Episode 11. Matheson proceeds to examine the rocks with a hand shovel and finds a piece of wood embedded in it, which he identifies as a timber. This find seems to verify that the rock structure is indeed manmade.

That night, the Fellowship of the Dig meets in the War Room, where they speculate as to the nature of the mysterious structure recently discovered at Smith's Cove. Marty Lagina, who attends the meeting via Skype, encourages his fellow treasures to dig up the structure and "get to the bottom" of it.

The next day, several members of the Oak Island team continue to excavate the structure at Smith's Cove. Billy Gerhardt removes a quantity of earth beside the supposed cobble, and Gary Drayton scans the fresh trench with his metal detector. Drayton quickly comes across a tapered wrought iron spike which bears great resemblance to one of the objects he discovered at Isaac's Point in the Season 7 premiere, which blacksmithing expert Carmen Legge identified as a hand point chisel. The object also bears some resemblance to the crib spike discovered on Lot 26 back in Season 6, Episode 3, as well as the crib spikes discovered near the Smith's Cove slipway back in Season 6, Episode 16. The

narrator then suggests that the artifact's discovery might constitute evidence that the recently-discovered wooden wall was constructed sometime in the 17th or 18th Centuries (the presumed age of the various crib spikes), apparently forgetting that the wall was found covered with 19th or 20th Century tar paper.

That night, the crew meets in the War Room with Oak Island theorist Corjan Mol. Mol presents his theory that classical French Baroque painter Nicolas Poussin included secret clues as to the location of the Oak Island treasure in two of his paintings, both of them entitled *Et in Arcadia ego* (also known as *The Shepherds of Arcadia*) and inspired by Italian Baroque painter il Guercino's earlier work of the same name. Poussin's first rendition of *The Shepherds of Arcadia*, painted in 1627, depicts two shepherds, a reclining man, and a shepherdess in a pastoral setting discovering an overgrown tomb and reading the inscription carved into its side: *"ET IN ARCADIA EGO"*. Mol suggests that the tomb's inscription might be an anagram for "GITE NEO ARCADIA", which, in Italian, means, "Excursion to New Arcadia".

The narrator then explains that Italian explorer Giovanni da Verrazano explored North America's Atlantic coast from North Carolina to Nova Scotia on behalf of King Francis I of France from 1523-24. During the voyage, Verrazano named the beautiful forested coastline north of Virginia "Arcadia" after a legendary pastoral paradise of Ancient Greek mythology. During this exposition, the show displays an old map bearing the title "Carte de l'Accadie", or "Map of Acadia" in French. Although there appears to be some implication that the map was drawn by Verrazano, the map displayed on the show was actually drawn by French geographer Jacques-Nicolas Bellin in 1757.

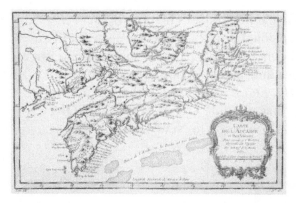

The narrator then explains that the name "Arcadia" gradually moved northeast until, in the early 1600s, it denoted a province of New France which covered an area that now comprises Canada's Maritime Provinces and much of the state of Maine. 17th Century French explorer Samuel de Champlain decided to omit the 'r' from "Arcadia" and call the region "Acadie", perhaps in an effort to make the word more congruent with native names for extant villages like Shubenacadie (located in Nova Scotia).

Back in the War Room, Corjan Mol shows the treasure hunters another painting by Nicolas Poussin entitled *Midas Washing at the Source of the Pactolus* (1627). This painting, Mol informs the treasure hunters, was made just after *The Shepherds of Arcadia*, and was intended to form a pendant painting with it (i.e. both paintings were meant to hang beside one another). The painting depicts a scene in the Classical Greek legend of King Midas of Phrygia. According to the legend, a satyr (a woodland deity) granted Midas' wish for the ability to turn everything he touched into gold. Unable to eat or drink as a result of his new ability, Midas prayed to the Greek god Dionysus (called "Bacchus" by the Romans) to reverse

the satyr's work. A sympathetic Dionysus ordered Midas to bathe in
the Pactolus River. In doing so, the Phrygian king cleansed himself
of his affliction, depositing gold dust into the riverbed in the process.
Mol puts forth the theory that Poussin's painting, which depicts
Midas bathing in the Pactolus River, is a reference to Nova Scotia's
Gold River- a gold-bearing waterway which empties into Mahone
Bay just northwest of Oak Island.

Corjan Mol further argues that Nicolas Poussin's second rendition
of *The Shepherds of Arcadia*, painted in 1637/38, was modeled on

a portion of a pentagram. He goes on to suggest that the painting and the pentagram on which it is modeled, when superimposed over top of Nolan's Cross, forms a treasure map indicating an area of interest near the tip of the Oak Island swamp. Mol finishes his presentation by suggesting that the Knights Templar buried the Ark of the Covenant on Oak Island, and that Nicolas Poussin somehow became privy to their secret.

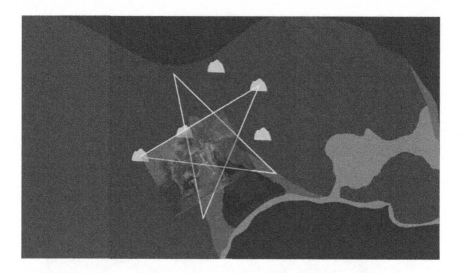

The next day, Rick Lagina, Steve Guptill, and Tony Sampson meet with GPR experts Don Johnston and Steve Watson at the Oak Island swamp. Using a dingy and a rope laid along gridlines which Guptill prescribed, the crew conducts a floating GPR scan of the swamp. During the process, Johnston and Watson detect a 6-metre-wide anomaly located three metres below the surface.

Later, Jack Begley and Gary Drayton continue to excavate the mysterious wooden structure at Smith's Cove by hand. Further excavation carried out off-camera has exposed four more log walls which appear to form two square shafts or boxes sitting side by side. The two men are later joined by other members of the team who assist in the excavation. At about three feet below the lip of one of the boxes, Doug Crowell discovers a platform of wooden beams. Despite this interesting development, Rick Lagina suggests that they stop excavating the boxes for the time being and explore more of the surrounding area first. In a later interview, Rick voices his fear that a rigorous investigation of the box-like structure may necessitate their digging a wider hole which might prevent them from accessing other areas of the bump-out with heavy equipment.

The following day, Jack Begley, Dave Blankenship, Doug Crowell, Terry Matheson, and Scott Barlow meet at the Money Pit area, where Choice Drilling is busy drilling an exploratory drillhole in search of another of the four walls of the 114-foot-deep Shaft 2 (one of Shaft 2's four walls may have been discovered at the end of the previous episode). The treasure hunters examine a core sample taken from a depth of 19-29 feet below the surface. To their delight, the sample contains a large piece of timber from 24-29 feet which appears to be a piece of a corner of Shaft 2. The narrator informs us that the team will need to intersect one more wall of the shaft in order to definitively determine the orientation of Shaft 2.

The Choice Drilling crew proceeds to sink another hole at one of the suspected locations of a Shaft 2 wall. A core sample taken from an undisclosed depth (later revealed to be 98.5-103.5 feet) in this hole contains a significant quantity of wood. "We've got three points now that can't be just one wall," says Doug Crowell of the discovery. "So we've got two walls." The crew then agrees to sink another hole in the hope of intersecting the 14-foot-long tunnel which once connected Shaft 2 with the original Money Pit, and to submit the recently-discovered wood samples for dendrochronological dating.

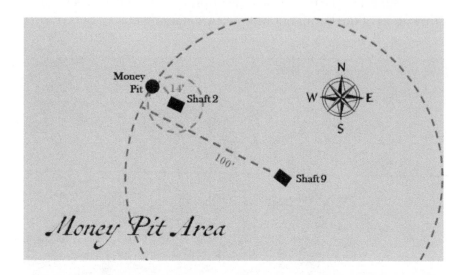

One week later, the crew meets in the War Room to hear the results of the aforementioned dendrochronological test. Craig Tester, who is in attendance via Skype, reveals that dendrochronologist Dr. Colin Laroque (who dated the wood from several Smith's Cove structures back in Season 6, Episode 21) dated the 98.5-103.5-foot-deep wood from the suspected Shaft 2 wall to 1796. Tester reminds the crew that Shaft 2 is believed to have been constructed in 1805, and remarks that the Laroque's dating fits perfectly with this. The narrator then remarks that, since it appears the crew has determined the location and orientation of Shaft 2, they finally know the precise location of the original Money Pit.

Plot Summary

GPR Scan of the Oak Island Swamp

In this episode, GPR experts Steve Watson and Don Johnston conducted a floating GPR scan of the Oak Island swamp using a dingy and ropes laid along gridlines prescribed by Steve Guptill.

This is not the first time a Ground Penetrating Radar scan has been conducted in the Oak Island swamp. Back in Season 2, Episode 8, Pat Campbell and Matt Savelle of Canadian Seabed Research Ltd. scanned the swamp's southeast corner, the Mercy Point, and the so-called Enochean Chamber area on the swamp's western edge with a GPR device. Although the scans indicated the presence of several underground anomalies, further investigation yielded little of interest.

Origin of the Name 'Acadia'

In this episode, theorist Corjan Mol attempted to draw a connection between the word "Arcadia", which is inscribed on tomb in Nicolas

Poussin's paintings *The Shepherds of Arcadia*, and Acadia, an old New French province made up of what is now Nova Scotia, New Brunswick, P.E.I., and much of the state of Maine.

In Classical Greek mythology, Arcadia is a pastoral paradise situated in the sparsely-populated mountainous interior of the Peloponnesian Peninsula. Named after Arcas, a legendary Greek demigod and hunter, the Arcadia of Greek mythology was said to be home to shepherds and nymphs who lived in harmony with nature, ruled over by the god Pan.

As was mentioned in this episode, Italian explorer Giovanni de Verrazano, during his 1523-24 voyage to North America on behalf of Francis I of France, applied the name "Arcadia" to the beautiful wooded Atlantic coast north of Virginia. According to Canadian

bibliographer William F.E. Morley in his 1979 article on Verrazano for the *Dictionary of Canadian Biography*, the word Arcadia made its first cartographical appearance on Italian cartographer Giacomo Gastaldi's 1548 map of North America's Atlantic Coast.

King Henry IV of France- who would become a great supporter and sponsor of Samuel de Champlain, the so-called Father of Acadia- referred to the Canadian Maritimes as "La Cadie" in a 1603 colonial license for French explorer Pierre Dugua, Sieur de Mons. Many historians believe that "La Cadie" has its origins in a native word picked up by French explorers, citing similar native place names like "Shubenacadie" and "Tracadie" as evidence. Samuel de Champlain apparently married Verrazano's "Arcadia" with King Henry's "La Cadie" by naming the Canadian Maritimes "L'Accadie", or "Acadia", in his writings and maps.

Corjan Mol's Theory

In this episode, researcher Corjan Mol presented his own Oak Island theory involving classical French Baroque painter Nicolas Poussin and his two renditions of *The Shepherds of Arcadia*. Specifically, Mol believes that the words "*Et in Arcadia ego*", which form the inscription on the tombs in Poussin's paintings, constitute an anagram for "*Gite Neo Arcadia*"- an Italian phrase which translates to "Excursion to New Arcadia". Mol contends that these words are intended to draw attention to a particular voyage to the Canadian Maritimes, or "New Arcadia"- perhaps the voyage which led to the interment of the Oak Island treasure.

Mol then showed the Oak Island crew another of Poussin's paintings entitled *Midas Washing at the Source of the Pactolus*. Mol informed the treasure hunters that Poussin created this painting in 1627, the same year in which he painted his first rendition of *The Shepherds of Arcadia*, and claimed that it was meant to hang alongside it. This claim is supported by the posthumous inventory of Cardinal Camillo Massimo, a 17th Century  Roman Church official and a major patron of the arts who owned both paintings, which referred to the items as "*due quadri compagni*", or "two fellow paintings".

The painting *Midas Washing at the Source of the Pactolus* depicts a scene from Classical Greek mythology and the Roman poet Ovid's masterwork *Metamorphoses*. Specifically, the scene depicts the climax of the legend of King Midas of Phrygia, whom a woodland deity had granted the ability to turn everything he touched into gold. Unable to eat or drink as a result of his new ability, Midas prayed to the Greek god Dionysus (called "Bacchus" by the Romans) and asked him to reverse the curse. The sympathetic deity ordered Midas to wash in the Pactolus River. In doing so, the king both cleansed himself of his affliction and deposited alluvial gold into the river. Mol argued that Poussin's painting of this scene was intended as a reference to Nova Scotia's Gold River- a gold-bearing waterway which empties into Mahone Bay just northwest of Oak Island.

Mol finished his presentation by putting forth the theory that Poussin's second rendition of *The Shepherds of Arcadia,* painted in 1636/37, is modeled around the shape of a pentagram. Mol appears to have borrowed this part of his theory from British screenwriter Henry Lincoln, co-author of the infamous 1982 book *The Holy Blood and the Holy Grail* (I will elaborate on this connection shortly). Mol further contended that this pentagram on which Poussin's painting was modeled, when superimposed over Nolan's Cross, forms a treasure map indicating an area of interest near the apex of the Oak Island swamp. He concluded by suggesting that the

Knights Templar buried the Ark of the Covenant on Oak Island, and that Nicolas Poussin somehow became privy to their secret and alluded to it in his work.

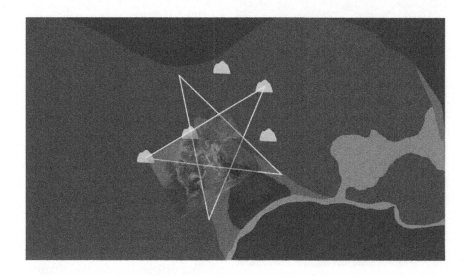

The Mystery of Nicolas Poussin and Rennes-le-Chateau

Corjan Mol is not the first researcher to include Nicolas Poussin in his Oak Island theory. In fact, the French painter appears so frequently in various Oak Island theories, as well as in hypotheses regarding other potentially-related mysteries, that a brief biography of the artist and an explanation of his place in some of the more popular of these theses may prove interesting to some readers.

Nicolas Poussin was born in Normandy, France, in 1594. Early on, Poussin displayed a natural aptitude for and interest in drawing. Contrary to his parents' wishes, he moved to Paris at the age of eighteen, whereupon he pursued a career as an artist. Poussin apprenticed with a variety of established Parisian painters and, in his early twenties, began receiving his own commissions from churches and convents.

In 1622, the Society of Jesus, also known as the Jesuit Order, hired Poussin to create six watercolor paintings depicting the miracles of

Saint Ignatius of Loyala and Saint Francis Xavier, the Order's founders, both of whom had just been canonized by the Catholic Church. These paintings were seen and admired by Giambattista Marino, a Napolitano poet. At that time, Marino served as court poet to Marie de' Medici, the mother of the reigning King Louis XIII. In the context of Oak Island, it might be worth noting that, although Marie de' Medici appeared to have little interest in the exploration of the Americas, her late husband, King Henry IV of France, had used the money she had inherited from her wealthy Florentine family to finance the voyages of explorer Samuel de Champlain, the so-called "Father of Acadia".

Impressed by Poussin's paintings, Marino commissioned the young French artist with making fifteen drawings, eleven of them depicting scenes from the Roman poet Ovid's

masterwork *Metamorphoses* and four of them depicting historic Roman battles. It seems likely that Poussin, who had received little formal education in his youth, first learned the story of King Midas during this period, as this legend features in Book XI of *Metamorphoses* (recall that the story of Midas is the subject of Poussin's *Midas Washing at the Source of the Pactolus* (1627), which formed a pendant painting with his first rendition of *The Shepherds of Arcadia*).

In 1623, Marino moved to Rome and invited Poussin to join him there. Poussin agreed to do so upon his completion of several major commissions for the residence of Marie de' Medici and the family chapel of Archbishop of Paris in the Cathedral of Notre-Dame.

In 1624, Nicolas Poussin relocated to Rome, where he would spend most of his professional life. For nearly four decades, the French artist painted hundreds of pieces for Roman cardinals and Italian

aristocrats in his own unique classical French Baroque style. In 1627, he painted his first rendition of *Et in Arcadia Ego*, which appears to be based on another painting of the same name by Italian Baroque artist Giovanni Barbiere, more popularly known as il Guercino.

Il Guercino's *Et in Arcadia ego*, painted between 1618 and 1622, depicts two shepherds in a rural setting staring at a skull resting on a *cippus,* a Roman milestone sometimes used as a funeral memorial. The bricks of the *cippus* are inscribed with the words *"Et in Arcadia Ego"*, or "Even in Arcadia I". As mentioned earlier, Arcadia is the name for the mountainous interior of the Peloponnesian Peninsula, which Classical Greek mythology contends was a paradise populated by shepherds and nymphs. The ambiguous Latin phrase inscribed on il Guercino's *cippus* appears to serve as a *momento mori*- a sobering reminder of our own mortality- asserting that Death is everywhere, even in the paradise of Arcadia.

Nicolas Poussin's 1627 rendition of *Et in Arcadia Ego* depicts two shepherds and a provocatively-dressed shepherdess examining an overgrown tomb in the wilderness. Like il Guercino's *cippus,* Poussin's tomb is inscribed with the phrase "*Et in Arcadia Ego*". In the foreground of the painting is a reclining man wearing a laurel wreath on his head, whom some art historians have interpreted as Alpheus, a river god of Greek mythology who happens to feature in Ovid's *Metamorphoses.* It is interesting to note that this figure bears great resemblance to Dionysus in Pouissin's 1627 painting *Midas Washing at the Source of the Pactolus,* which was meant to serve as a companion to *Et in Arcadia Ego.*

Nearly ten years later, from 1637-38, Poussin painted a second rendition of *Et in Arcadia Ego* for Cardinal Giulio Rospigliosi, an Italian Church leader who would go on to become Pope Clement IX. This painting differs from Poussin's earlier version in several ways, including the more dignified dress and bearing of the shepherdess and the letter of the inscription at which one of the shepherds is pointing; in the 1627 painting, a shepherd points to the letter 'D', while in the later painting, a shepherd points to the letter 'R'.

Nicolas Poussin's forty year residency in Rome was punctuated by an illustrious two-year stint in Paris; in late 1640, the French painter returned to his home country to serve as First Painter to King Louis XIII. For two years, Poussin created paintings for French churches, religious organizations, and the famous "Red Eminence", Cardinal Richelieu.

Poussin returned to Rome in December 1642, where he spent the rest of his life painting for a number of patrons he had acquired back in France. He passed away in Rome on November 19, 1665, and was buried in Rome's Basilica of San Lorenzo in Lucina.

For centuries, an aura of mystery and intrigue has surrounded Nicolas Poussin and his work. This sentiment is epitomized in a cryptic inscription on the artist's tomb, which lies below a sculpted relief depicting Poussin's second version of *Et in Arcadia Ego,* crafted in 1832. When translated from Latin to English, the inscription reads:

"Spare your pious tears. Poussin lives in this urn. He had given his life without knowing how to die. In this place Poussin is silent, but if you would like to hear him speak, it is surprising- he lives and speaks through his paintings."

The notion that the great French artist may have been privy to some important secret first appeared in April 17th, 1656, in a letter written by Abbe Louis Fouquet (the future bishop of a region in southern France called Agde) to his elder brother, Nicolas Fouquet, the Superintendent of Finances at the court of the French King Louis XIV. Louis was one of Poussin's patrons and lived in Rome at the time. To his elder brother in Paris, he wrote, in French:

"I have delivered to M. Poussin the letter which you have done him the honour of writing to him; he has read it with all imaginable joy. You would not believe, Monsieur, either the pains he takes for your service, the affection with which he takes them, or the merit and probity he brings in all things.

"He and I have planned certain things, of which I shall be able to talk to you in depth, which will give you by M. Poussin advantages (if you do not wish to despise them) that Kings would have great difficulty in drawing from him, and that after him perhaps no one in the world will ever recover in the centuries to come; and, what is more, this could be done without much expense and could even turn to profit, and these are things so hard to discover that no one, no matter who, upon this earth today could have better fortune or perhaps equal..."

This cryptic letter is doubly intriguing in light of certain events which succeeded it. In the early autumn of 1661, Nicolas Fouquet was arrested by the Captain of the King's Musketeers and charged with embezzlement. After an unfair trial which lasted nearly three years, Fouquet was convicted and sentenced to imprisonment for life. The former finance minister spent the rest of his days locked away in the Fortress of Pignerol (located in what is now the town of Pinerolo, Italy). As he was a man of high birth, Fouquet was assigned a valet,

or manservant, during his incarceration. Interestingly, whenever Fouquet's regular valet was indisposed, he was substituted by the so-called "Man in the Iron Mask", a mysterious unidentified prisoner who was otherwise held in solitary confinement and forced at all times to wear a mask of either iron or velvet.

Five years after Nicolas Fouquet's death in 1680, King Louis XIV purchased a number of Nicolas Poussin's paintings, including his second rendition of the *Shepherds of Arcadia,* and added them to the French Royal Collection. Ten years later, the *Shepherds of*

Arcadia was displayed in the Palace of Versailles, where it remained until its relocation to the Louvre Museum in 1806. Strangely, the painting is said to have disappeared sometime between its introduction to Versailles and relocation to Paris; it curiously failed to appear in a 1750 exhibition of the Royal French Collection in Luxembourg.

Around that same time, in the mid-18th Century, a wealthy British MP named Thomas Anson- the elder brother of Admiral George Anson of the Royal British Navy who circumnavigated the globe in the 1740s; who features in Gary Clayton's Oak Island theory, which was presented back in Season 4, Episode 13- decorated the yard of Shugborough Hall, his family's ancestral home in Staffordshire, England, with eight custom-made megalithic monuments. Among the strangest of these is the so-called Shepherd's Monument- a rustic arch in which is set a mirror-image relief copy of Poussin's second rendition of *The Shepherds of Arcadia*, crafted by Flemish sculptor Peter Scheemakers. The Monument also contains the carved bald head of a smiling man, a carved head with goat-like horns resembling the god Pan of Greek mythology (the ruler of Arcadia), and eight Roman letters flanked by a 'D' to the lower left and an 'M' to the lower right. The sequence of letters on the Shepherd's Monument, also known as the Shugborough Inscription, appears to form some sort of code. Although many cryptographers have put forth a variety of possible solutions to the code, none of these has been universally accepted.

Some researchers believe that the Shugborough Monument is related in some way to the Oak Island mystery. Many of them point to the fact that one of the shepherds in the Monument's sculpture has his index finger placed on the letter 'R' of 'ET IN ARCADIA EGO', almost as if to cover it up. Removing the 'R' from 'Arcadia' makes 'Acadia', the name old French province in the Canadian Maritimes in which Oak Island is located. When this tantalizing possibility is considered in the context of the rest of the scene, the sculpture appears to imply that something important is entombed in Acadia, or Nova Scotia.

One proponent of theory that the Shugborough Monument is connected in some way to the Oak Island mystery is Swedish art director Peter Oberg. Oberg believes that the letters on the Shugborough Inscription stand for numbers which, when added up, equal 2,810- the distance in miles from the Shepherd's Monument to Oak Island's Money Pit. He arrives at these numbers by calculating the diameter of circles drawn on the monument's engraving, and by interpreting some letters as Roman numerals.

Another Scandinavian who believes in a connection between the Shugborough Inscription and the Oak Island mystery is Norwegian organist and cryptographer Petter Amundsen, who presented his own Oak Island theory back in Season 1, Episode 4. Amundsen believes that the inscription forms a three-level cipher. On the first level, the letters form some sort of anagram which, when some letters are switched to their Greek forms, appears to suggest the name 'Thomas Anson', the man who commissioned the Shepherd's Monument. The second cipher level- decoded using a key in a poem, Greek mythology, and astronomy- allegedly creates a celestial map which leads to Oak Island. The third alleged cipher level- first discovered by another Norwegian named Oystein Bruno Larson- involves turning the inscription letters into geographic co-ordinates which lead to a location 1.5 nautical miles from Oak Island. Amundsen presented his theory in the book he co-wrote with Norwegian novelist Erlend Loe, entitled *Organisten*, or *The Organist*.

When one considers the mystique that Nicolas Poussin and his paintings have garnered over the years as a result of the Shugborough Monument and the cryptic inscription that adorns his tomb, it is easy to understand how the French painter and his famous second rendition of *The Shepherds of Arcadia* found their way into the heart of a clever, sinister 20th Century hoax upon which an entire genre of misguided Oak Island theories are based. The story of this hoax begins in 1969, when British screenwriter Henry Lincoln picked up a copy of the recently-published book *Le Tresor Maudit de Rennes-le-Chateau*, or "The Accursed Treasure of Rennes-le-Chateau", by French author Gerard de Sede. The book puts a twist on a little local legend endemic to a sleepy town on southern France called Rennes-le-Chateau.

The original legend on which de Sede based his book was first proliferated in the mid-1950s by a local restaurateur named Noel Corbu, and dealt with a former local character named Father Berenger Sauniere. Sauniere was a Roman Catholic priest who was appointed to Rennes-le-Chateau's Church of Saint Mary Magdalene in 1885. In the late 1800s, Sauniere renovated his dilapidated parish and built a castle-like library and villa for himself, paying for the costly projects with mysteriously-acquired money. The Catholic Church conducted an investigation into Sauniere's mysterious wealth and eventually charged him with simony- the fraudulent sale of religious favours. Specifically, the Church accused the priest of pressuring people into making donations he did not need and accepting payments for hundreds of Masses he never intended to say (in the Catholic Church, it is common for parishioners to ask a priest to offer a Mass for a specific intention, like the repose of a recently deceased relative). According to Noel Corbu, however, the source of Sauniere's wealth was not simony, but rather the lost treasure of the 13th Century French Queen Blanche de Castile, who raised ransom money for her son, Prince (and later Saint) Louis IX, after his capture by Egyptian Saracens in the Seventh Crusade at the Battle of Al Mansurah. Sauniere located this treasure by following clues laid out in parchments he discovered in a particular pillar in his church during the renovations he financed in the late 1800s.

The French author Gerard de Sede put a different spin on the legend of Berenger Sauniere. In his book, he wrote that the priest, during his renovation of the Church of Saint Mary Magdalene, discovered four parchments in a pillar which supported the altar. De Sede included what purported to be photocopies of these parchments in his book. Two of the parchments contained genealogies which stretched back to the days of the Frankish Merovingian dynasty. The other two contained passages from the Gospels written in Latin. According to de Sede, Sauniere suspected that the parchments contained coded messages within their texts, and took them to Paris to have them deciphered. During his Parisian excursion, the French priest visited the Louvre Museum, where he purchased prints of three paintings, one of them Nicolas Poussin's *The Shepherds of Arcadia.* Upon his return to Rennes-le-Chateau, Sauniere began spending an extraordinary amount of money on various building projects, having become inexplicably and spontaneously wealthy. De Sede implies in his book that Sauniere, aided by the codes in the parchments, must have discovered some sort of treasure in Rennes-le-Chateau.

During this time, locals observed that Sauniere spent many a night in the church cemetery engaged in some strange and mysterious business, moving tombstones and effacing epitaphs. One of the graves which the priest defaced was that of Marie de Blanchefort, a local aristocrat who died in 1781. Fortunately, the markings on de Blanchefort's grave had already been recorded in a booklet entitled *Les Pierres Gravees du Languedoc*, or "The Engraved Stones in Languedoc", written by a man named Eugene Stublein in 1884. De Sede included photocopies of Stublein's interpretations of these markings- which included those inscribed on de Blanchefort's headstone as well as words carved into a rectangular stone set perpendicular to it- in his book.

In 1969, while vacationing in the Pyrenees, an English screenwriter named Henry Lincoln purchased a copy of de Sede's book. While examining a photocopy of one of the parchments Sauniere is said to have discovered hidden in a pillar in his church, he noticed that some of the Latin letters dipped below the others. To his astonishment, Lincoln found that these anomalous letters, when put together, formed a message in French. When translated to English, the message reads: "To Dagobert II, King, and to Sion belongs this treasure and he is there dead."

Fascinated, Lincoln believed that de Sede's story of Sauniere and the mysterious treasure of Rennes-le-Chateau would make for an excellent BBC documentary. He said as much to a certain BBC producer, who agreed with him and sent him to Paris to interview Gerard de Sede. Ever since he deciphered the code in the parchment, Lincoln had suspected that the French author had discovered the secret message as well, and was curious as to why he failed to include the decipherment in his book. He said as much to de Sede in his interview, to which the author replied, "Because we thought it might interest someone like you to find it for yourself". De Sede's use of the word "we" troubled Lincoln, as it implied the presence of some shadowy association behind the mystery of Rennes-le-Chateau.

As the BBC prepared their documentary on the tale of Berenger Sauniere, Henry Lincoln received a letter from Gerard de Sede in which the French author disclosed the solution to the code in another of the parchments discovered in the Church of Mary Magdalene. When translated from French to English, the coded message reads:

"SHEPHERDESS NO TEMPTATION THAT

POUSSIN TENIERS HOLD THE KEY

PEACE 681 BY THE CROSS AND THIS

HORSE OF GOD I COMPLETE THIS

DAEMON GUARDIAN AT MIDDAY

BLUE APPLES"

The words "Shepherdess" and "Poussin" reminded Lincoln that, in de Sede's book, Sauniere is said to have purchased a print of Nicolas' Poussin's 1637 painting *The Shepherds of Arcadia*. With this in mind, Lincoln looked at the various photocopies in de Sede's book and made an extraordinary discovery. One of the inscriptions on the tomb of Marie de Blanchefort is flanked by columns of letters, some from the Latin alphabet and others from the Greek alphabet. When the letters from the Greek alphabet are exchanged for their Latin counterparts, a Latin phrase emerges: "Et in Arcadia Ego"- another clear connection between Nicolas Poussin and the mystery of Rennes le Chateau.

Around this time, Lincoln received another letter from Gerard de Sede. In the letter, the French author claimed that he and his shadowy associates, to which he alluded earlier, had discovered a tomb near Rennes-le-Chateau which bore remarkable resemblance to that depicted in Poussin's painting. Using the directions that de Sede provided, Lincoln found this tomb on the side of the road between the villages of Serre and Arques, just a few miles from Rennes-le-Chateau. Indeed the tomb and its setting was nearly identical to that in Poussin's *The Shepherds of Arcadia,* down to the foliage in the background and a rock which rests at the base of the sarcophagus. Even more startling were the similarities between the surrounding landscape and the backdrop of *Et in Arcadia Ego.* Lincoln quickly identified four mountaintops in Poussin's painting which corresponded almost perfectly in both shape and placement with those surrounding this roadside sarcophagus. It seemed clear that Nicolas Poussin had painted this particular tomb and its surroundings in *The Shepherds of Arcadia,* either having visited the location or worked off of detailed sketches.

Henry Lincoln spent the next seven years attempting to solve the mystery of Rennes-le-Chateau, assisted on occasion by tips he received from the author de Sede and his mysterious associates. Lincoln produced three films for the BBC which documented his progress: *The Lost Treasure of Jerusalem,* produced in 1971; *The*

Priest, the Painter, and the Devil, produced in 1972; and *The Shadow of the Templars,* produced in 1979. In his second film, he consulted Professor Christopher Cornford of London's Royal College of Art. Cornford analyzed *The Shepherds of Arcadia* and determined that it appeared to be modeled around a portion of a pentagram. The professor attempted to explain the presence of this pentagram by suggesting that its inclusion implied Poussin's attempt to connect his painting with the occult, or with the Cult of Pythagoras- an ancient Greco-Italian religion which revolved around geometry, mathematics, and Classical Greek mythology. Corjan Mol, who presented his own theory in this episode of *The Curse of Oak Island,* appears to have borrowed this part of Lincoln's work.

Following the publication of *The Shadow of the Templars* in 1971, Henry Lincoln teamed up with New Zealander Michael Baigent and New Jerseyite Richard Leigh- researchers who shared his interest in the Knights Templar. Together, the three men began to research the mystery of Rennes-le-Chateau. Shortly after the formation of this alliance, Lincoln was contacted again by Gerard de Sede, who directed him to a particular document in the *Bibliotheque Nationale,* the national library of France. This document, called the *Dossiers Secret d'Henri Lobineau,* or the "Secret Files of Henri Lobineau", contained, among other things, diagrams depicting the genealogy of the Merovingian dynasty and references to an ancient

secret society called the Priory of Sion. The Priory of Sion, the
document contented, was formed in the year 1099 by descendants
of the Merovingian dynasty. Following the First Crusade, it formed
the Knights Templar as its military arm and financial branch. Over
the years, it has been led by men of status and acclaim, including
Leonardo da Vinci, Sir Isaac Newton, and Victor Hugo. Its motto
is *"Et in Arcadia ego"*, and its stated mission is the reinstallation of a
Merovingian king on the throne of France. De Sede later confessed
to Henry Lincoln that he was a member of the Priory of Sion, and
that the organization's current Grandmaster was a Frenchman
named Pierre Plantard, who was the heir to the Merovingian
dynasty.

Using the *Dossiers Secret* as one of their major sources, Lincoln,
Baigent, and Leigh wrote a book entitled *The Holy Blood and the
Holy Grail*, which was published in 1982. The book revolves
around an offensive thesis which I will not dignify here with an
exposition. One of the many propositions put forth in the book is
that the phrase *"Et in Arcadia Ego"* could be considered an anagram
for *"I! Tego Arcana Dei"* - Latin for "Begone! I Conceal the Secrets
of God". This proposal appears to have inspired Corjan Mol's own
interpretation of *"Et in Arcadia Ego"* as an anagram for *"Gite Neo
Arcadia"*, or "Excursion to New Arcadia".

Due to its controversial nature, *The Holy Blood and the Holy
Grail* was commercially successful, prompting its three authors to
pen a sequel to it entitled the *Messianic Legacy.* In 2003, American
writer Dan Brown wrote an enormously successful mystery thriller
novel entitled *The Da Vinci Code*, which appears to be based on
the thesis outlined in *The Holy Blood and the Holy Grail.* Three
years later, Brown's novel was adapted into a controversial
Hollywood movie featuring actor Tom Hanks, bringing the mystery
of Rennes-le-Chateau, in a roundabout way, to an international
audience.

For decades, a number of researchers- foremost among them
French journalist Jean-Luc Chaumeil- have chipped away at the
story of Rennes-le-Chateau and the Priory of Sion. Beneath a façade

of mystery and intrigue, they have uncovered evidence of an extraordinarily complex hoax concocted by three men: the writer Gerard de Sede; the Priory of Sion's supposed Grandmaster, Pierre Plantard; and a French surrealist named Phillipe de Cherisey. Plantard, the mastermind of the plot, conceived the story of the Priory of Sion, a medieval secret society with roots in the Merovingian dynasty responsible for the formation of the Knights Templar, whose Grandmasters included the movers and shakers of European culture. A fifty-year-old tomb near Rennes-le-Chateau which bore remarkable resemblance to that depicted in *Et in Arcadia Ego* prompted him to give Nicolas Poussin and his famous painting places of prominence in the story. Phillipe de Cherisey then created 'evidence' for the organization's existence by fabricating a number of historical documents, including the parchments which Sauniere purportedly discovered in his church; the 1884 booklet of Languedoc engravings by Eugene Stublein; and the all-important *Dossier Secret*, which Plantard submitted to the *Bibliotheque Nationale* in 1967. Gerard de Sede completed the hoax by writing his book *The Accursed Treasure of Rennes-le-Chateau*, a colourful spin on a local legend, including photocopies of several of de Cherisey's forged documents therein, and waiting for someone like Henry Lincoln to stumble upon it and take the bait.

Although the alleged connection between Nicolas Poussin and the Priory of Sion has been debunked, the unsolved Shugborough Inscription and cryptic inscription on Poussin's tomb hint at the possibility that the French painter was privy to some sort of secret, clues to which he embedded in his paintings.

Season 7, Episode 9

An Eye for an Eye

Plot Summary

The Fellowship of the Dig meets in the War Room to discuss their next course of action in light of their recent discovery of Shaft 2. The treasure hunters agree that they ought to search for the remnants of the 14-foot-long tunnel said to have connected Shaft 2 with the original Money Pit. In a later interview, Rick Lagina elaborates on their reasoning, saying, "Now the critical piece of missing information is 'what is the orientation of the tunnel?'. Does it go west by southwest, or does it go west by northwest? Where does it lie?"

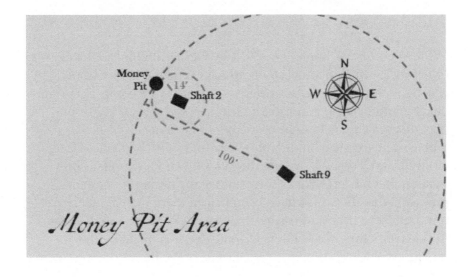

Doug Crowell and Steve Guptill proceed to the Money Pit area, where they mark a location at which they suspect that Shaft 2 tunnel might be located. Colton Robinson and Mike Tedford of Choice Drilling then prepare to sink a hole at the prescribed location.

Meanwhile, Gary Drayton, and Peter Fornetti head to the bump-out of the Smith's Cove cofferdam, where they search for metallic artifacts in earth that has been freshly turned by Billy Gerhardt. First, Drayton unearths a clump of earth which appears to contain iron. "[There] might be a goodie hidden inside," Drayton suggests, before putting the object to the side.

While the treasure hunters work, Billy Gerhardt points out a cluster of flat rocks which he unearthed, which evoke the flat rocks of which the Smith's Cove box drains were said to be comprised. The heavy equipment operator digs in the area with his excavator and unearths what appears to be a fragment of a vertically-aligned timber. The treasure hunters show the find to Rick Lagina, Doug Crowell, and Terry Matheson, the latter of whom expresses his opinion that the large rocks surrounding the timber lie in such profusion that they must have been placed there by man. Gerhardt removes more rock and earth surrounding the timber, revealing a wooden structure which Doug Crowell suggests might be the remains of a wharf or pier. In a later interview, Rick Lagina puts forth the notion that this new structure might simply be an extension of the slipway, or perhaps a much older structure on top of which the slipway was constructed.

Later that day, Terry Matheson and Dave Blankenship head to the Money Pit area, where Choice Drilling is busy sinking Borehole F-14 in the hope of intersecting the Shaft 2 tunnel. Matheson explains that they hope to encounter the tunnel somewhere between 89-105 feet below the surface. The drill reaches a depth of 89 feet without encountering anything other than in-situ soil, just as expected. The treasure hunters then examine a core sample taken from a depth of 99-105 feet- their target depth. Sure enough, the sample contains a large chunk of wood at the 100-foot level, which Matheson suggests must constitute a piece of either the floor or ceiling of the Shaft 2 tunnel. Elated, the treasure hunters agree that they must locate at least one more piece of the Shaft 2 tunnel in order to fully determine its orientation, and subsequently the location of the original Money Pit.

The next day, the Fellowship of the Dig meets in the War Room with Corjan Mol, who presented his own Oak Island theory the previous episode, and with his fellow researcher, Chris Morford. Mol and Morford show the treasure hunters a 1650 self-portrait of classical French Baroque painter Nicolas Poussin and point out an illustration of a painting in its background. This painting depicts a lady wearing a hat in which is set the image of a human eye. Mol and Morford propose that this lady is the shepherdess who features in Poussin's 1637 rendition of *Et in Arcadia Ego*.

S7E9: An Eye for an Eye

In the previous episode, Mol demonstrated that Poussins 1637 painting *Et in Arcadia Ego* appears to have been modeled on a portion of a pentagram, and showed the treasure hunters a map of Nolan's Cross on which the painting and its pentagram were overlaid. In this episode, he demonstrates that the centre of the pentagram on which *Et in Arcadia Ego* was modeled appears to be the forehead of the shepherdess- the same place over which the third eye appears on the hat of the lady in Poussin's self-portrait. Furthermore, Mol and Morford demonstrate that the centre of *Et in Arcadia Ego,* when the painting is superimposed overtop of Nolan's Cross, appears to lie just southwest of the so-called 'Eye of the Swamp'- a pond located at the tip of the Oak Island swamp around which geoscientist Dr. Ian Spooner discovered a ring of flat stones in Season 7, Episode 3. The treasure hunters express some surprise at this connection between the eye on the lady's hat in Poussin's self-portrait and the name which Marty Lagina dubbed the pond. The narrator then attempts to connect Poussin's painting and the pond to the "All-Seeing Eye", a symbol of Freemasonry and the United States mentioned back in Season 4, Episode 2, when Tony Sampson discovered a rock in a water well in the town of New Ross, Nova Scotia, bearing what he suggested might be a representation of the symbol. The treasure hunters, along with a skeptical Marty Lagina, thank the researchers for their time and agree to investigate the point of interest which they have prescribed.

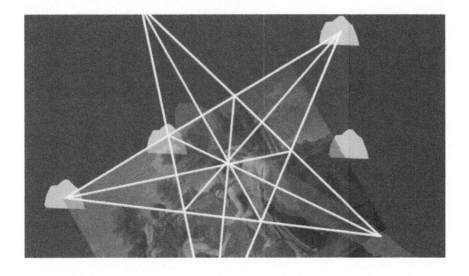

The next day, Steve Guptill meets with geoscientist Dr. Ian Spooner and three of his student assistants from Acadia University (namely Lauren Ruff, Chelsea Renaud, and Julia Crews) at the Oak Island swamp. Guptill and his students head out to the Eye of the Swamp in a dingy and collect several core samples of the swamp floor using a vibracore drill.

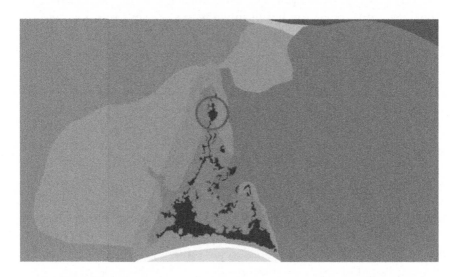

Meanwhile, Rick Lagina, Peter Fornetti, Gary Drayton, and Billy Gerhardt continue the excavation of the bump-out area at Smith's Cove. Not far from the cofferdam wall, the treasure hunters unearth a massive wooden structure consisting of large parallel and perpendicularly-aligned logs attached by saddle-notches, along with a handful of wooden pegs. Drayton remarks that the only other place they have found wooden pegs on the island was in the U-shaped structure, and suggests that this new structure they unearthed may be connected to it in some way.

Rick Lagina notes that the structure appears to be surrounded by packed clay, prompting the narrator to remind us that puddled clay was said to have been found on one or more of the nine oak log platforms unearthed at regular 10-foot intervals in the Money Pit. The treasure hunters reluctantly agree to postpone their excavation of the structure and wait for an assessment by archaeologist Laird Niven.

The next day, the Fellowship of the Dig meets in the War Room with Tom Nolan and Dr. Ian Spooner. Spooner, who has analyzed the samples that he and his students extracted from the Eye of the Swamp, shows the treasure hunters a diagram of one of the samples and informs them that lower end of the sample contains what appears to be disturbed earth. "How do I know it's disturbed?" Spooner asks rhetorically. "It's because we've got interlayered organic matter and till. You just can't get that [naturally]." The geoscientist goes on to explain how he carbon dated a sample of wood found overtop of the disturbed earth from 1600 to 1700.

"So what you're saying," clarifies Marty Lagina, "is in [the year] 16-something, somebody dug a hole there."

"Right," Spooner confirms.

Spooner then shows the treasure hunters a twig he extracted from another core sample, which he carbon dated from 1674-1778. This data, coupled with the carbon dating of the wood from the previous core sample, led him to deduce that the aforementioned swamp excavation must have taken place between 1674 and 1700- a date range which corresponds with many Oak Island discoveries made over the years, particularly those made throughout Season 5.

Season 5 Discoveries

- Human Bones = Ⓐ
- British Coins = Ⓑ
- Garnet Brooch = Ⓒ
- Lead Cross = Ⓓ
- Leather = Ⓔ
- Parchment = Ⓕ

When prompted by Rick Lagina, Tom Nolan discloses that his father, Fred Nolan, had a particular interest in the Eye of the Swamp due to the fact that, no matter how much water he pumped from it, it always remained wet.

Before concluding his presentation, Dr. Spooner informs the team that the carbon dating of another twig located near the bottom of one of his core samples appeared to indicate that the swamp first formed around 1220 A.D. Marty Lagina remarks that this theory corresponds with the popular notion that the medieval Knights Templar are behind the Oak Island mystery.

Finally, Rick Lagina shows Dr. Spooner Zena Halpern's mysterious map of Oak Island, first introduced back on the Season 4 premiere, and its reference to a Templar voyage to the island in 1179 A.D. The geoscientist says that he would "like to look at [the map] more closely to just see how it matches up with what [he and the crew] think might have existed at that time."

Analysis

The Wharf

In this episode, the Fellowship of the Dig discovered an enormous wooden structure within the bump-out area of the Smith's Cove cofferdam containing large logs and wooden pegs- the same

materials of which the U-shaped structure is comprised. Doug Crowell and Laird Niven opined that the structure bears some resemblance to a wharf or pier.

S7E9: An Eye for an Eye

Dr. Spooner's Second Analysis of the Swamp

In this episode, geoscientist Dr. Ian Spooner of Acadia University, along with three student assistants, collected core samples of the Eye of the Swamp- the pond located at the Oak Island swamp's northern tip. In a War Room meeting at the end of the episode, Dr. Spooner informed the Oak Island crew that the samples contain evidence that the swamp first formed around 1220 A.D., and that the floor of the Eye of the Swamp was disturbed by man sometime between 1674 and 1700- the latter being a date range which corresponds with many Oak Island discoveries made over the years, and the former corresponding with the popular theory that the Knights Templar are behind the Oak Island mystery.

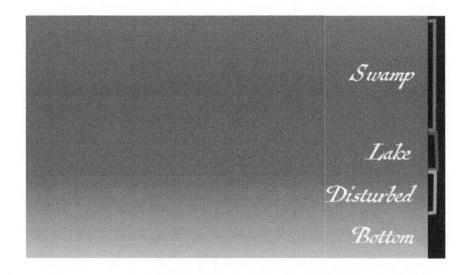

As Spooner acknowledged in this episode, his analysis of the Eye of the Swamp core samples differs from a previous assessment he made back in Season 7, Episode 3, when he extracted core samples from the 'Ship Anomaly' in the Oak Island swamp. In the earlier episode, Spooner concluded that the swamp was only three or four hundred years old, and supported trees and other forms of terrestrial vegetation prior to its transformation into a wetland.

Season 7, Episode 10

Gary Strikes Again

Plot Summary

The episode begins at the bump-out area of the Smith's Cove cofferdam, where the boys discovered the wharf-like structure the previous episode. Rick Lagina, Gary Drayton, and Peter Fornetti make a cursory examination of the partially-uncovered structure and fail to find any Roman numerals carved into it, Roman numerals being the markings that were found inscribed on the U-shaped structure. Archaeologist Laird Niven then arrives on the scene and examines the object. "My initial impression," says Niven, "is that I would associate that with the slipway." The archaeologist gives the treasure hunters the green light to hand-excavate the structure and search for any artifacts that might be found on top of or around it.

Before proceeding with the excavation, Gary Drayton scans the structure and its vicinity with his metal detector. In doing so, he comes across a strip of metal, which he suspects might be silver, perforated by a single hole. "It looks like some kind of silver tag," he ventures, before suggestion a potential connection between this object and the lead cross he discovered on the Smith's Cove beach back in Season 5, Episode 10.

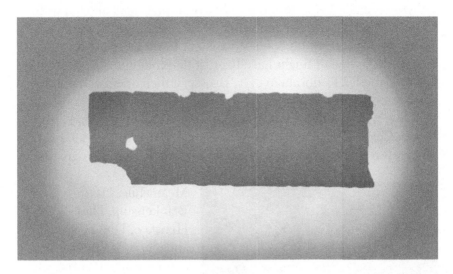

Meanwhile, Craig Tester, Jack Begley, and Scott Barlow begin draining the Oak Island swamp, having obtained permits from the provincial government to excavate certain areas of interest within the wetland. The next day, Rick Lagina and Tom Nolan meet at the swamp with John Skierka of Great Excavations Inc. We learn that the treasure hunters are considering hiring Skierka to excavate their areas of interest in the swamp, apparently having disposed of the services of contractor Shawn Wilson, whom they invited to perform a similar job through the use of a "trench cage", or "dig box", back in Season 7, Episode 3. Skierka informs the team that he plans to excavate the areas of interest with a "swamp excavator"- a specialized piece of heavy equipment specifically designed for use in swamp-like environments.

Later, the Oak Island team meets in the War Room and calls up Dr. Christa Brosseau of Halifax's St. Mary's University, who has analyzed the silver tag that Gary Drayton found near

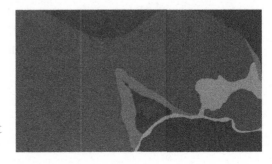

the wharf-like object in Smith's Cove. Dr. Brosseau informs the crew that the object is not composed of silver or pewter as Gary Drayton initially suspected, but rather of impure lead alloyed with small amounts of tin and antimony. She further states that tin and antimony are commonly found in ancient lead objects, and suggests that the trace metals might have been added intentionally in order to improve the lead's durability. Dr. Brosseau then advises that, if the team wants to learn more about the artifact, they ought to subject it to a laser ablation test (similar to that carried out on the lead cross by Dr. Chris McFarlane of the University of New Brunswick back in the Season 6 premiere), which will determine its isotopic signature.

Meanwhile, Dave Blankenship, Dan Henskee, Doug Crowell, and Terry Matheson meet at the Money Pit area, where Choice Drilling is busy sinking an exploratory drillhole called FG-13 in search of a second piece of the Shaft 2 tunnel. Sure enough, while examining a core sample taken from a depth of 98.5-108.5 feet, the treasure hunters find a large piece of hand-sawn lumber, which they hope constitutes the coveted second piece of the tunnel in question. Matheson also points out layers of sand and clay within the core sample, which he says would make a perfect conduit for water from the Smith's Cove flood tunnel to the Shaft 2 tunnel. The narrator then reminds us of the sand the crew discovered in a 99-109-foot core sample taken from a hole drilled in the Cave-In Pit area back in Season 7, Episode 5, and of the theory introduced in that episode that the sand might constitute the remains of the Smith's Cove flood tunnel.

82'
91'
99'
109'

The treasure hunters are soon joined by Rick, Marty, and Alex
Lagina, who congratulate them on their success in determining the
orientation of the Shaft 2 tunnel. In a later interview, Marty remarks
upon the layer of sand that Terry Matheson identified in the FG-13
core sample and explains that the geologist believes the sand to be
naturally-occurring material which facilitated the flooding of the
Shaft 2 tunnel back in 1805. Marty also expresses his own opinion
that the sand may have been placed intentionally by the creators of
the Smith's Cove flood tunnel, as "sand will transmit a lot of water".
Back at the Money Pit site, the treasure hunters agree to sink one
more hole in order to further confirm that they have indeed
determined location and orientation of the Shaft 2 tunnel.

Later that afternoon, Rick and Marty Lagina, Tom Nolan, and Dave Blankenship watch as representatives of Great Excavations Inc. transport John Skierka's swamp excavator across the Oak Island causeway.

The next morning, the Fellowship in the Dig meets in the War Room with Dr. Chris McFarlane, the geochemistry professor who conducted the laser ablation test of the lead cross back in the Season 6 premiere. McFarlane, who has conducted a similar test on the lead tag recently discovered beneath Smith's Cove, informs the team that the tag has the highest tin ratio he has ever seen in a lead artifact. He then discloses that "the slipway artifact is clearly not of North American origin," and suggests that the lead of which it is comprised was probably mined somewhere in the Mediterranean regions of Italy, France, or Spain.

Later, the boys head to the Oak Island swamp, which is now almost entirely drained. Heavy equipment operator Billy Gerhardt gets into the driver's seat of John Skierka's swamp excavator, and Marty Lagina, taking a position in the passenger seat, comes along for the ride. Gerhardt drives the excavator to what has been dubbed the "Paved Wharf"- the pattern of stones which Tony Sampson discovered on the swamp floor back in Season 7, Episode 1. The episode ends as the treasure hunters begin excavating the area.

Analysis

The Lead Tag

In this episode, Gary Drayton discovered a tag-like strip of metal in
Smith's Cove near the wharf-like structure discovered the previous
episode. Although Drayton initially suspected the artifact to be
made of lead, Dr. Christa Brosseau determined that it was made of
impure lead alloyed with 2% tin and 2% antimony.

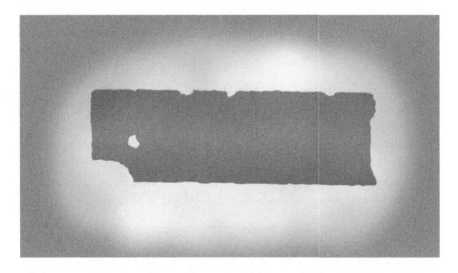

Dr. Chris McFarlane later conducted a laser ablation test on the
object and determined that the lead from which it is comprised was
likely mined somewhere in the Mediterranean regions of Spain,
France, or Italy. McFarlane also stated that the artifact possessed a
higher concentration of tin than any other lead object he has
analyzed.

Season 7, Episode 11

The Eye of the Storm

Plot Summary

The episode begins at the freshly-drained swamp, where Marty Lagina and Billy Gerhardt are using the swamp excavator to dig up the "Paved Wharf"– a pattern of stones on the swamp floor discovered by Tony Sampson in Season 7, Episode 1. While the treasure hunters work, the narrator informs us that Hurricane Dorian, one of the most powerful hurricanes ever recorded in the Atlantic Ocean, is expected to hit Oak Island in several days.

PAVED WHARF

Marty and Billy uncover a large boulder with the swamp excavator and decide to leave it where it lies. Rick Lagina, who had been hitherto observing the operation, asks his younger brother to stop digging in order to allow him to search through the spoils that Marty has already removed. Rick quickly discovers a wooden stake lying in the muck and finds that its point had been sharpened with six cuts. The treasure hunters agree that this artifact must be one of the line of wooden survey markers which Fred Nolan found during his own swamp excavation in 1969. Marty resumes the excavation and unearths another wooden stake nearly identical to the first.

Meanwhile, Jack Begley and Gary Drayton do some metal detecting in the area surrounding the wharf-like structure at Smith's Cove, where Drayton discovered a lead tag the previous episode. The pair soon uncovers a thin wrought-iron rod which Drayton tentatively identifies as a crib spike on account of its resemblance to similar artifacts found nearby in Season 7, Episode 8, and Season 6, Episode 16. Despite this interesting find, the treasure hunters both express some disappointment at the relative scarcity of artifacts in the bump-out area.

Meanwhile, at the Money Pit area, various members of the Oak Island team stand by as Choice Drilling sinks borehole FG-12 in search of a third piece of the Shaft 2 tunnel. The treasure hunters inexplicably decide to inspect a core sample taken from a depth of 18.5 feet. As might be reasonably expected, the core sample contains disturbed earth interspersed with bits of wood.

Back at the swamp, Rick and Marty Lagina, Craig Tester, and Scott Barlow, in order to allow the swamp excavator (operated by Billy Gerhardt) access to another section of the 'Paved Wharf', remove a succession of plywood sheets which had previously served as a walkway from the swamp shore to that particular area of interest. That accomplished, Gerhardt drives the excavator into the area and proceeds to dig a large hole in search of the rocks that Sampson had discovered. Since the bottom of the hole is obscured by a rapidly-growing puddle of muddy water, Rick and Craig decide to examine it manually; they slide into the hole and find that its bottom is indeed lined with what feel like flat rocks. In order to remove the water so that they might better observe the rocks beneath, the treasure hunters dig a trench nearby, create a channel connecting the two holes, and begin pumping water from the trench.

Back at the Money Pit area, the treasure hunters dissect several more core samples from FG-12, finding large chunks of wood at depths of 74 and 106 feet, respectively. The 106-foot-deep wood appears to be older than the other, and bears markings which appear to have been made with an axe. Although its depth roughly corresponds with that of the Shaft 2 tunnel, Doug Crowell and Marty Lagina speculate that the 106-foot-deep wood might be a part of the original Money Pit.

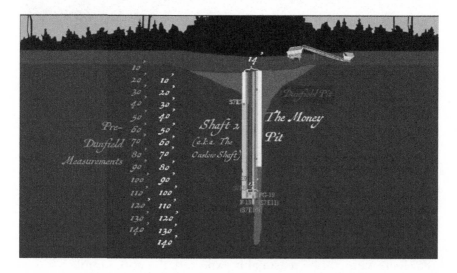

The next day, Alex Lagina and Gary Drayton drive to the Ross Farm Museum in New Ross, Nova Scotia. There, they show blacksmithing expert Carmen Legge several of the wrought-iron rods they discovered in the area of the Smith's Cove slipway, including the artifact they found earlier this episode; the tapered spike unearthed in Season 7, Episode 8; and the mysterious curved artifact unearthed in the same area in Season 7, Episode 6. Legge identifies the artifacts as pins which would have been "inserted near a post or a heavy rod to make a heavy, thick wall", and dates them from 1600-1820. He then elaborates on the artifacts' function, saying that they would have been formed around anchor pins driven into bedrock and then covered with clay, limestone, or cement, serving as primitive rebar for the concrete base of a dry dock at which ships would have been repaired. "Best guess," he concludes, "is it's for reinforcing a wall that was built along the edge of the water."

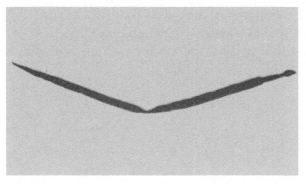

Later, various members of the Oak Island team dismantle and dismember the newly-discovered Smith's Cove wharf for the purpose of subjecting it to dendrochronological testing.

Meanwhile, the Fellowship of the Dig heads to the 'Paved Wharf' hole in the Oak Island swamp, which is now relatively dry and exposed. Marty Lagina examines the stones which lie on the hole's floor and decides that they are too round to be flagstones, as some of the treasure hunters had hoped they might be. The stones are still too deeply buried in the muck for the treasure hunters to confidently diagnose their nature, and Marty Lagina laments that it seems unlikely that the crew will be able to adequately uncover them before Hurricane Dorian reaches Oak Island. Resigned to this reality, the treasure hunters begin gathering up plywood and moving pieces of equipment in preparation for the upcoming storm.

By 6:05 P.M., Hurricane Dorian has arrived at Oak Island. Footage of the Island beset by high winds and pouring rain is interposed with clips of Global News Halifax' coverage of the storm. In an interview, Marty Lagina suggests that the inopportune timing of the hurricane brings to mind the supposed curse said to hang over Oak Island and its treasure.

Two days after the storm, Rick Lagina, Scott Barlow, and Billy Gerhardt drive to Oak Island to assess the damage. They find that the edge of the causeway connecting Oak Island with the mainland has been severely eroded, precluding the transportation of any heavy equipment to the Island until its repair. Further down the road, they find that the swamp has refilled entirely with water. Mercifully, the hurricane appears to have inflicted minimal damage on Smith's Cove and its cofferdam. Rick tasks Billy with clearing some of the damaged trees and assigns Scott and himself the task of re-draining the swamp. The episode ends as the clean-up operation commences.

Analysis

The Stake in the Swamp

Near the beginning of the episode, Rick Lagina, Marty Lagina, and Billy Gerhardt discovered two wooden stakes in the 'Paved Wharf' area of the Oak Island swamp. The stake bore six cut marks which appeared to have been made with an axe. The crew agreed that these artifacts must be members of the line of survey markers discovered by Fred Nolan in 1969. Nolan had one of these stakes carbon dated to 1550, while Dan Blankenship had another carbon dated from 1490-1660.

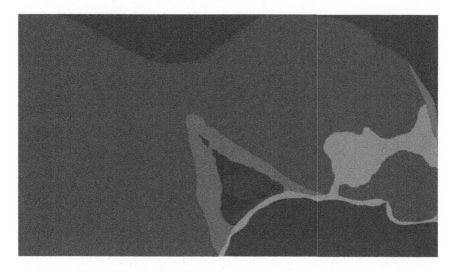

This is not the first time that Oak Island Tours Inc. unearthed a wooden stake matching the description of the mysterious survey markers that Nolan first discovered in 1969. Back in Season 5, Episode 13, while metal detecting in the northern section of the swamp, Rick Lagina discovered a similar axe-sharpened wooden stake. Although it likely has little connection with the stakes in the swamp, it is interesting to note that, back in Season 3, Episode 7, Marty Lagina discovered a thick, saw-cut spruce stake about 10 feet underground at a point dubbed the 'Nolan Site', where Fred Nolan had previously discovered what he believed to be a subterranean cave.

Primitive Rebar

In this episode, Gary Drayton and Jack Begley unearthed a thin wrought-iron rod near the wharf-like structure discovered in the bump-out area of the Smith's Cove cofferdam back in Season 7, Episode 9. Later, Drayton and Alex Lagina presented this artifact- along with the tapered wrought-iron spike discovered at Smith's Cove in Season 7, Episode 8; the mysterious curved artifact unearthed in the same area in Season 7, Episode 6; and other similar artifacts presumably discovered nearby off-screen- to blacksmithing expert Carmen Legge. Legge identified the artifacts as piece of primitive rebar used to reinforce the cement base of a dry dock at which ships would have been repaired.

Borehole FG-12

At the Money Pit area, the Fellowship of the Dig stands by as Choice Drilling sinks borehole FG-12 in search of a third piece of the Shaft 2 tunnel. The treasure hunters dissect a number of core samples and find large chunks of wood at depths of 74 and 106 feet, respectively. The 106-foot-deep wood appears to be older than the 74-foot piece, and bears markings which appear to have been made with an axe. Although its depth roughly corresponds with that of the Shaft 2 tunnel, Doug Crowell and Marty Lagina speculate that the 106-foot-deep wood might have been a part of the original Money Pit, namely a piece of one of the wooden platforms which lay in the Pit at 10-foot intervals or undiscovered cribbing which initially lay below the 100-foot level. If the wood is indeed a part of the original Money Pit, then its depth and precise location are irrelevant; since treasure hunter Robert Dunfield destroyed the Money Pit while digging his infamous 140-foot-deep crater in the area, any fragment of the Money Pit found at a depth of 106 feet would constitute loose backfill.

[See 'Carbon Dating of the Wood from the Money Pit' in Season 7, Episode 13]

Hurricane Dorian

At the very beginning of the episode, we were informed of the impending arrival of Hurricane Dorian, one of the most powerful hurricanes ever recorded in the Atlantic Ocean. The rest of the episode was punctuated by clips of Global News Halifax' coverage of the storm's progress. The hurricane finally hit the Island near the end of the episode, flooding the swamp and damaging the causeway, yet failing to do any serious damage to either the Money Pit area or the Smith's Cove cofferdam.

Hurricane Dorian is the second major storm to hit Oak Island during the lifetime of this TV show. In the winter of 2016/17, which separated Season 4 from Season 5, the island was ravaged by a series of violent windstorms which uprooted trees and all but obliterated the South Shore road which skirts the Oak Island swamp.

Season 7, Episode 12

Fortified

———————◆———————

Plot Summary

Rick Lagina and Chris Barlow pay a visit to the Oak Island swamp, which Hurricane Dorian refilled with water the previous episode. Rick estimates that it will take the crew two or three days to re-drain the swamp and resume their excavations of the areas of interest therein, and suggests that they ought to prioritize the excavation of the Paved Wharf.

Later that day, the Fellowship of the Dig meets in the War Room. There, Craig Tester reveals the results of the dendrochronological testing of the wharf in Smith's Cove, samples from which were extracted in the previous episode. According to dendrochronologist Dr. Colin Laroque, who analyzed one of the samples, the wharf is made of red spruce felled in 1741. The treasure hunters express some surprise at this result, as many of them had expected the wharf to be contemporaneous with the nearby slipway, which is believed to have been constructed around 1769. Doug Crowell observes that the most momentous event to take place in the area proximate to the year 1741 was the first Siege of Louisbourg, which lasted throughout the spring and summer of 1745. This prompts Marty Lagina to remark that the wood's date evokes Naval historian Chipp Reid's theory, introduced back in Season 7, Episode 5, that the wooden structures beneath Smith's Cove constitute the remains of an early 18th Century French artillery battery. The treasure hunters all agree that, in light of this most recent piece of evidence, a trip to the Fortress of Louisbourg is in order.

The next day, Rick Lagina and Doug Crowell drive to the Fortress of Louisbourg on Cape Breton Island. On the way, the treasure hunters discuss the tunnels which run beneath Louisbourg, which evoke the Smith's Cove flood tunnel, and the fact that the body of the Duc d'Anville- a French military leader associated with another Oak Island theory- lies buried beneath Louisbourg, having been moved from its previous resting place on an island in Halifax Harbour.

Meanwhile, Jack Begley, Peter Fornetti, and Gary Drayton go metal detecting on Oak Island's Lot 27, where the three of them discovered a rusted iron chisel back in Season 7, Episode 5. In this episode, the treasure hunters unearth a lead artifact which Drayton identifies as scrap metal from a sprue- a channel by which molten metal enters a mold. In this case, the sprue appears to be from a musket ball mold. The treasure hunters work their way from the forest down to the beach, where they unearth what appears to be an axe head encased in an agglomerate of rocks and sediment. Drayton suspects that the artifact might be the remains of a rigging axe, or a hatchet with a hammer on the blunt end, and dates it to the 18th Century or earlier.

Meanwhile, Rick Lagina and Doug Crowell arrive at the Fortress of Louisbourg- a living history museum revolving around a reconstruction of a quarter of the original French fortress. There, they meet with historian Sarah MacInnes, who takes them to the Louisbourg chapel, the final resting place of the Duc d'Anville. Inside the chapel, MacInnes explains that in 1749, following the Treaty of Aix-la-Chapelle which returned the fortress to the French, d'Anville's corpse was exhumed from its grave on Georges Island in Halifax Harbour and reinterred beneath the altar in the Louisbourg chapel.

MacInnes then takes the treasure hunters to Louisbourg's bomb-proof casements, one of the only original French structures that survived Britain's systematic destruction of the fortress from 1760-1768. Inside one of the casements is a stone drain system which reminds Doug Crowell of Oak Island's flood tunnels.

MacInnes proceeds to show Rick and Doug the countermine tunnel, another original French structure consisting of an underground tunnel with stone walls and a vaulted stone roof, which was intended to intercept any British mines that were dug beneath the fortress' walls during an invasion. The historian informs the treasure hunters that the tunnel was dug through marshy terrain, and that its builders would have needed to manipulate the surrounding water during its construction. "Could it be," the narrator asks, "that the same engineering knowledge used to build the countermine tunnel in the surrounding swamp at Louisbourg was also employed in the construction of Oak Island's elaborate network of booby-trapped flood tunnels?"

At Doug Crowell's suggestion, Sarah MacInnes and her associate, Ruby Fougere, show Rick and Doug the blueprints of the Fortress of Louisbourg. They point out the plans for the countermine tunnel, which is revealed to be 180 feet long and shaped like a cross. Doug then draws a parallel between the cross-shaped tunnel and Nolan's Cross on Oak Island, suggesting that there might be some sort of connection between the two. MacInnes then shows the treasure hunters a photo taken inside the tunnel, revealing a perfectly straight arched passageway lined with rough masonry.

The next day, Rick Lagina, Alex Lagina, and Billy Gerhardt resume the excavation of the Paved Wharf in the freshly re-drained swamp. After uncovering the boulders of which the structure is comprised,

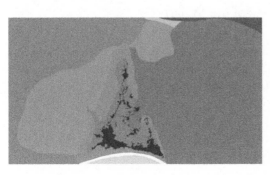

the crew is joined by Terry Matheson. The geologist identifies the boulders as clastic rocks, making a point to distinguish them from limestone and gypsum bedrock. "I'm surprised," he says, "to see what I think I would not encounter until about 120 feet down in the Money Pit area".

The following day, Rick Lagina, Alex Lagina, and Dr. Ian Spooner stand by as Billy Gerhardt washes the Paved Wharf with buckets of swamp water. Dr. Spooner states that the mass of rocks of which the feature is composed is not characteristic of wetland environments, suggesting that "it's almost as if the rocks were brought in." The geoscientist later elaborates on his analysis, saying "There's these layers of stone above the till that have no clay around them and yet have swamp sediment around them. It has to be manipulated. I can't find a natural process that would have led to this. It's a manipulated site." The treasure hunters are then joined by archaeologist Laird Niven, who states that the rocks do not seem to be naturally arranged, and appear to have "been introduced" by man. Rick phones up Marty Lagina and informs him of the find. When Marty asks what purpose might have been fulfilled by such a structure, Dr. Spooner observes that the Eye of the Swamp, the Paved Wharf, and the deepest part of the swamp all align, suggesting that the swamp was once an inlet connected to the ocean, and that the Paved Wharf was a work surface used for unloading material from ships which entered this inlet.

Analysis

Dendrochronological Dating of the Wharf

In this episode, we learned that the wood from the wharf discovered at Smith's Cove in Season 7, Episode 9 was dendrochronologically dated to 1741, predating the wood from the nearby slipway by about three decades. Interestingly, this date corresponds best with the theory that the Oak Island treasure consists of the contents of a French pay ship bound for the Fortress of Louisbourg around the time of the First Siege of Louisbourg in 1745.

The Rigging Axe

In this episode, Jack Begley, Peter Fornetti, and Gary Drayton discovered a rusted axe head on the beach of Oak Island's Lot 27, which Drayton suggested might be the remains of a rigging axe.

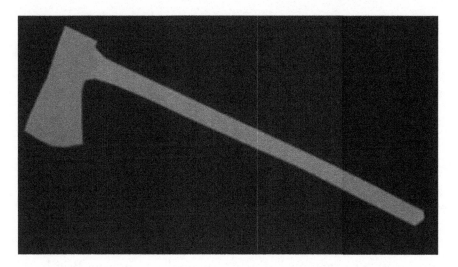

This is not the first axe to be found on Oak Island. In 1931, Chappells Limited discovered an axe in the Chappell Shaft at a depth of around 116 feet with a wide blade and a three-foot-long wooden handle. Treasure hunter Frederick Blair observed that this artifact resembled a 17th Century Acadian axe head that he had seen at the museum at Annapolis Royal. Others identified the artifact as an "old Anglo-American felling axe". On his website, Gary Drayton claimed to have discovered the heads of two early 18th Century iron trade axes in the Money Pit area in the summer of 2014. In Season 5, Episode 1, Gary Drayton and Peter Fornetti discovered a woodcutter's axe at Isaac's Point, at the easternmost end of Oak Island.

Louisbourg Connections

In this episode, Rick Lagina and Doug Crowell paid a visit to the Fortress of Louisbourg, where they learned about several feats of French engineering which prove that the 18th Century French Royal Army were capable of constructing Oak Island's supposed underground workings. The first of these are stone casements, or bomb-proof storage rooms, which contain a stone drainage system evocative of the Smith's Cove flood tunnel.

Another structure reminiscent of the flood tunnel is Louisbourg's stone countermine tunnel, which was intended to prevent British sappers from tunneling beneath the fortress. Interestingly, this tunnel was built through marshy terrain, evoking the Oak Island swamp and the alleged construction projects associated with it. Even more intriguingly, the tunnel was built in the shape of a cross, evoking Nolan's Cross.

Another interesting piece of trivia imparted in this episode is that Jean-Baptiste de la Rochefoucault- a French military commander connected with a related Oak Island theory- is buried beneath the altar of the Louisbourg chapel.

Paved Wharf Analysis

In this episode, the Oak Island crew fully uncovered the Paved Wharf in the Oak Island swamp. Geoscientist Dr. Ian Spooner, geologist Terry Matheson, and archaeologist Laird Niven all agreed that the rocks of which the feature was comprised must have been placed there by man.

Season 7, Episode 13

Bromancing the Stones

Plot Summary

Rick Lagina takes Tom Nolan to Oak Island's recently-drained swamp and shows him the stones that make up the Paved Wharf. "Oh, there's no way that's natural, Rick," Nolan says. "Look at it. It's just layered right on top... It's like you're standing on a paved road in the middle of a bog."

Later, the Oak Island crew congregates in the War Room. There, Rick Lagina and Doug Crowell show their fellow treasure hunters photos of the casements and the countermine tunnel at the Fortress of Louisbourg, which they visited the previous episode, and discuss their evocation of the Smith's Cove flood tunnel. Crowell then shows the crew an old photo given to him by a Louisbourg historian which depicts a stratum of rocks lying on top of a layer of earth. This structure, which Crowell says is an original piece of Louisbourg

flooring, bears remarkable resemblance to the Paved Wharf in the swamp.

Later, Rick Lagina and Billy Gerhardt meet Dr. Ian Spooner at the Paved Wharf.

Upon examining the formation, the geoscientist finds a stick crushed between two rocks, which he claims to be an indication that the feature could not have been formed by a glacier. When Rick asks Dr. Spooner to estimate the date at which the stones were laid down, the geoscientist suggests that they carbon date the stick he found between the rocks, implying that the stones were laid when the stick was green.

The next day, Billy Gerhardt excavates more of the swamp in the area of the Paved Wharf in an effort to define the extent of the structure. As the heavy duty equipment operator goes about his work, Jack Begley and Gary Drayton search for metallic objects in the spoils that he removes. After digging through dirt and detritus for some time, Gerhardt uncovers another layer of rocks nearby, which Gary suggests might constitute an extension of the Paved Wharf. The treasure hunters are then joined by Rick Lagina, Craig Tester, and Steve Guptill, the former of whom tasks the latter with determining the depth of this new rock layer and comparing it with that of the Paved Wharf. The new rocks prove to lie one foot below sea level- a foot higher than the Paved Wharf.

Later that day, Craig Tester, Charles Barkhouse, and Terry Matheson meet at the Money Pit area, where the Choice Drilling crew is busy sinking exploratory boreholes in the area at which the team now believes the original Money Pit once lay. While extracting a core sample from a depth of 109-119 feet, drillers Mike Tedford and Colton Robinson claim that their drill fell into some sort of subterranean void. The core sample appears to contain undisturbed soil and crumbly limestone, which Craig interprets as an indication that the drill failed to intercept the original Money Pit. Craig suggests that they sink another hole about a foot and a half away.

The next day, Rick Lagina, Billy Gerhardt, and Laird Niven drive to the Dartmouth Heritage Museum in Dartmouth, Nova Scotia, having acquired a permit to excavate the museum's yard in search of the supposed 90-foot stone which they learned might be buried there in Season 7, Episode 7. Billy Gerhardt begins digging 20'x20' hole in the yard with a backhoe. Despite finding a number of bricks and a large boulder, he fails to unearth anything resembling the legendary 90-foot-stone. The boys are then joined by Kevin Rideout, the area local who had previously informed them of the stone's existence, a tour guide having pointed it out to him decades before. Rideout says that he believes the treasure hunters are looking in the right place, but notes that the surrounding area is more elevated than he remembered it to be in the past, suggesting that the stone may have been covered up in some sort of landscaping project carried out years ago. Accordingly, Billy Gerhardt digs the hole a little deeper, yet fails to unearth anything of interest.

Meanwhile, Gary Drayton and Jack Begley go metal detecting on the shores of the Eye of the Swamp. The treasure hunters quickly unearth the iron head of a pickaxe, which Gary suggests is an old pick used for tunneling. Several feet away, they find what appears to be the rusted head of a round point shovel.

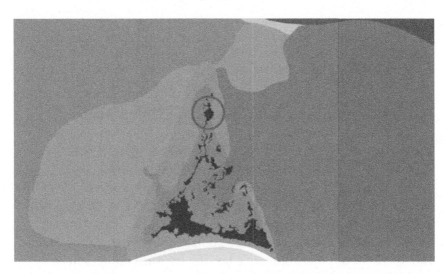

Later that night, the Fellowship of the Dig meets in the War Room to learn the results of the carbon dating of the 106-foot-deep wood found in Borehole FG-12 in Season 7, Episode 11, which some of the crew members suspected might be a fragment of the original Money Pit. Craig Tester reveals that the wood was dated from 1626-1680- a date range which roughly corresponds with many of the artifacts discovered in the Money Pit area throughout Season 5. Marty Lagina remarks that the upper range of the wood's carbon dating is also consistent with that of the twigs which Dr. Ian Spooner and his graduate students discovered in core samples taken from the Eye of the Swamp in Season 7, Episode 9.

Season 5 Discoveries

1650-1750

A B

C

D

E F

Pre-1650   Post-1750

- Human Bones - Ⓐ
- British Coins - Ⓑ
- Garnet Brooch - Ⓒ
- Lead Cross - Ⓓ
- Leather - Ⓔ
- Parchment- Ⓕ

"I wonder what was happening in the area [in the] late 1600s, early 1700s," muses Gary Drayton.

"Yeah, that's the question," Marty replies.

Analysis

Follow-Up on the Stone at the Dartmouth Heritage Museum

In this episode, Rick Lagina, Billy Gerhardt, and Laird Niven followed the lead introduced by Kevin Rideout introduced in Season 7, Episode 7, indicating that Oak Island's legendary 90-foot-stone might lie in the yard of the Evergreen House in Darmouth, Nova Scotia- now the home of the Dartmouth Heritage Museum. Despite digging a deep 20-foot by 20-foot hole in the spot at which Rideout believed the stone once lay, the treasure hunters were unable to unearth anything of interest.

Carbon Dating of the Wood from the Money Pit

In this video, we learn that the wood brought up from Borehole FG-12 in Season 7, Episode 11, which some of the crew members suspected might be a piece of the original Money Pit, was carbon dated from 1626-1680. This date range corresponds with a number of Oak Island theories, including the French theory, the English theory, the Spanish theory, the Knights Baronets, theory, and the notion that New English treasure hunter and later politician Sir William Phips is the man behind the Oak Island mystery.

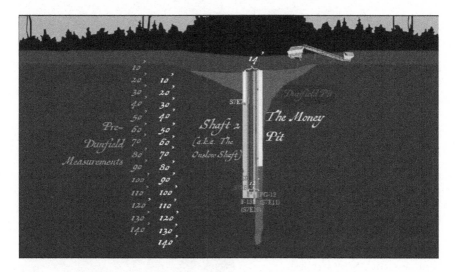

The Acadian Theatre of the Nine Years' War

In this episode, the wood from the Money Pit area brought up from Borehole FG-12 in Season 7, Episode 11 was carbon dated from 1626-1680, prompting Gary Drayton and Marty Lagina to wonder aloud what was happening in the area in the late 1600s. The answer is that the Atlantic Northeast was teetering precariously on the precipice of war- namely the Nine Years' War, known as King William's War in Canada and the United States.

The first few years of King William's War were characterized by Wabanaki and French-Canadian raids against New English settlements, many of these led by Jean Vincent de Saint-Castin and a French Sulpician missionary named Father Louis-Pierre Thury. In

1690, the New Englanders began to hit back, launching their own counteroffensives into Acadia. The first of these campaigns was led by Benjamin Church, a veteran of King Philip's War (a conflict fought in the 1670s between Native Americans and New Englanders) who trained his own soldiers in the guerilla tactics of the East Coast Native Americans, forming his own unit of special light infantrymen who constituted the first regiment of what would one day become the U.S. Army Rangers. Church's first expedition into Acadia culminated in a battle near what is now Portland, Maine.

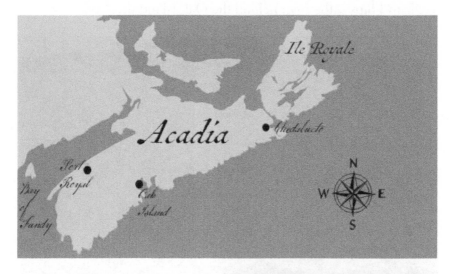

The second New English offensive against Acadia was led by Sir William Phips, a character who features in an interesting Oak Island theory presented by engineers Graham Harris and Les MacPhie in their book *Oak Island and its Lost Treasure*.

William Phips was considered something of a homegrown hero in New England. A lowborn shipwright and lumber merchant from the colony of Massachusetts, he had allowed his hard-won livelihood to literally go up in flames in order to save the lives of the residents of a particular village during a Wabanaki raid that took place during King Philip's War. More recently, he had been awarded a knighthood by King James II for salvaging the contents of a sunken Spanish treasure galleon in the Caribbean, a portion of which Harris and MacPhie contend lies at the bottom of the Money Pit. Despite Phips' complete lack of military experience, the Massachusetts militia promoted him to the rank of Major General in the spring of 1690 and gave him command of the naval expedition against New France.

First, Phips launched an attack against Port Royal, the capital of Acadia, situated on the southwestern shores of the Acadian Peninsula. To his delight, Phips found that Port Royal's ninety soldiers were actually in the process of dismantling their fortifications so that stronger ones could be built in their place. None of the fort's cannons were presently functional, and to top it off, the village's armory housed a total of nineteen muskets at that time. The garrison surrendered without a fight.

About a month after his capture of Port Royal, Sir William Phips tasked one of his officers with raiding the Acadian village of Chedabucto, situated at the tip of the Acadian Peninsula just across the Chedabucto Bay from Ile Royale (i.e. Cape Breton Island). In addition to housing a French military post called Fort Saint Louis, Chedabucto served as the headquarters of the Company of Acadia, an important French fishing company.

On June 3rd, 1690, Phips' captain and eighty-eight New English soldiers stormed Fort Saint Louis. Although they were heavily outnumbered, the twelve Acadian soldiers who manned the fort put up a fierce six-hour defense. When the New Englanders began to firebomb the fort, the French defenders realized that future resistance would be futile. They surrendered to the New English captain, who allowed them to retreat across the Gulf of St Lawrence to the French colony of Plaisance, on the island of Newfoundland.

That fall, Phips launched a third offensive against the French, this one targeting the city of Quebec, the heart of New France. Accompanied by 2,300 Massachusetts militiamen, Phips sailed from

Boston up the Atlantic Coast and further up the St. Lawrence River. The New English army reached the New French capital on October 16th, 1690, whereupon Phips sent an envoy into the city to deliver his terms of surrender. The French commander, Governor Frontenac, had the emissary blindfolded and brought to his residence, the Chateau St. Louis, where his war council was assembled. There, the envoy delivered Phips terms of surrender, telling Frontenac that he had one hour to reply. The enraged Governor famously retorted that the only reply Phips would receive would be from the mouths of his cannons.

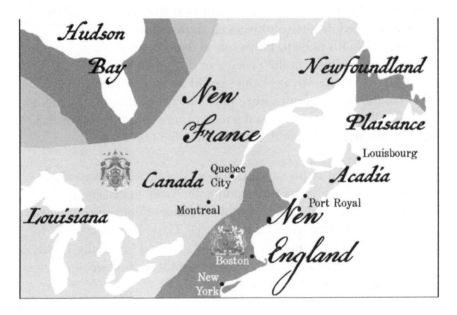

That evening, the New Englanders launched their assault on Quebec. From the very start, it was clear that their enterprise was doomed to fail. Members of the 1,200-man landing party were prevented from disembarking on the wooded shores outside the city by French-Canadian soldiers and First Nations warriors who fired at them from concealment in the trees. Meanwhile, Phips' three main warships barraged the city with cannon fire, only to be pounded in turn by Quebec's shore batteries which exceeded them in firepower. Following a futile attempt to overcome the French shore defensives, the besiegers returned to Boston in defeat.

S7E13: Bromancing the Stones

In the years that followed Phips' failed assault on Quebec, a number of battles between the French and the English and their respective First Nations allies took place in the borderlands between Acadia and New England. Benjamin Church launched two more offensives into what is now Maine, New English sailors made another assault on Port Royal, and French and English mariners engaged in a naval battle in the Bay of Fundy.

In 1696, the French and their native allies captured Fort William Henry, a large stone fortress situated near what is now Bristol, Maine, which had been built on the orders of Sir William Phips. The attackers returned up the Atlantic Coast and preceded to destroy nearly every English settlement in Newfoundland. In response, Benjamin Church led a number of brutal raids on Mi'kmaq and Acadian settlements throughout what is now the province of New Brunswick.

The Nine Years War finally ended in 1697, and its belligerents signed the Treaty of Ryswick- a document which, among other things, restored the pre-war borders in North America. Peace would reign in Acadia for another four years, until the death of the heirless Spanish king and the subsequent War of Spanish Succession, but that's a story for another time.

Season 7, Episode 14

Burnt Offerings

Plot Summary

In a continuation of the last scene of the previous episode, this episode begins in the War Room, where Craig Tester has just revealed that the 106-foot-deep wood found in Borehole FG-12 in Season 7, Episode 11 was carbon dated from 1626-1680. The crew members agree that this discovery warrants the sinking of the first caisson of the season overtop of FG-12. In an aside, the narrator informs us that FG-12 is located 25 feet northwest of Borehole H8, which yielded fragments of parchment and human bone back in Season 5.

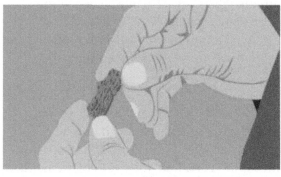

Later that day, several members of the Oak Island team meet at Smith's Cove with Laird Niven. The archaeologist tells the treasure hunters that the box-like structure discovered in the bump-out area back in Season 7, Episode 7 is probably not of cultural significance, implying that it was likely built by previous treasure hunters rather than the builders of the slipway, and gives them the green light to excavate the structure as they please. Billy Gerhardt proceeds to expose one side of the structure with his backhoe while Craig Tester and Jack Begley strip away the remaining dirt by hand. During this

process, Jack has a brush with the island's curse when a large rock breaks free from some nearby dirt and slams into his shoulder. Shortly thereafter, half of the structure collapses.

The next day, Rick Lagina and Jack Begley stand by as Gary Drayton conducts a metal detecting operation in the northern section of the swamp. After finding a modern nail, Gary comes across a hefty strip of iron with a sharp 90 degree bend at one end, which he tentatively identifies as some sort of bracket or a strap "that went around a chest or a box". The artifact reminds Rick of the wrought iron hinge which Gary discovered near the Smith's Cove slipway back in Season 6, Episode 16. The treasure hunters phone up Laird Niven and inform him of the discovery. Shortly thereafter, the archaeologist arrives on the scene and examines the piece. "It is old, isn't it?" he remarks. He goes on to suggest that it might have been used to reinforce a large timber, and advises the treasure hunters to show it to blacksmithing expert Carmen Legge.

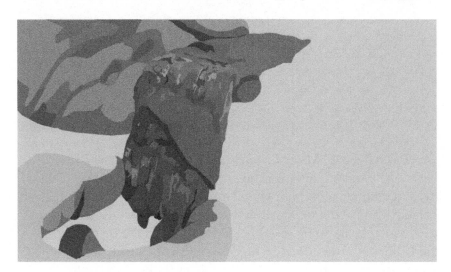

Later, Marty and Alex Lagina accompany Gary Drayton to the so-called Uplands- the area between Smith's Cove and the Money Pit, beneath which the Smith's Cove flood tunnel is believed to lie. Hoping that they might intercept the flood tunnel, the treasure hunters begin to excavate and examine the area, Marty removing earth with a backhoe and Alex assisting Gary as he sifts through the spoils with a metal detector. Several feet below the surface, the boys discover a handful of square timbers which appear to be part of some sort of shaft or tunnel.

The treasure hunters are soon joined by other members of the team. While Steve Guptill determines the coordinates of the newly-discovered Uplands structure, Marty Lagina remarks that the find evokes the wooden shafts discovered nearby, beneath the erstwhile Smith's Cove crane pad, in Season 6, Episodes 19 and 20. These structures are believed to be the exploratory shafts which Robert and Bobby Restall sank at Smith's Cove in the mid-1960s.

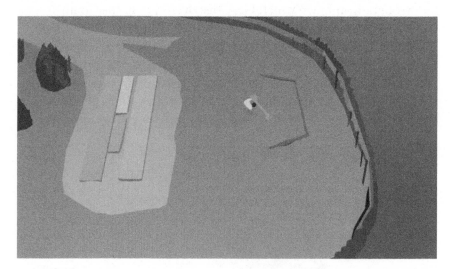

The following day, Marty Lagina shows Rick Lagina and Laird Niven the structure he unearthed in the Uplands area. There, the treasure hunters meet with Gary Drayton, Billy Gerhardt, and Alex Lagina, who have since excavated more of the structure, uncovering a log which bears some resemblance to those which comprised the U-Shaped structure. The boys keep digging, unearthing an old square nail which Drayton tentatively dates to the early 1800s.

Charles Barkhouse then appears on the scene and, when shown the nail, suggests that the structure might constitute undocumented work by the Truro Syndicate. Below the nail, the treasure hunters come across a massive log which rivals the diameter of any of the logs discovered at Smith's Cove.

Later that day, Marty Lagina, Alex Lagina, and Gary Daryton drive to the Ross Farm Museum, where they meet with Carmen Legge. The treasure hunters show the blacksmithing expert the metal strap they found in the swamp, as well as the pick and spade head that Jack Begley and Gary Drayton discovered near the Eye of the Swamp in the previous episode. Legge opines that the spade head is not a spade head at all, but rather a piece of sheet metal which might have been used to cover the inside of a wall or box. He declares the pickaxe head to be hand-wrought, says that it was intended for mining or tunneling, and dates it form the mid to late 1700s. Finally, Legge identifies the metal strap as a piece of a sailing ship used to hold timbers together, much to the pleasure of Gary Drayton. He measures the artifact and finds it to be nine inches long- a length, he says, which was common for such items between 1710 and 1790. He concludes his assessment by declaring that the strap was subjected to a hot sustained fire, finding charred material embedded in the fibre of the iron. The treasure hunters take this as potential evidence that the ship which they hope lies in the swamp was burned in an effort to conceal its presence.

Analysis

The Bracket

In this episode, Gary Drayton discovered a wrought-iron metal bracket in the northern section of the Oak Island swamp. Blacksmithing expert Carmen Legge later measured this artifact, found it to be nine inches in length, and subsequently identified it as a strap used to hold together the timbers of a ship. He dated the artifact from 1710 to 1790, and added that it bore evidence of having been subjected to a hot and sustained fire.

Following Legge's interpretation, several members of the Oak Island team took this artifact as potential proof of the theory that a ship once existed in the swamp. Legge's statement that the bracket was subjected to fire implies a new twist on this theory, namely that the ship in the swamp was burned, perhaps in an attempt to conceal evidence of its existence.

Season 7, Episode 15

Surely Templar

Plot Summary

In light of Gary Drayton's discovery of an iron bracket in the swamp in the previous episode, the Oak Island crew members return their attention towards the so-called Ship Anomaly, hoping once again that this feature might be the site of a buried ship. The narrator reveals that the depth of the Ship Anomaly is not uniform, with the northern end lying at a depth of 15 feet and the southern end lying at a depth of 55 feet. Accordingly, the crew decides to dig a fifteen-foot-deep exploratory trench at the Anomaly's northern end. Several feet below the surface, they discover an axe-cut wooden stake similar to those discovered in Season 7, Episode 11.

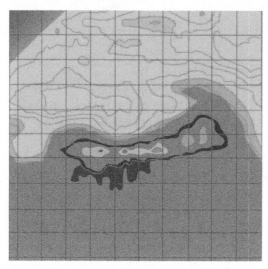

Meanwhile, in Traverse City, Michigan, Marty Lagina and Craig Tester have a Skype meeting with Vanessa Lucido of ROC Equipment, during which they ask the CEO the dimensions of the largest caisson ROC is capable of sinking. Lucido replies that, although the previous custom-made caisson used on Oak Island throughout Seasons 5 and 6 measured 50 inches in diameter, the ROC oscillator is capable of handling 8-foot (96-inch) caissons. The treasure hunters arrange for Lucido to bring the larger caisson to Oak Island.

Back in the swamp, while heavy equipment operator Billy Gerhardt is busy digging the trench at the tip of the Ship Anomaly, Gary Drayton conducts a metal detecting operation in the surrounding area. He quickly comes across a metallic object buried beside a cone-shaped rock. This artifact proves to be a pointy metal cone in which a broken wooden dowel appears to be embedded. "Initially," says Rick Lagina in a later interview, "it looked like a spear point... or a lance point, rather. But then we turn it about, and it appears hollow..."

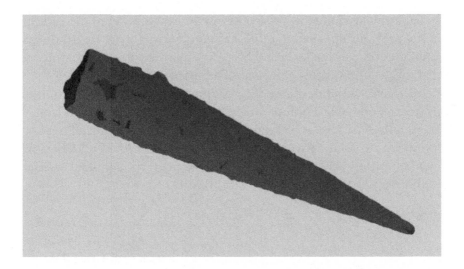

Meanwhile, Gerhardt is precluded from digging his trench to the planned depth of 15 feet due to the hardness of the clay. Fearful that they might damage their backhoe if they persist, the crew decides to terminate the operation.

That night, the crew congregates in the War Room, where they meet with author James McQuiston, who presented his Oak Island theory back in Season 6, Episode 20. In his previous War Room meeting with the Oak Island team, McQuiston had put forth the theory that members of the Knights Baronets of Nova Scotia- a

17th Century Scottish chivalric order associated with the short-lived Scottish colony of Nova Scotia- had buried the treasure of the Knights Templar on Oak Island sometime in the 1630s. In this episode, he expands on that theory by claiming that Sir William Alexander, the founder of the Nova Scotian colony, was the leader of a secret proto-Masonic society. "The bottom line," he summarizes, "is that it's more than apparent that the Scottish clan leaders who became the Knights Baronets of Nova Scotia had a lot of links to the Freemasons," Freemasonic symbolism having been associated with a number of discoveries made on Oak Island over the past two centuries. McQuiston goes on to point out that John Smith, one of the co-discoverers of the Money Pit, was related to one James McLean, whom he claims succeeded William Alexander as the leader of aforementioned secret society. He further suggests that John Smith knew about the existence of the Money Pit through his connection to James McLean and deliberately searched for it on Oak Island.

The next day, Marty Lagina, Charles Barkhouse, Laird Niven, Steve Guptill, and Peter Fornetti head to the foundation of the McGinnis family home on Oak Island's Lot 21. The narrator informs us that the team has acquired a permit to excavate the anomalies surrounding the foundation, these anomalies having been discovered by GPR experts Steve Watson and Don Johnston back in Season 7, Episode 5. Under Niven's direction, the treasure hunters use pins and string to mark off the locations of the test pits which they plan to dig and begin to excavate these sections with trowels. Each load of earth removed is then filtered on a sifting screen and minutely scrutinized. "Under Laird's supervision," Rick explains in a later interview, "we will conduct a proper archaeological dig of the foundation and the surrounding area..."

Later, Billy Gerhardt, Jack Begley, and Gary Drayton resume the excavation of the trench in the Uplands area between Smith's Cove and the Money Pit area, in which several large timbers were discovered in the previous episode. They soon intersect what appears to be the collapsed remains of a wood-shored shaft or tunnel. Near the structure, Jack Begley discovers a wad of what appears to be coconut fibre. The treasure hunters find more of the substance nearby and collect it for future analysis.

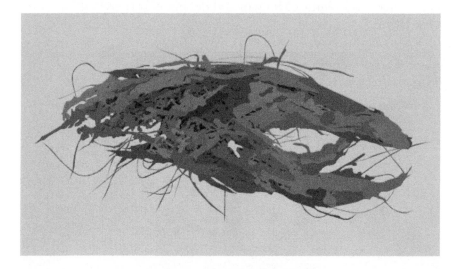

The next day, Marty Lagina, Alex Lagina, and Gary Drayton drive to the Ross Farm Museum in New Ross, Nova Scotia. There, they show blacksmithing expert Carmen Legge the conical metal object they discovered in the swamp near the northern tip of the Ship Anomaly. "Well," says Legge while turning the object over in his hands, "it's a hollow point. Two rivets on each side. Obviously it would have a wooden handle inserted in there and riveted into place." After dating the artifact from 1710 to 1790, the blacksmithing expert identifies the object as the tip of a pike pole and declares that it must have come off a sailing ship. "I know that they use a lot of these on ships," he explains, "to maneuver ships in really, really close spaces." Following Legge's analysis, some of the treasure hunters take the artifact as evidence of the theory that a ship, burnt or otherwise, lies interred within the Oak Island swamp.

Following their meeting with Carmen Legge, the treasure hunters resume their excavation of the trench in the Uplands. While incrementally 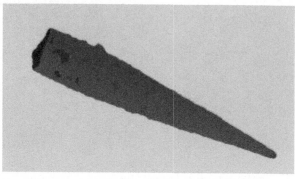 picking away at the recently-discovered wooden structure with his backhoe, Billy Gerhardt intersects a vein of water. Immediately, the trench begins to flood. The water flow quickly slows to a trickle, allowing the treasure hunters to examine the area from which the water erupted. Curiously, the water appears to have issued from the space between two large boulders which, as Jack Begley remarks, bear great resemblance to those discovered on Smith's Cove in Season 6, Episode 10, which Doug Crowell suspected might be the remains of one of the box drains. Rick Lagina inserts the end of his shovel into the cavity and finds it to be oriented vertically, and to be deeper than the shaft of his spade. Jack Begley voices his opinion that the boulders might constitute the remains of the Smith's Cove flood tunnel, and that the wooden structure nearby might constitute the remains of a searcher shaft called Shaft 5.

The narrator then explains that Shaft 5 was sunk by members of the Truro Company in the summer of 1850 about 100 feet from the Smith's Cove beach for the purpose of intersecting the Smith's Cove flood tunnel. At depth of about 35 feet, labourers had encountered a boulder. When they removed it, water began to flood the pit. The 19th Century treasure hunters, suspecting that they had indeed intersected the flood tunnel, promptly clogged the booby trap with clay and wood pilings before fruitlessly attempting to bail water from the Money Pit.

The next day, the Fellowship of the Dig meets in the War Room and calls up Dr. Ian Spooner, who has had a chance to examine the supposed coconut fibre found in the Uplands trench. The geoscientist confirms that the substance is indeed coconut fibre, as suspected.

Analysis

The Pike Pole Point

In this episode, Gary Drayton discovered a conical metal object buried beside a cone-shaped rock near the northern tip of the Ship Anomaly in the Oak Island swamp. Embedded within the object was a broken wooden dowel held in place by two rivets. Later, blacksmithing expert Carmen Legge examined the artifact and identified it as the tip of a pike pole- a tool used maneuver large wooden objects- and dated it from 1710 to 1790, similar to the bracket found in the previous episode. He further opined that the object was used to finely maneuver a sailing ship, bolstering the theory that the remains of a ship lie buried in the swamp.

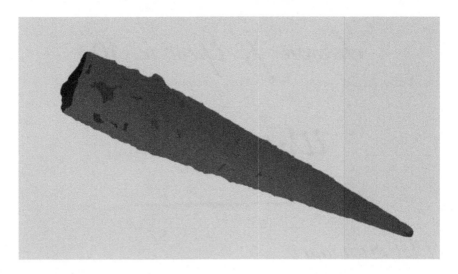

The Uplands Structure: Shaft 5?

Near the end of this episode, members of the Oak Island team resumed the excavation of the trench in the Uplands area between Smith's Cove and the Money Pit area which commenced at the end of the previous episode. The treasure hunters uncovered the remains of some sort of shaft or tunnel. Nearby, they came across several wads of what was later determined to be coconut fibre. Further below, they uncovered two large boulders between which issued a stream of water.

Following that discovery, some of the treasure hunters theorized that the wooden timbers in the trench constitute the remains of Shaft 5- a shaft dug by members of the Truro Syndicate in 1850 for the purpose of intersecting the Smith's Cove flood tunnel. At a depth of 35 feet, the Truro treasure hunters encountered a boulder which, when removed, allowed water from below to rise up and flood the shaft. Believing that they had indeed intersected the flood tunnel, they attempted to clog the supposed booby trap with clay and wood pilings. That accomplished, they tried to bail water from the Money Pit, but to no avail, leading some of the treasure hunters to believe that they had not completely plugged the flood tunnel, and others to suspect that there might be more than one flood tunnel feeding the Money Pit.

Season 7, Episode 16

Water Logged

Plot Summary

The episode begins in the Uplands area between Smith's Cove and the Money Pit, where Billy Gerhardt is busy uncovering what is believed to be the remains of Shaft 5. While the heavy equipment operator goes about his job, Gary Drayton scans the fresh spoils with a metal detector. Gary quickly comes across two large iron spikes, both of which he dates to the 1700s. The narrator remarks that, if the artifacts indeed date to the 18th Century, they were probably left by the builders of the Smith's Cove flood tunnel rather than members of the Truro Company, the latter having constructed Shaft 5 in 1850.

Later that day, the Fellowship of the Dig meets in the War Room, Marty Lagina and Craig Tester in attendance via Skype. Marty and Craig inform the team that they recently met with Jeremy Church, a geophysicist employed by the seismic exploration company Eagle Canada who appeared on the show in Season 6, Episodes 1 and 3. Church and the rest of the Eagle Canada crew have finally processed the data from the massive seismic scan of the eastern half of Oak Island which they performed back in Season 7, Episode 6. The data indicates the presence of an underground anomaly near the southeastern end of the Cave-In Pit at a depth of about 60 feet. The anomaly is linear and appears to run in the direction of the Money Pit, strongly evoking the Smith's Cove flood tunnel. Recall that GPR experts Steve Watson and Don Johnston, back in Season 7, Episode 2, also discovered some underground anomalies near the Cave-In Pit during their ground penetrating radar scan of the area, one of them lying at a depth of 82 feet and the other lying at a depth of 91 feet. A subsequent exploratory drilling operation (conducted in Season 7, Episode 5) revealed the presence of four feet of sand somewhere between 99-109 feet below the surface- deeper, it must be mentioned, than either of the two GPR anomalies.

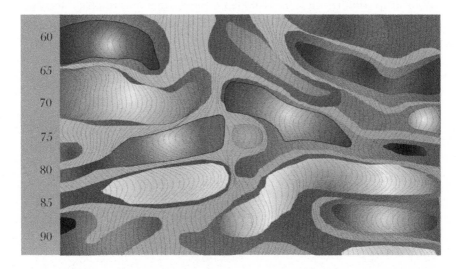

The narrator then reminds us that, back in Season 7, Episode 4, the team discovered fragments of wood at a depth of around 52 feet in Borehole OITC-6, located on Smith's Cove's upper beach. These fragments were later dated from 1735-1784. The narrator suggests that these pieces of wood and the 60-foot-deep seismic anomaly located southeast of the Cave-in Pit may both be part of the Smith's Cove flood tunnel.

Two days later, Devin Matchett of Delway Enterprises delivers an enormous long-armed excavator to the island. Matchett explains to Rick and Marty Lagina that this piece of equipment differs from other excavators in that its boom is 60 feet long, while those on regular excavators rarely exceed a length of 35 feet. Once the machine is unloaded, Marty Lagina jumps in the cab and drives to the Uplands pit, which Billy Gerhardt then proceeds to excavate (using the new equipment). After several bucket-loads of earth are removed, water begins pouring into the pit. While the treasure hunters admire the spectacle, a huge wall of earth breaks free from the side of the pit and crashes into the water below. The hole slowly starts to cave in, prompting the treasure hunters to backfill it for safety purposes and agree to abandon the excavation for the time being.

The next day, members of the Oak Island team meet at the Eye of the Swamp, determined to investigate the stones that encircle its perimeter, around each of which Gary Drayton discovered the presence of some mysterious iron objects in Season 7, Episode 3. The treasure hunters begin draining the pond with pumps, and Marty Lagina and Billy Gerhardt supplement the effort by removing water with their new excavator.

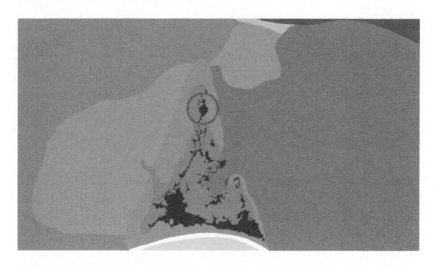

While the Eye of the Swamp is being drained, Rick Lagina and Gary Drayton do some metal detecting on the beach of Oak Island's Lot 17. There, they come across a large misshapen chunk of scrap lead. Rick suggests that they subject the artifact to a laser ablation test similar to those previously conducted on the lead cross and the cloisonné).

The next morning, the Oak Island team resumes the excavation of the Eye of the Swamp, which is not yet completely dry. One of the first buckets of sludge which Marty Lagina removes from the feature with the excavator contains a rock, which Jack Begley and Gary Drayton proceed to examine. The show neglects to inform us whether this rock contains any trace of the mysterious iron which Gary discovered back in Episode 3 of this season. While liberating the rock from the muck surrounding it, Jack Begley observes that the mud is mixed with what appears to be blue clay- a substance of which other sections of the swamp are devoid.

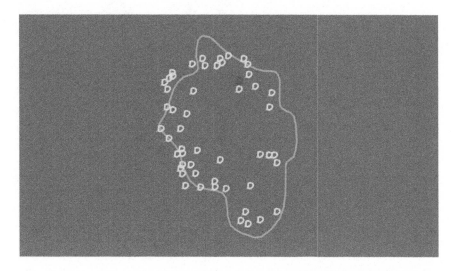

Shortly thereafter, the treasure hunters uncover the remains of three large tree stumps rooted to the swamp floor, reminiscent of the various oak stumps discovered in the swamp over the years, including those dredged up in Season 2, Episode 1; and Season 4, Episode 3. "These stumps should not be there," says Rick Lagina in a later interview, "unless there was a transition from dry to wet conditions." Marty Lagina then elaborates on his elder brother's remark, stating, "It just is so obvious that something changed radically between when those trees were growing and today, and if that's a natural process, OK. Doesn't mean anything. If it's man-made, it sure means something."

Gary Drayton examines one of the stump with his metal detector and discovers an iron rod embedded in the wood. This find evokes another discovery made in Season 4, Episode 3, when Tony Sampson discovered a metal object encased in a large stump rooted to the floor of the Mercy Point area in the Oak Island swamp. Sampson had pried that object loose, revealing it to be a survey marker placed decades ago by treasure hunter Fred Nolan.

The next day, Craig Tester, Alex Lagina, and Charles Barkhouse head to St. Mary's University in Halifax, Nova Scotia. There, they present Associate Professor of Chemistry Dr. Christa Brosseau with the iron spikes recently discovered in the Uplands pit. With the help of research instrument technician Dr. Xiang Yang, Dr. Brosseau examines the nails under an electron microscope and finds that they both contain phosphorus, which she says is an indication that they were forged sometime prior to the 1840s. She

also states that old iron objects rich in phosphorus are commonly found in Britain and Northern Europe. Alex Lagina then remarks that, if the artifacts were indeed manufactured prior to 1840, they may have been left by the builders of the Smith's Cove flood tunnel.

Later, the Fellowship of the Dig meets at the Mug & Anchor Pub in the town of Mahone Bay, Nova Scotia. There, Alex Lagina presents his fellow treasure hunters with the nails from the Upland pit and informs them of Dr. Brosseau's analysis. In light of the news that the spikes might have been left by the original depositors, the treasure hunters agree that they ought to resume the excavation of the Uplands pit.

The next day, Tom Nolan assists Rick Lagina, Gary Drayton, and Billy Gerhardt in their excavation of the Eye of the Swamp. While digging at the centre of the feature, Billy Gerhardt uncovers a stack of enormous boulders comparable in size to those which comprise Nolan's Cross. The treasure hunters agree that they ought to have the boulders analyzed by geoscientist Dr. Ian Spooner.

Plot Summary

The Cave-In Pit Anomaly

Near the beginning of this episode, we learned that the seismic survey of the eastern half of Oak Island carried out in Season 7, Episode 6, indicated the presence of a tantalizing anomaly southeast of the Cave-In Pit at a depth of 60 feet. The anomaly is linear and runs towards the Money Pit area, evoking the Smith's Cove flood tunnel.

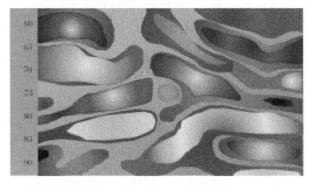

This discovery is reminiscent of the anomalies discovered by GPR experts Steve Watson and Don Johnston during their ground penetrating radar scan of the Cave-In Pit area in Season 7, Episode 2. Specifically, these anomalies were located at depths of 82 and 91 feet, respectively. A subsequent exploratory drilling operation failed to determine the nature of these anomalies, although it did yield four feet of sand somewhere between the depth of 99 and 109 feet.

As the narrator mentioned in this episode, the 60-foot-deep anomaly indicated by the seismic survey data also calls to mind the fragments of wood discovered between 50-53 feet in Borehole OITC-6- an exploratory drillhole punched at Smith's Cove's upper beach in Season 7, Episode 4. These fragments were later carbon dated from 1735-1784.

Metal Rods in Stumps in the Swamp

In this episode, the Oak Island team uncovered several large tree stumps on the outer perimeter of the Eye of the Swamp. While examining the area with a metal detector, Gary Drayton discovered what appeared to be an iron rod embedded in one of these stumps.

This find evokes another discovery made in Season 4, Episode 3, when diver Tony Sampson discovered a stump in the Mercy Point area in the swamp. Sampson discovered the presence of some sort of metal object in the swamp which proved to be an iron survey marker placed decades ago by treasure hunter Fred Nolan.

Nails from the Uplands Pit

In this episode, the crew discovers two square-shanked rosehead nails in their exploratory pit in the Uplands area. At the end of the episode, Dr. Christa Brosseau 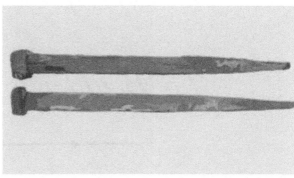 and Dr. Xiang Yang of St. Mary's University in Halifax examine the artifacts under an electron microscope and find that both of them contain significant quantities of phosphorus. Dr. Brosseau explains that this is an indication that the nails were crafted prior to 1840, and that they were probably made in either England or Northern Europe.

Season 7, Episode 17

To Boulderly Go

Plot Summary

Rick Lagina takes Dr. Ian Spooner to the Eye of the Swamp, where a stack of boulders was uncovered at the end of the previous episode. As the geoscientist examines the feature, Rick remarks that formation bears great resemblance to the subterranean makeup of the so-called "Paved Wharf", beneath which layers of large rocks were discovered in Season 7, Episode 12. Spooner concurs with his assessment, and concludes that the formation must be artificial. The treasure hunters are soon joined by Laird Niven, who observes that the feature resembles filled-in cellars that he has examined in the past.

Meanwhile, at Mari Vineyards in Traverse City, Michigan, Marty Lagina has a video call with Mike Monahan of Irving Equipment Ltd. Marty reveals that Oak Island Tours Inc.'s cofferdam permit will expire in about a month, and asks Monahan whether Irving will be able to dismantle the cofferdam and restore Smith's Cove to its original condition in accordance with provincial environmental law. Monahan replies that his team is capable of such an operation and will require three weeks to complete it.

The next day, Billy Gerhardt, under Rick Lagina's direction, reopens the Uplands pit abandoned the previous episode in the hopes of intersecting the Smith's Cove flood tunnel. About six feet below the surface, Billy uncovers a handful of wooden planks and boards which Rick suggests might be the remains of a shaft wall, the shaft presumably being Shaft 5.

Later, Alex Lagina and Peter Fornetti head to Oak Island's Lot 21, where Laird Niven and conservator Kelly Bourassa are busy digging archaeological trenches around the foundations of the McGinnis family cabin, in the areas where the GPR scan conducted in Season 7, Episode 5 indicated the presence of underground anomalies. Laird shows the cousins the remains of a stone wall which he discovered in one of the trenches, which old photographs indicate constitute the foundation of a shed.

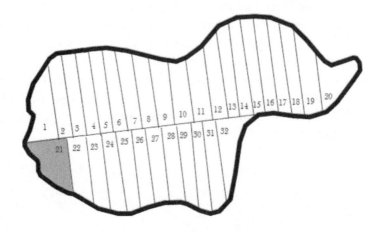

That evening, the Fellowship of the Dig meets in the War Room to learn the results of a laser ablation test to which the lump of lead discovered on the beach of Lot 18 in the previous episode was

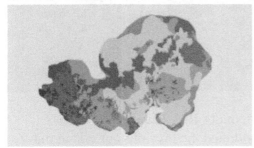

subjected. The crew members call up geochemistry professor Dr. Chris McFarlane, who performed the test. McFarlane informs the team that the lead contains mercury and tin, and opines that the mercury must have been introduced after smelting. "Mercury is one of the most volatile elements," he explains, "so if you heat it up to 8[00 or] 900 degrees to smelt it, the mercury would be gone. So it had to have been introduced by some other process. I've never seen anything like it, honestly." Jack Begley then remarks that mercury features in Petter Amundsen's Oak Island theory, presented back in Season 1, Episode 4, which contends that Elizabethan-Jacobean scientist and nobleman Sir Francis Bacon is the man behind the

Oak Island mystery. Jack explains that, in his 1626 book *Sylva Sylvarum*, Bacon described a preservation technique in which the object to be preserved is dipped in mercury. Interestingly, a number of artifacts discovered on Oak Island over the years, including fragments of broken pottery found in 1937 on Joudrey's Cove and a fragment of parchment brought up from the Money Pit area in 1897, are said to have borne traces of mercury. After Jack's exposition, Dr. McFarlane, in response to a question from Doug Crowell, states that the artifact's isotopic signature suggests that the lead was mined in the Greek mainland, the Aegean Islands, Cyprus, or Turkey. Gary Drayton remarks that each of the places that McFarlane mentioned were known to have been frequented by the Knights Templar.

The next day, Rick Lagina and Craig Tester head to the foundations of the McGinnis cabin on Lot 21, where Laird Niven is busy excavating by hand. The archaeologist shows the treasure hunters evidence of what he believes might be a trap door in the cellar. He also shows Rick and Craig a decorated bone handle of a knife which he discovered in the cellar area, which he dates to the latter half of the 18th Century. The narrator then informs us that Laird will be unable to excavate the foundations further without first acquiring another permit from the Nova Scotian government.

That afternoon, Rick Lagina and Terry Matheson stand by as Billy Gerhardt excavates the Uplands pit. Billy brings up several large timbers bearing notches which Terry observes appear to have been fashioned with an axe. Terry also notices a hole drilled in one of the notches, which he remarks bears great resemblance to drilled holes found in the U-Shaped structure.

When Billy Gerhardt uncovers potential evidence of a tunnel, Rick Lagina decides to examine the supposed structure with his own eyes. He climbs into the bucket of the excavator and Billy Gerhardt lowers him into the hole, much to the consternation of Terry Matheson, who expresses some concern that the hole could cave in. Rick is unable to tell whether truly constitutes a tunnel or not, and Billy brings him back to the surface.

The next day, Marty Lagina and Craig Tester join the rest of the crew at the Uplands pit. There, Rick Lagina shows his younger brother the notched and drilled beam recently recovered from the hole. Marty expresses his belief that the beam is at least two hundred years old and suggests that they have it dendrochronologically tested.

Billy Gerhardt proceeds to remove several more buckets of earth from the hole and hits what he believes to be a boulder. In order to verify the nature of the obstruction, Marty Lagina peers over the edge of the pit, secured to the surface by a rope and harness. Marty spies the opening of what he suspects might be an underground tunnel near the bottom of the hole. In order to get a better look at the feature, the treasure hunters attach a camera to the excavator bucket and lower it into the pit. The feature proves to be a large indentation in the side of the pit surrounded by planks running in all directions, apparently having been torn from their original positions by the excavator. Lodged in the middle of the cavity are what appear to be several large boulders. Marty expresses his opinion that the feature is indeed a tunnel.

That evening, the treasure hunters convene in the War Room, where they review the footage taken in the Uplands pit. Marty Lagina, Paul Troutman, and Billy Gerhardt all express their opinion that the aforementioned feature appears to be the remains of an underground tunnel. Marty remarks that a dendrochronological test of the wood removed from the pit will shed light on the nature of the structure.

The next day, Rick Lagina and Scott Barlow meet at Smith's Cove with Mike Jardine of Irving Equipment Ltd. The treasure hunters watch as Jardine's crew begins to dismantle the cofferdam, ending this season's excavations at Smith's Cove.

Analysis

The Mercury-Tinged Lead

In this episode, Dr. Chris McFarlane of the University of New Brunswick released the results of the laser ablation test of the lead blob discovered on the beach of Oak Island's Lot 18 in Season 7, Episode 16. McFarlane disclosed that the artifact contains significant quantities of tin and mercury, and postulated that the latter was somehow introduced after the ore from which the lead derives was smelted. He also opined that the ore from which the lead derives was likely mined on the Greek mainland, the Aegean Islands, Cyprus, or Turkey.

After learning the results of the laser ablation tests, Jack Begley remarked that the presence of mercury in the lead artifact evokes Petter Amundsen's theory, mercury immersion being one of the conservational techniques described in the writings of Sir Francis Bacon, who features prominently in Amundsen's theory.

The Tunnel in the Uplands Pit

In this episode, Oak Island Tours Inc. reopened the Uplands pit, which was backfilled in the previous episode. In addition to unearthing a variety of timbers, one of them reminiscent of the U-Shaped structure, the crew discovered the remains of what appears to be an underground tunnel. Several crewmembers suggested that the feature might be the remains of the Smith's Cove flood tunnel, and all agreed that a dendrochronological test of the timbers of which it is comprised is in order.

Season 7, Episode 18

The Turning Point

Plot Summary

The Lagina brothers and Dave Blankenship stand by as Irving Equipment Ltd. and ROC Equipment deliver 8-foot-wide caissons, an oscillator, and a crane to Oak Island. The trio meets with Vanessa Lucido, Jared Busby and Danny Smith, who inform them that they have brought 210 feet of caisson to Oak Island, and will be able to sink 202-foot-deep shafts.

While ROC and Irving set up their equipment in the Money Pit area, Rick Lagina, Gary Drayton, Steve Guptill, and Dr. Ian Spooner resume their excavations at the Eye of the Swamp. Dr.

Spooner, who has been examining the geological makeup of the dig site with a trowel, shows Rick a sample of material he extracted from beneath one of the boulders uncovered in Season 7, Episode 16, and cites it as proof that the boulders constitute relatively recent additions to the swamp. While the dig resumes, Spooner informs Rick that the vibracore samples of the Eye of the Swamp which he and his graduate students extracted in Season 7, Episode 9 contained high concentrations of mercury and lead near their bottoms, which he takes as an indication of human activity. In a later interview, Rick Lagina remarks that the presence of mercury in the swamp evokes Petter Amundsen's theory that Francis Bacon is the man behind the Oak Island mystery, and that the lost manuscripts of William Shakespeare, written in Bacon's hand and preserved in mercury, lie buried on Oak Island. Although the show fails to mention it, Spooner's disclosure also brings to mind the lump of scrap lead which Gray Drayton discovered in Season 7, Episode 16, on the beach of Oak Island's Lot 18, which Dr. Chris McFarlane, in the previous episode, revealed contains a significant quantity of mercury.

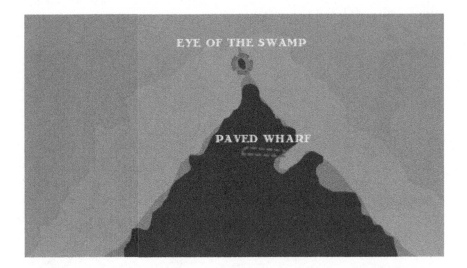

The next day, the Oak Island team meets at the swamp with archaeologist Aaron Taylor, a colleague of Dr. Spooner's who teaches archaeology at St. Mary's University in Halifax. Taylor examines some of the stones in the swamp and opines that they were not deposited by glaciers. "In archaeology," he says, "we have an expression: 'when in doubt, excavate'". He then suggests that the crew subject a section of the swamp's stone formations to a formal archaeological excavation. When pressed by Marty Lagina, he admits that he believes the stones were placed by man.

Following Aaron Taylor's preliminary analysis, Dr. Spooner proffers his own theory that the Eye of the Swamp constitutes the remains of a 300-year-old clay mine, considering the significant quantities of blue clay which Jack Begley discovered at the site in Season 7, Episode 16. Taylor concurs with his theory and elaborates on it by suggesting that, if the Eye of the Swamp is indeed the site of a clay mine, the Paved Wharf might have been constructed as a roadway by which clay could be transported from the mine to the beach, where it could be loaded onto ships.

That evening, the Fellowship of the Dig congregates in the Mug & Anchor Pub in Mahone Bay, Nova Scotia. There, the treasure hunters discuss Ian Spooner and Aaron Taylor's theory that the Eye of the Swamp is the site of an old blue clay mine. Rick Lagina concludes the meeting by making the toast: "To the swamp!", to which Marty Lagina, who has made no secret of his aversion to the swamp, refuses to raise his glass.

The next day, Rick Lagina, Doug Crowell, and Steve Guptill meet with Vanessa Lucido and Mike Jardine at the Money Pit area. The narrator informs us that the team plans to sink a caisson at a site dubbed 'OC1'. While the oscillator is moved into position, Lucido remarks that this custom-built piece of machinery weighs 110,000 pounds- nearly double the weight of the oscillator used in prior seasons, which weighed 64,000 pounds.

Later that day, Rick Lagina, Jack Begley, Gary Drayton, and Billy Gerhardt excavate the edges of the Paved Wharf in the hopes of better determining the extent of the structure. The treasure hunters observe a rapid influx of water into one of the trenches they dig and speculate as to the water's sources, of which there appear to be two. Jack notes that some of the water appears to be issuing from a cluster of rocks, which he suggests might be part of the Paved Area (the "Paved Area" being a term which some of the treasure hunters now sometimes use in reference to what was formerly called the "Paved Wharf"). "It's very simple," says Rick in a later interview. "If you have a pile of rocks, water will flow through, certainly. Was it a way to conduct water from one area to another? It's possible. It'd be great if it were a French drain [see Season 4, Episode 13 in *The Oak Island Encyclopedia*] or part of the flood tunnel system, but as of yet, we have not been able to ascertain its purpose." The treasure hunters are soon joined by Craig Tester, who observes that some of the water appears to be flowing into the trench from the direction of the beach, and suggests that they ought to try to take samples of each apparent water source in order to determine whether they are fresh or salty. Billy extracts some of the water with the bucket of his excavator, the runoff from which Rick collects in a bottle and tastes (to the visible disgust of Craig Tester). Rick declares that the water tastes brackish, or slightly salty- an indication that one of the water sources might be Smith's Cove.

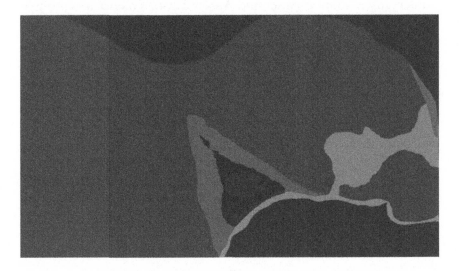

The next day, Charles Barkhouse, Doug Crowell, and Laird Niven meet with GPR experts Steve Watson and Don Johnston at Oak Island's Lot 25, where Samuel Ball's home once stood. The narrator informs us that, although the foundation of Ball's cabin is a protected heritage site, and that treasure hunters are precluded from excavating within 200 feet of the ruins, Laird Niven has secured a special permit to allow Watson and Johnston to conduct a GPR scan of the area.

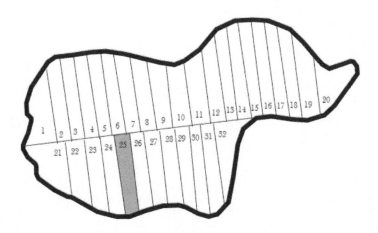

As the GPR experts prepare to carry out their scan, Rick Lagina shows Ian Spooner the recently-dug trench in the Oak Island swamp which appears to be fed by multiple sources of water. Rick and Dr. Spooner watch as Billy Gerhardt drains the trench, which is now full of water, with his backhoe.

Back on Lot 25, Steve Watson and Don Johnston discover what appears to be an underground wall near the Ball foundations with their GPR scanner. Shortly thereafter, they come across another anomaly which appears to lie 1.5 feet below the surface. When the GPR experts complete their survey, Laird Niven states that he thinks they now have sufficient data to apply for an excavation permit from the Nova Scotian government.

Later, Rick Lagina, Dan Henskee, and Dave Blankenship drive to the Money Pit area, where they find the rest of the crew in attendance. The treasure hunters stand by while Dave Blankenship and Dan Hensee start up the oscillator which is now in place, initiating the sinking of the massive caisson dubbed 'OC1'.

Analysis

The Clay Mine Theory

In this episode, Dr. Ian Spooner put forth the theory that the Eye of the Swamp might constitute the remains of a 300-year-old clay mine, considering the significant quantities of blue clay which Jack Begley discovered at the site in Season 7, Episode 16. His colleague, Aaron Taylor, who teaches archaeology at St. Mary's University in Halifax, concurred with his assessment.

Dr. Spooner is not the first to hypothesize that Oak Island was once the site of a clay mine. Back in Season 3, Episode 6, miner John O'Brien outlined his own theory that pre-Conquista Mayans discovered palygorskite clay on Oak Island in around 800 A.D. Palygorskite is a rare type of clay arguably most famous for being a key constituent of Maya blue, a bright blue pigment used by members of the Maya civilization. Essentially a mixture of palygorskite and indigo dye, Maya blue was employed as a colorant in ceramics, murals, sculptures, and illuminated codices, and was used to paint sacrificial human victims during Mayan rituals. Mysteriously, palygorkite clay is not known to exist in any substantial

natural deposits in Mesoamerica. John O'Brien believes that the
"blue clay" discovered at depth on Oak Island over the years is, in
fact, a rare form of naturally blue palygorskite clay. He maintains
that this substance, having a natural blue pigmentation, would have
been especially valuable to the Maya. O'Brien contends that Maya
miners sank shafts on and dug tunnels beneath Oak Island
throughout the Middle Ages in search of this material. He also
believes that, during the *Conquista* of Hernan Cortes, members of
the dying Aztec Empire secreted their most valuable treasures out of
Mexico and entombed them on Oak Island, in the old Mayan mine
shafts.

Anomalies by the Samuel Ball Foundation

In this episode, GPR experts Steve Watson and Don Johnston
discovered the presence of two underground anomalies near the
foundations of the home of one-time Oak Island landowner Samuel
Ball. One of these anomalies appeared to be an underground while,
while the other appeared to lie 1.5 feet below the surface.

[For the results of the excavation of these anomalies, see 'The Lot
25 Tunnel' in Season 7, Episode 22]

Season 7, Episode 19

Lords of the Ring

───────•─◆─•───────

Plot Summary

The episode begins at the Money Pit area, where the excavation of
caisson OC1 is underway. At a depth of 50 feet, the caisson
intersects what appears to be the remains of the Hedden Shaft. The
treasure hunters stand by as the hammergrab brings up load after
load of timber.

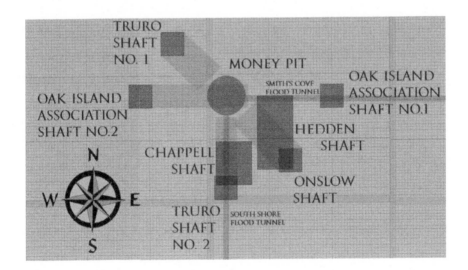

Later, Rick Lagina and Gary Drayton do some metal detecting along
the southern lip of the Oak Island swamp. After unearthing the lid
of a tin can, they come across an old ring on which a flower and

other decorations have been engraved. Visibly pleased with this new discovery, Gary designates the ring a "top pocket find" and puts it away for future analysis.

Rick and Gary proceed to the Oak Island Research Centre, where they show the ring to Marty Lagina, Laird Niven, and Kelly Bourassa. Marty and Laird observe that the ring is quite small- an indication that it was probably intended for a woman. Laird examines the artifact under a Grobet digital microscope, revealing a silver inlay in the grooves that make up the ring's central flower motif. Bourassa points out that the artifact contains two different types of corrosion, one of them green and the other reddish, which he suggests might be an indication that the ring is composed of a copper alloy. While pondering ring's implications, Rick refers to the artifact's central ornament as a "starburst", evoking the 18th Century

silver laminate dandy button which Gary Drayton and Charles Barkhouse discovered at Isaac's Point in Season 7, Episode

1. Marty concludes the preliminary inspection by suggesting that they show the ring to gemologist and master goldsmith Charles Lewton-Brain, who analyzed Lot 8 and Lot 21 brooches back in Season 6, Episode 2.

The next day, Rick Lagina, Craig Tester, and Terry Matheson meet with oscillator operator Danny Smith at the Money Pit area, where they learn that OC1 has reached a depth of about 105 feet. Craig remarks that everything extracted below this point is of potential interest and will need to be examined. Rick asks Smith to inform him and the team if anything unusual occurs henceforth in the excavation.

The ROC and Irving Equipment Ltd. crews continue to excavate OC1, pausing after every hammergrab scoop to allow the treasure hunters to process the spoils. The Fellowship searches through each hammergrab load with a metal detector, manually extricates every large timber or piece of wood, and transfers the rest of the muck to the wash plant for sifting. In a later interview, Marty Lagina declares his intention to submit some of the wood extracted from OC1 for dendrochronological testing.

The treasure hunters watch as the hammergrab emerges from the caisson with a large metal object in its jaws. Although the artifact brings to mind the metal artifacts brought up from the GAL1 caisson in Season 4, Episode 15, Craig Tester declares that the object must be the "Hedden shield"- a notion with which his fellow treasure hunters immediately concur. "That hasn't seen the light of day since 1936," Doug Crowell says. The narrator then explains that this artifact is almost certainly the 6-foot-tall metal brace of "shield" with which the Hedden Shaft was reinforced back in the 1930s.

Later that day, the treasure hunters examine the OC1 spoils which the wash plant has sorted. Paul Troutman finds several fragments of glass and pottery with which Rick Lagina is unimpressed. Paul then comes across a large piece of what appears to be bone- perhaps human bone- which had lain at a depth of about 120 feet. The narrator reminds us that, back in Season 5, Episodes 5 and 6, 17th Century human bones were discovered in Borehole H8. These bones, however, were discovered at a depth of 160-165 feet.

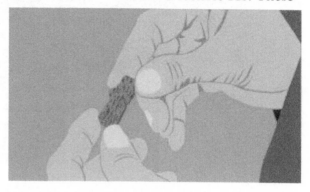

That same afternoon, the Oak Island team congregates in the War Room and calls up Charles Lewton-Brain, who has had a chance to examine photographs of the ring found at the southern edge of the swamp. The gemologist and master goldsmith tells the crew that he observed evidence of crude repairs made to the ring, their purposes being to make the ring "much bigger" and "a little smaller", respectively. These repairs were made with silver, while Lewton-Brain suspects that the rest of the ring is composed of either bronze or a copper-silver alloy. The goldsmith states that the ring's floral design appears to have been hand-chiseled, which he claims is potential evidence that the artifact was crafted prior to the 1730s. "Saw blades," he explains, "don't really become available to jewelers until the 1730s, 1750s, and so, prior to that, you would be cutting the metal out with a chisel." Lewton-Brain goes on to identify the style as European, and possibly Spanish.

The next day, the crew resumes the excavation of OC1. Somewhere below 120 feet, the hammergrab picks up half of a circular wooden sheet which Terry Matheson identifies as "the top or bottom of a barrel". In the same load, the treasure hunters find a short wooden slat which Matheson identifies as a stave of the same barrel. These artifacts reminds Doug Crowell of the yellow-painted wooden disk discovered by the Oak Island Association at a depth of 118 feet in 1861.

At a depth of about 147 feet, the hammergrab brings up an axe-cut beam. As the treasure hunters are unaware of any wood-cribbed searcher shafts or tunnels having been constructed at that depth, they deduce that the wood must be part of the original Money Pit. Disappointingly, the next few hammergrab loads contain nothing of interest. The treasure hunters decide to abandon the shaft at a depth of 158 feet in order to avoid destroying the caisson's teeth on the bedrock below.

The next day, Rick Lagina, Dave Blankenship, and Doug Crowell drive to the home of the late Dan Blankenship. There, they are greeted by Dave's sister, Linda Flowers, who now owns the house. Linda takes the boys to Dan's old office, where the veteran treasure hunter kept his records, and leaves them to search through the papers for any clue which might help them select the location of their next Money Pit shaft.

The next day, Rick Lagina meets in the Oak Island Research Centre with Charles Barkouse, Doug Crowell, Laird Niven, and Steve Guptill. Rick assigns his fellow treasure hunters the task of determining the location of their next shaft in the Money Pit area. "We've got a lot of data [which] keeps on pointing in a similar area," Steve says, "but that area isn't tight enough." Doug then produces a sheet of paper he discovered in the archive of Dan Blankenship, which he asks his fellow crewmembers to take a look at. Doug explains that this document was produced by Erwin Hamilton, who looked for treasure on Oak Island from 1938-1941, and contains a birds-eye diagram depicting the old searcher tunnels which Hamilton re-excavated during his Oak Island tenure. In a later interview, Rick Lagina expresses his hope that this document will help the team more accurately determine the location and orientation of the Shaft 6 tunnel, which constituted one of their primary goals throughout Season 6. Steve Guptill agrees to compare the diagram with the coordinates he has already plotted.

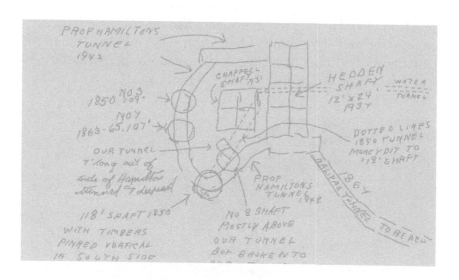

The next day, the crew meets at the Money Pit area, where the sinking of a new shaft called '8A' is about to commence. The narrator informs us that, aided by Hamilton's diagram, Steve Guptill was able to pinpoint what he believes to be the location of Shaft 6 and its tunnel. Similar to Shaft S6, which was excavated in Season 6, Episodes 17 and 18, 8A will be sunk at the suspected junction of the

Shaft 6 tunnel and the Money Pit- a site located about 20 feet southwest of OC1. The treasure hunters express their optimism in the project as the 8A caisson begins its descent into the earth.

Analysis

The Ring in the Swamp

In this episode, Gary Drayton and Rick Lagina discovered a metal ring engraved with a floral motif at the southern edge of the Oak Island swamp. Gemologist and master goldsmith Charles Lewton-Brain of the Alberta College of Art and Design examined photos of this artifact and observed that its central motif appears to have been hand-chiseled. He took this as evidence that the ring might date prior to the mid-18th Century, when jewelers began cutting out metal with saw blades rather than chisels. He tentatively identified the engraving's style as European, and possibly Spanish.

In the days following this episode's first airing, at least two fans of *The Curse of Oak Island* posted photos of very similar rings to various Oak Island-related Facebook groups, these baubles being identical in every respect to the artifact found in the swamp save for their coloration and lack of tarnish or corrosion. One of these fans, whose ring has a bright silver colour, claimed to have found his own trinket in 2015, in a farmer's field in Wisconsin. Another, whose ring is bronze-coloured, claimed to have been given this ring by her mother forty years ago. In a Facebook thread attached to a photo of the bronze-coloured ring, a specialist who has appeared on the show in the past declared that, although he is not a jewelry expert, this object looks "like stamped costume jewelry with a silvered copper alloy core".

SWAMP RING

FAN RING #1

FAN RING #2

If the bronze-coloured ring is indeed a piece of modern costume jewelry, and if the ring found in the swamp is a piece from the same batch, as it appears to be, then it seems likely that the artifact discovered in this episode is a relatively modern item which was deposited in the swamp sometime in the last century. This possibility evokes the so-called "Swordgate" scandal in which archaeologist Andy White and writer Jason Colavito demonstrated that the supposed Roman *gladius* showcased in Season 3, Episodes 10 and 11 of *The Curse of Oak Island* is not a genuine Roman artifact but rather a relatively modern souvenir item of a type once sold to tourists in Italy.

About a week after the first ring owners came forth with their jewelry, an American Oak Island researcher named John Frick announced on various Oak Island-related Facebook groups that he had determined the swamp ring's manufacturer to be Joseph Esposito, a jewelry manufacturing company established in 1910. Frick purchased a ring of the same model on Ebay and found that, allowing for tarnish and corrosion, it was virtually identical to the ring found in the swamp. Although Frick's claims drew some harassment from fans of the show, a respected expert who has appeared on *The Curse of Oak Island* in the past came to his defense, writing the following as a reply to his post:

A photo of Oak Island researcher John Frick's 'Joseph Esposito' ring, courtesy of John Frick.

"John Frick did his homework well. Scientific analysis results on the metals that comprise the ring, performed after the filming wrapped and which I read constantly, pointed to a unique plating method that was developed after 1930. Knowing this, even though the earlier opinion that the fabrication method could allow the ring to be much older, it became obvious this year that it was not. What you don't often see on TV is the real lag time in receiving test results. The show tells the story of the hunt, and sometimes test results come in too late to be of impact to the show."

The Barrel Bottom

In this episode, the Oak Island crew discovered a piece of what appears to be the head or bottom of a barrel, along with what might be a stave of that barrel, below a depth of 120 feet in Borehole OC1. These artifacts reminded Doug Crowell of a similar object discovered by the Oak Island Association at a depth of 118 feet in 1861.

That summer, the Oak Island Association sank the 118-foot-deep Shaft 6 eighteen feet west of the Money Pit. That accomplished, they tunneled towards the Money Pit, hoping to circumvent the Smith's Cove flood tunnel (Oak Island Tours Inc. mapped this tunnel via exploration drilling throughout Season 6). Much to their pleasure, the Association men reached the Money Pit without being flooded out; the circumvention was a success. With the elusive treasure nowhere to be seen at that 118-foot-depth, the treasure hunters proceeded to dig through the Money Pit's eastern wall. As soon as they did, water began to seep in from the east, and in no time, both Shaft 6 and the Money Pit were both completely flooded with seawater. The Association men proceeded to bail water from Shaft 6. That accomplished, they began to clear the tunnel of the mud and debris which had filled it. The first pieces of debris they removed, which presumably slid into the tunnel from the Money Pit during the flooding, included fragments of age-blackened wood, a spruce slab perforated by an auger hole, a hand-cut branch of juniper, and a round yellow-painted object resembling a dish or the bottom of a barrel. The barrel bottom recovered from OC1 reminds Doug Crowell of the latter artifact.

No sooner had the labourers begun the job of clearing the tunnel than, according to foreman Jotham McCully, "they heard a tremendous crash in the Money Pit and barely escaped being caught by the rush of mud which followed them into the West pit and filled it up 7 feet in less than three minutes."

Season 7, Episode 20

Springing the Trap

Plot Summary

The episode begins at the Money Pit area, where the sinking of caisson 8A is underway. The shaft reaches a depth of 78 feet without incident, passing through what appears to be *in situ* soil.

Meanwhile, Alex Lagina, Gary Drayton, and Billy Gerhardt dig an exploratory trench between the Eye of the Swamp and the Paved Wharf. Less than a foot below the surface, they uncover a layer of large rocks embedded in clay, which Gary suggests might be a continuation of the Paved Area. The boys then do some metal detecting in the trench and come across two long, thin iron rods bearing resemblance to the pieces of primitive rebar found near the slipway in Season 7, Episode 11, and to the crib spikes discovered at Smith's Cove throughout Seasons 6 and 7. Gary remarks that these artifacts, which are the first of their kind to be discovered in the Oak Island swamp, constitute evidence of tunneling or shaft-building in the area, similar to the pickaxe head found at the Eye of the Swamp in Season 7, Episode 13. He then suggests that they show the artifacts to Carmen Legge.

Alex, Gary, and Billy continue digging and quickly come across several pieces of charred wood. The narrator then reminds us of the theory, introduced in Season 7, Episode 14, following the discovery of the scorched metal bracket in the northern section of the swamp, that a sailing ship was burned centuries ago in the swamp. Gary

Drayton suggests that they show the wood to Dr. Ian Spooner, while Alex Lagina suggests that they have the pieces carbon dated.

The three treasure hunters then call over Rick and Marty Lagina and show them their recent swamp discoveries. Marty confidently identifies one of the metal rods as a crib spike, concurring with Gary Drayton's earlier assessment, and expresses surprise that such an object would be found in the swamp. "What does it mean?" he asks, clearly frustrated by the discoveries' mysterious implications.

The next morning, the Oak Island crew congregates at the Money Pit area to watch the sinking of Borehole 8A. At a depth of about 103 feet- five feet shy of the approximate target depth, the suspected location of the Shaft 6 tunnel- the caisson encounters some resistant material which caisson operator Danny Smith believes to be wood. The next hammergrab load indeed contains a handful of splintered wood, to Danny's obvious delight. Certain that 8A has intersected the Shaft 6 tunnel, the treasure hunters extract several more

hammergrab loads from the caisson, which they scan with a metal detector before washing by hand. The spoils yield many tiny scraps of leather, evoking the leather fragments recovered from

Borehole H8 throughout Seasons 5 and 6, as well as the leather piece found in Borehole S6 in Season 6, Episode 17. The narrator then reveals that 8A lies ten feet southeast of H8.

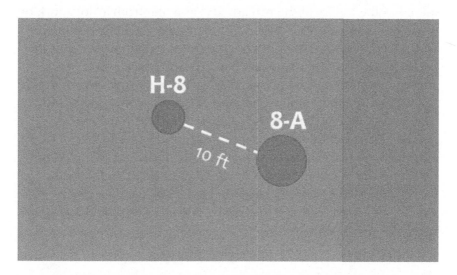

The crew continues to excavate 8A, finding a large hand-cut piece of oak at a depth of 114 feet. Gary Drayton then examines the spoils with his metal detector. "Talk about finding a needle in a haystack," he says as he retrieves what he identifies as a sail cloth needle from the muck.

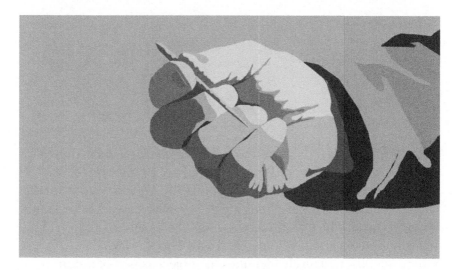

The next day, Marty Lagina, Alex Lagina, and Gary Drayton drive to the Ross Farm Museum, where they show Carmen Legge the thin iron rods they found in the swamp. The blacksmithing expert identifies the longer of the two artifacts as a tine from a "long fork or a seaweed fork or a moss fork". He then suggests that the shorter rod, which is tapered at both ends, might be a marlinspike- a tool used for nautical rope work and rope repair. The narrator subsequently attempts to connect the possible marlinespike with the theory that a sailing ship was burned or buried centuries ago in the Oak Island swamp. Finally, the treasure hunters show Legge the needle-like object found at a depth of 114 in Borehole 8A. Although the blacksmithing expert initially declares that he has no idea what the object is or what it was doing at depth in the Money Pit area, he later opines that it is too large to be a sailing cloth needle, and suggests that it might have served as a spike in a *trou de loup*-type booby trap.

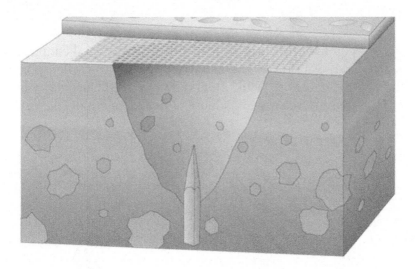

Later, while the Oak Island crew gathers at the Money Pit area to oversee the completion of Borehole 8A, Jack Begley and Steve Guptill manually wash some of the spoils already extracted from the shaft at a wash table. Steve finds a piece of what appears to be hand-wrought metal, which Jack suggests might be a piece of a hinge. The treasure hunters are then joined by Laird Niven, who independently, tentatively identifies the object as part of a strap hinge.

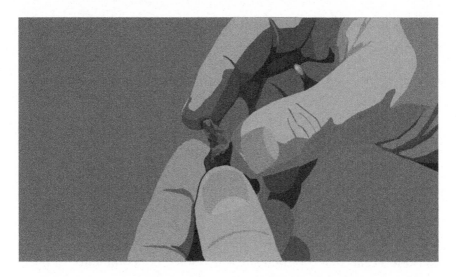

Back at the Money Pit area, the treasure hunters sink the 8A caisson to a depth of about 165 feet. The last few hammergrab loads contain nothing but water, prompting the Fellowship to abandon the hole.

Analysis

The Fork Tine and the Marlinspike

In this episode, Gary Drayton and Alex Lagina discovered two thin iron objects in the Oak Island swamp between the Eye of the

Swamp and the Paved Wharf. Although the objects bear some resemblance to the crib spikes found at Smith's Cove throughout Seasons 6 and 7, and to the rebar found near the slipway in Season 7, Episode 11, blacksmithing expert Carmen Legge identified one of them as the tine of a long fork, and the other as a marlinespike- a tool used for nautical rope work and rope repair.

Leather in the Money Pit

In this episode, Oak Island Tours Inc. recovered many tiny scraps of leather from a depth of 103 feet in Borehole 8A, the suspected location of the junction of the Money Pit and the Shaft 6 tunnel.

These are not the first pieces of leather to be found on Oak Island. Throughout Seasons 5 and 6, the crew discovered fragments of leather in Borehole H8, some of them at a depth of 162 feet. At least one of these fragments was determined to be vegetable-tanned book binding through which fibres of sheepskin parchment were woven. Strikingly similar to the events of this episode, the crew also found leather at a depth of 101 feet in Borehole S6 in Season 6, Episode 17, at what was then suspected to be the confluence of the Money Pit and the Shaft 6 tunnel.

The Booby Trap Spike

In this episode, the crew discovered an iron needle at a depth of 114 feet in Borehole 8A. Although Gary Drayton initially identified the artifact as a sail cloth needle, blacksmithing expert Carmen Legge suggested that the artifact might have served as a spike in a *trou de loup*-type booby trap at the bottom of the Money Pit.

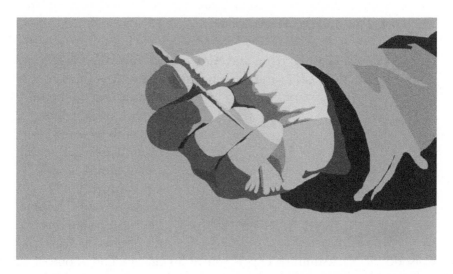

Season 7, Episode 21

A Leaf of Faith

Plot Summary

While the Irving Equipment Ltd. crew fills in Borehole 8A, which was terminated in the previous episode, the Oak Island crew meets in the War Room with geophysicist Jeremy Church of Eagle Canada. Church, who has had the opportunity to study the data collected during the seismic scan carried out in Season 7, Episode 6, shows the crew diagrams depicting various underground anomalies on the eastern half of Oak Island. First, the geoscientist shows the crew a representation of the Money Pit area on a screen. "Each one of these..." Church says, hovering his cursor over various irregularities, "these are all little disturbances- probably searcher tunnels. But within there, there's a subtle, little anomaly." Church then indicates a 13' x 13' feature located at the centre of the Money Pit area at a depth of 160 feet. He calls this feature the "Teardrop", and reveals that the H8 shaft intersected its southern end. The narrator then remarks that this feature brings to mind the original Money Pit, which was said to have a diameter of 13 feet, and attempts to equate it with the Chappell Vault, which H8 is believed to have grazed and possibly pushed to the side.

Upon hearing Church's report, Rick Lagina expresses pleasant surprise and suggests that the crew sink a caisson overtop of the Teardrop anomaly. Marty Lagina expresses similar sentiments and concludes the meeting.

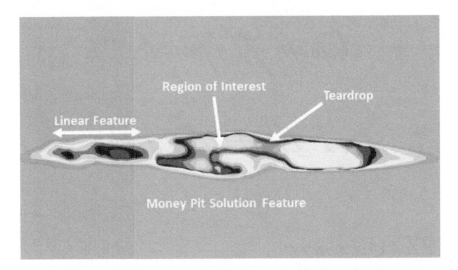

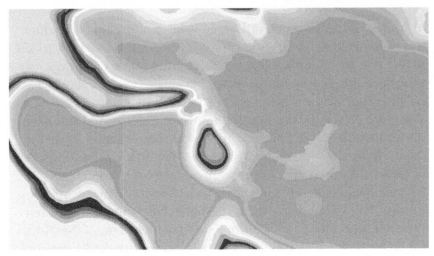

Later that day, Rick Lagina, Doug Crowell, Billy Gerhardt, and Scott Barlow meet with botanist Dr. Roger Evans of Acadia University at the Eye of the Swamp. There, they show the scientist the largest of the three oak stumps unearthed in the area in Season 7, Episode 16. Dr. Evans extracts some bark from the stump and promises to examine it at his lab, remarking that the ease with which he removed the material from the wood reminds him of cork oak, a tree native to Portugal. The narrator proceeds to suggest that Portuguese explorers, or perhaps the Portuguese Knights of Christ- groups around which various Oak Island theories revolve- may have planted cork oak trees on Oak Island for some purpose. Scott

Barlow then discloses that he has always believed the mysterious oak trees which once grew on Oak Island were intentionally planted as markers by the original treasure depositors.

The next day, the Oak Island crew meets in the War Room with Lee Lamb and Richard Restall, the children and siblings, respectively, of former Oak Island treasure hunters Robert and Bobby Restall. The Lagina brothers show the Restall siblings a variety of artifacts they discovered on the island over the years which seem to indicate human activity predating the 1795 discovery of the Money Pit. Lee then tells the treasure hunters about an incident which took place during her family's Oak Island tenure. As Lee tells it, Robert and Bobby Restall's first operation on Oak Island was the excavation of a trench on Smith's Cove. On the morning following their first day of digging, the Restall father and son found their trench filled with water. Floating on the water's surface was a leaf and a cluster of acorns. For some reason, Robert Restall formed the opinion that the leaf was not from one of the so-called "canopy oaks" for which the island was named, but rather a piece of the mysterious coconut fibre-eelgrass filtration system believed to prevent the Smith's Cove box drains from becoming flooded with sand and debris. "It was part of the filtration system," Lee says, "and it was coming from underneath. They used eelgrass, coconut fibre... and sometimes branches." Lee then presents the treasure hunters with two envelopes, one of them containing the leaf in question, which the Restalls had pressed so as to preserve it, and the other containing some of the acorns which Robert and Bobby had recovered from Smith's Cove. Marty Lagina thanks Lee and Richard for bringing the specimens and informs them that the team will have them analyzed by Dr. Roger Evans.

Following the War Room meeting, Rick Lagina drives Richard Restall to the dilapidated remains of the old Restall shack, which Fred Nolan transported years ago onto his own property. Inside the ruins, Richard describes the bygone furnishings which once transformed the former tool shed into his family's Oak Island home, pointing out the corner where the radio once stood and the spot where his bunk used to be. "That was the sum total of our existence," he concludes, after describing how he would spend his evenings reading while his brother, Bobby, wrote letters or entries in his journal. "That was it. It was pretty Spartan."

Following Richard Restall's tour, Doug Crowell and Scott Barlow, who have since joined the two Ricks, reveal that they intend to refurbish the shack and return it to the state in which it existed while it served as the Restall family home. "Keep it as sparse as you can," Richard advises, "because there was nothing fancy about that shack."

The next day, the Lagina brothers, Craig Tester, and Dr. Roger
Evans meet with Lee Lamb and Richard Restall in the Oak Island
Research Centre. There, the treasure hunters show Dr. Evans the
leaf and acorns with which the Restall siblings provided them during
their War Room meeting. The botanist compares the Restall acorns
with local red oak acorns and concludes that the two derive from
different species of oak, conceding the possibility that the Restall
acorns may have derived from a type of oak which someone
brought to Oak Island and planted long ago. When prompted by
Richard Restall, Dr. Evans expresses his belief that the Restall
acorns could not have floated across the Atlantic Ocean from
Europe or Africa due to their poor resistance to the deleterious
effects of salt water. Unfortunately, the botanist declares that it is
unlikely the team will be able to extract any DNA from the Restall
acorns for identification purposes due to their advanced age.

Rick and Marty Lagina then drive the Restall siblings to the Money
Pit area, where the rest of the team is preparing to sink a caisson on
the Teardrop anomaly introduced earlier in the episode. Rick
informs Lee and Richard that the team has decided to name this
caisson 'RF1', an acronym for "Restall Family 1", in honour of the
Restall family's extraordinary contributions towards the Oak Island
treasure hunt. The treasure hunters look on as Lee and Richard
start up the oscillator, initiating the sinking of RF1.

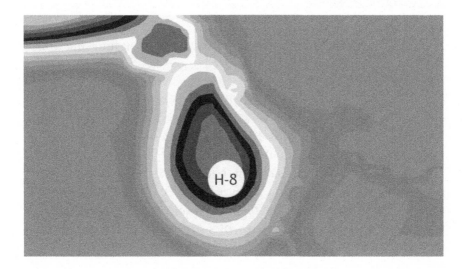

The Fellowship of the Dig resumes the excavation of RF1 the following day. At a depth of 86 feet, the shaft encounters timbers, which Craig Tester suggests are part of the Chappell Shaft. When the shaft reaches a depth of 100 feet, Gary Drayton begins examining each load of material removed from the caisson with his metal detector. Following Gary's preliminary examination, the spoils are transferred to a wash table, where they are manually washed and sifted through by Jack Begley and Steve Guptill. At the wash table, Steve Guptill finds a shard of red pottery. "That's really old pottery, Steve," Jack says. "Look at how thick it is! The thicker, the older, too, and that's the thickest pottery I've seen at this wash table."

Shortly after Steve Guptill's discovery, Gary Drayton finds the upper half of an old pickaxe in a batch of RF1 spoils brought up from a depth of 90 feet. Gary shows Terry Matheson his find before calling over Rick and Marty Lagina. Gary remarks that this artifact appears to have the same style as the pickaxe he discovered at the Eye of the Swamp in Season 7, Episode 13, which Carmen Legge, in Season 7, Episode 14, dated from the mid to late 1700s. "It's a cool artifact," says Marty of the pick in a later interview. "I can tell you without going to the venerable Carmen Legge. It was probably built long ago." Unfortunately, since the pick was found at a depth of 90 feet, it probably constitutes the leavings of a previous searcher rather than that of an original depositor.

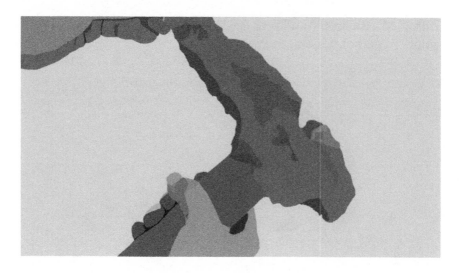

Below the 100-foot depth, the hammergrab brings up loads of large hand-cut timbers, which the treasure hunters set to the side. One of these timbers has a wooden dowel protruding from its end, evoking the wooden pegs found in the U-shaped structure. The artifact's resemblance to the Smith's Cove feature is further enhanced when Gary Drayton discovers what appears to be the Roman numeral 'II' carved into the wood. The treasure hunters speculate that this timber and the others like it might have been left by the original Money Pit depositors and agree to have them dendrochronologically tested.

Analysis

The Teardrop

In this episode, geoscientist Jeremy Church of Eagle Canada showed the Oak Island crew the results of the seismic survey carried out by Eagle Canada in Season 7, Episode 6. On a diagram of the Money Pit area, he pointed out a 160-foot-deep 13'x13' anomaly he calls the "Teardrop", and revealed that Borehole H8 intersected the southern end of this feature.

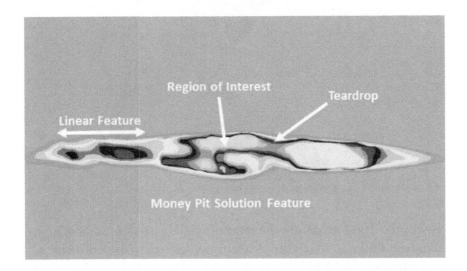

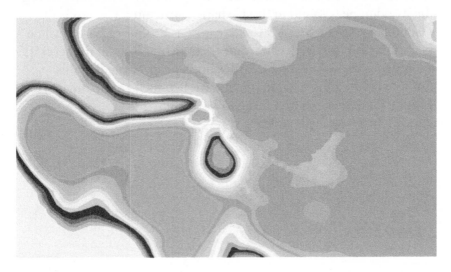

This scene is reminiscent of Season 6, Episode 3, in which Jeremy Church showed Rick and Marty various diagrams based off seismic survey data collected in Season 6, Episode 1. In that episode, Church pointed out a 10-foot-tall anomaly in the Money Pit area which lay at a depth of 160 to 170 feet- essentially, the same feature as the "Teardrop" anomaly introduced in this episode. The feature appeared to be a cavern in the hard limestone, the edge of which Borehole H8 apparently clipped. Oak Island Tours Inc. searched for this supposed cavern via exploration drilling in Season 6, Episode 4 and recovered a fragment of possible coconut fibre and a piece of axe-hewn wood at a depth of 170 feet from a drillhole called H7.5.

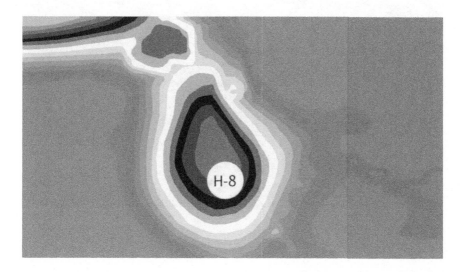

In Season 6, Episode 12, Mike Roberts and Joey Rolfe of Divetech Ltd. lowered a camera-equipped ROV into H8, with which they conducted a sonar scan of the anomaly. At a depth of 170 feet- the bottom of the alleged cavity- the scanner picked up what appeared to be the right-angled corner of a void. Before the operation could be completed, the scanner and camera malfunctioned and the ROV filled with water, becoming the most recent additions to a long list of unexplainable equipment failures on Oak Island.

The Oak Leaf and Acorns

In this episode, Lee Lamb and Richard Restall showed the Oak Island team a pressed oak leaf and a handful of acorns which their father had retrieved from a flooded exploratory trench he dug at Smith's Cove. According to Lee, Robert Restall believed that these items did not come from a local red oak, but had rather floated up from the Smith's Cove filter. Botanist Dr. Roger Evans examined these specimens and concluded that they do not belong to the same species of red oak endemic to that part of Nova Scotia.

Season 7, Episode 22

Marks X the Spot

Plot Summary

The episode begins at the Money Pit area, where the excavation of Borehole RF1 is underway. The Fellowship of the Dig works feverishly to process the spoils, extracting old timbers and transporting the rest of the muck to the wash table. Some of the timbers are inscribed with Roman numerals, evoking the U-shaped structure. In a later interview, Rick and Marty Lagina explain that the large timbers extracted from RF1 are unlike those which comprise the Chappell or Hedden Shafts.

In RF1 spoils taken from a depth of about 120 feet, Gary Drayton discovers a strange iron crowbar-like device with a sharp hook on one end, which Rick Lagina suggests might have been used to maneuver timbers. The treasure hunters agree that they ought to show the artifact to Carmen Legge.

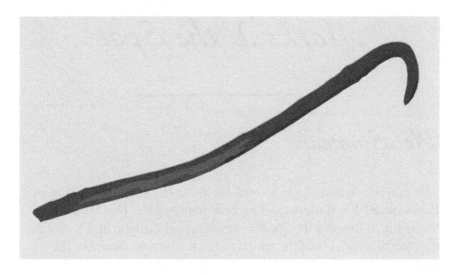

The next morning, Craig Tester and Alex Lagina drive to the Ross Farm Museum, where they show Carmen Legge some of the items they discovered in RF1. First, the blacksmithing expert examines the crowbar-like object and finds a "wear mark" on one side of the hooked end. "So, that tells me," he says, "that it was sort of anchored into the wall of a rock formation... These would be driven into the roof or wall of a cave, and then lanterns or other working

equipment like hoists and pulleys would be anchored *on" the hook. When prompted by Craig* Tester, Legge dates the artifact to the 1700s.

Next, Carmen Legge takes a look at the pickaxe found at a depth of 90 feet in RF1 the previous episode. The blacksmithing expert identifies the artifact as a "very typical rock hammer" which would have been used in a tunnel or a cave, and declares that such an object could have been made as far back as the Middle Ages.

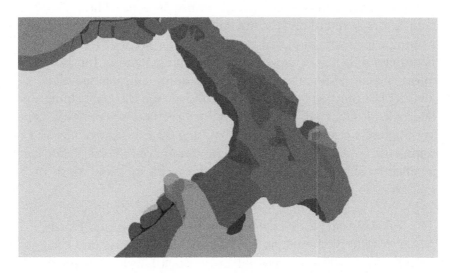

Back on Oak Island, Jack Begley and Steve Guptill search through 120-foot-deep RF1 spoils at a wash table. Jack picks out what appears to be a piece of rope. Shortly thereafter, he comes across a clump of coconut fibre. The treasure hunters are joined by Dan Henskee, whereupon Steve finds a mysterious black object, one side of which appears to be caked in concrete.

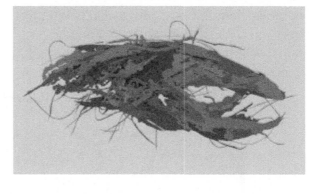

At the Money Pit area, the RF1 caisson reaches a depth of 160 feet- the neighbourhood of the Teardrop anomaly introduced in the previous episode. The hammergrab emerges from the caisson bearing a crumpled piece of sheet metal in its jaws. Doug Crowell identifies the object as a "shield" used in 1931 to protect the builders of the Chappell Shaft from falling debris.

As soon as the caisson begins its descent into uncharted territory below the Chappell Shaft, one of the brackets securing the oscillator to the hammergrab crane snaps due to the pressure. The contractors spend the rest of the day repairing the damage before resuming the excavation that evening. At a depth of 181 feet, the hammergrab brings up little aside from water. Vanessa Lucido informs the boys that the caisson is now advancing at a rate of 4 inches per hour due to some nether obstruction- probably limestone bedrock. "I have a super unconventional method we could try," she says, before suggesting that they try raising the caisson five feet and setting the 50,000-pound hammergrab on top of the obstruction in an effort to slowly sink it deeper into the earth. Rick and Marty Lagina agree to the proposal.

The following day, Rick Lagina, Charles Barkhouse, and Laird Niven drive to the foundations of Samuel Ball's house on Oak Island's Lot 25. The narrator informs us that Laird has acquired a permit to excavate the site in an archaeological manner, for which he said he would apply back in Season 7, Episode 18. After taking photographs of the site, the treasure hunters begin excavating the designated perimeters of the test pits with trowels. They are soon joined by Kelly Bourassa, Gary Drayton, and Jack Begley, who assist in the operation. Less than an inch below the surface, Bourassa uncovers a metal strip, which he identifies as hinge belonging to a building or a chest, as well as a metal bracket.

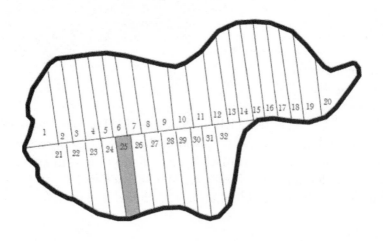

The next day, Alex Lagina, Billy Gerhardt, and Dr. Ian Spooner do some work in the Swamp's Paved Area. Dr. Spooner extracts some wood taken from beneath the stones, which he hopes to carbon date. "This stick," he says, "will tell me when that stone was placed".

Back on Lot 25, Jack Begley, Charles Barkhouse, and Laird Niven dig on the GPR anomaly discovered in Season 7, Episode 18. Several feet below the surface, Jack Begley hits a layer of stacked stones which appear to lie atop some sort of cavity- apparently, the anomaly indicated by the GPR scan. The treasure hunters are soon joined by Rick Lagina and Billy Gerhardt, the former of whom enthusiastically designates this potential tunnel on the Ball foundation the long-coveted "one thing... for the Ball foundation".

The next day, the boys excavate more of the cavity before showing it to Marty and Alex Lagina. The treasure hunters proceed to invite Derek Hale, the owner of a company called 'The Septic Doctor', to Oak Island. Hale produces a hose with a small camera on the end from his truck, telling the crew that he and his employees use this device to "scope sewer lines". Hale lowers the camera into the cavity, revealing a long, narrow stone tunnel. At an undisclosed distance from the cavity's entrance, the camera's progress is impeded by a rock lying in the middle of the tunnel. The treasure hunters agree that they ought to excavate the tunnel by hand in order to find out where it leads. "It's a complete mystery what this is," says Marty Lagina, "but it can't be a tunnel to nowhere. It just can't be. Nobody would do that."

Analysis

The Lot 25 Tunnel

In this episode, the Oak Island crew excavated the foundation of Samuel Ball's home on Oak Island's Lot 25, where GPR experts Steve Watson and Don Johnston discovered the presence of underground anomalies in Season 7, Episode 18. During the excavation, the treasure hunters uncovered a mysterious underground rock-lined tunnel which they plan to fully uncover in the future.

Season 7, Episode 23

Timeline

———————◆———————

Plot Summary

Mike Jardine meets with Craig Tester and Gary Drayton at the Money Pit area, where caisson RF1 had encountered a 180-foot-deep obstruction the previous episode. Mike informs the treasure hunters that Vanessa Lucido's idea of leaving the hammergrab atop the obstruction overnight appears to have moved the offending object five feet. The treasure hunters then use the hammergrab to remove the obstruction, which appears to be gravel they previously used to backfill Borehole H8, before encountering what oscillator operator Danny Smith declares "feels like a void" at a depth of 202 feet. Despite this tantalizing development, the hammergrab proceeds to bring up more gravel backfill, prompting the treasure hunters to reluctantly terminate the shaft for safety purposes.

The next day, the Oak Island crew uses an excavator to extract some of the stones from the Paved Area in the swamp. While they work, the treasure hunters are approached by Doug Crowell and Dr. Ian Spooner. Dr. Spooner informs the treasure hunters that the stick which he extracted from beneath the Paved Area the previous episode was carbon dated to around 1200 A.D. – a date consistent with the Knights Templar theory. The geoscientists declares this to be evidence that the Paved Wharf, which multiple experts have opined was created by the hand of man, was formed around 1200 A.D. The treasure hunters decide to convene in the War Room in light of this startling development.

The crew members file into the War Room the following day, where they find a visual timeline laid out on the table. This display, created by Charles Barkhouse, stretches from 1100 A.D. to the present day. There is a thick line of demarcation at 1795, the date in which the Money Pit was first discovered. Various artifacts recovered on Oak Island over the years have been placed on the timeline in the respective centuries during which they are believed to have been created or deposited. A cluster of coins, nails, and buttons lie between 1650 and 1795, in the midst of which are the labels 'Golden Age of Piracy' at 1700 and 'Crown Jewels Theory' at 1793. The burnt iron bracket found in the swamp lies at around 1700, and the rhodolite garnet brooch found on Lot 8 lies at around 1650. The Spanish maravedis sits at 1652, and the conical pike pole point found in the swamp is located at 1600 (despite Carmen Legge's dating the artifact from 1710 to 1790), overtop the labels 'Rosicrucians' and 'Francis Bacon'. In the middle of the 1500s, we see two large rusted iron strips presumably recovered from Smith's Cove. At 1500 is the label 'French Exploration', and at 1400 is the label 'Portuguese Exploration', below which lies the hand-point chisel found at Isaac's Point. Somewhere in the 1400s, we see the swage blocks discovered on Lot 21. At 1300 is the label 'Order of Christ', overtop of which sits a clump of coconut fibre. The lead cross and the swamp stick extracted by Dr. Spooner have been placed in the late 1200s. The year 1200 bears the label 'Norsemen Exploration'. At the beginning of the timeline, at the year 1100, we

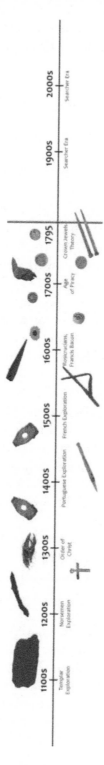

see a blackened piece of wood- perhaps one of the pieces of burnt wood found in the swamp. Below this item is the label 'Templar Exploration'.

The treasure hunters proceed to discuss the implications of the finds. Jack Begley points out that the data seems to point to multiple operations that took place at different times. "We know, during specific dates," he says, "that large amounts of work went on on Oak Island in at least two different clumps of time. You've got the 1600s," he says, pointing to artifacts which date to that time period, "which fits with the Rosicrucians and the Francis Bacon theories. You've got the 11-1400s, which fits right in with the Templar theories. And we have dendro information from the slipway that someone was there doing a lot of work before searchers." Doug Crowell echoes that notion, saying, "All of this changes the mystery as we know it... because it was supposed to be an uninhabited island in 1795 when the treasure hunt began as we know it, but this has shown us that there was a story, and there was activity going on here much earlier, and on possibly a very continual basis, whether it's the same group or not."

During the discussion, Jack Begley and Gary Drayton express their belief that some of the artifacts bolster the Knights Templar theory. Craig Tester, on the other hand, remarks that much of the evidence points to an event that took place in the late 1600s. Gary Drayton suggests that, based on the swage blocks found on Lot 21 and the pick head found at the Eye of the Swamp, tunnels may run beneath Oak Island in places other than the Money Pit area. Surveyor Steve Guptill then discloses that data collected during "strategic digs" indicates that the Paved Area measures 170'x 80', and that, according to Dr. Ian Spooner, it may have lain at the edge of open water in the 1200s.

Once each of the treasure hunters have said their piece, Marty Lagina withdraws a modern toonie, or $2 Canadian coin, from his pocket and places it at the right end of the timeline. "That's my toonie," he says. "That's the one I put down H8". The narrator then reminds us that, back in Season 5, Episode 8, Marty threw a coin down H8 for good luck, saying "Go find your brother." In the War

Room, Marty observes that the PVC casing he tossed the toonie down was located about ten feet from the centre of RF1, indicating that the toonie drifted about ten feet underground. In light of this new evidence, the treasure hunters discuss the possibility that the Money Pit treasure similarly drifted underground from its original position, perhaps both vertically and horizontally.

Marty Lagina then asks the Fellowship whether they believe treasure still lies hidden somewhere on Oak Island. Every crew member but Alex Lagina, Laird Niven, and Dan Henskee express their belief that there is probably still treasure to be found on the island. Marty himself states that he believes there to be a 40% possibility that Oak Island was ever the depository of treasure, and a 20% possibility that treasure remains to be found. "But that's way farther than I ever was before," he continues. "My leading theory, when I first came on this island, was that it was just collective madness."

Next, the treasure hunters bring up the subject of the "Big Dig"- a long-discussed comprehensive excavation of the Money Pit area, which Marty Lagina estimates would cost tens of millions of dollars and take as long as three years to complete. The narrator then explains that the Big Dig would either involve the "construction a massive concrete shaft around the entire Money Pit area so that access to the vault would be unhampered by flooding," or the drilling of a 100-foot-wide ring of boreholes which would be pumped full of some freezing agent, allowing the treasure hunters to excavate the Money Pit area without having to contend with floodwater.

"The Big Dig has been kind of hanging out there for a long time," Marty Lagina summarizes in a later interview. "It's almost like a child's dream. The science is relatively simple. It's just basically trying to make a solid ring around the Money Pit, and then plug the bottom of it, and then excavate that." Rick Lagina then adds, "It's enormously expensive from a financial [perspective, and] commitment of time and resources, but at the end of the day, you dig an 80 foot, 100-foot-in-diameter circle, we all know within that resides the original Money Pit. I think it's ultimately the only way to really get to the bottom of what happened here on Oak Island."

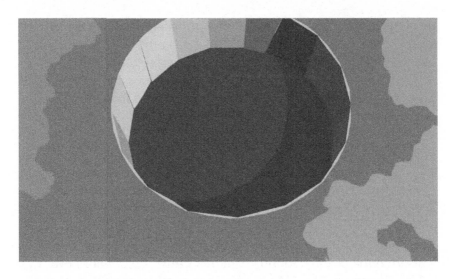

The Fellowship of the Dig concludes the War Room meeting and heads to Borehole 10-X, where a commemorative plaque honouring Dan Blankenship has been erected. The plaque reads:

"Daniel Christian Blankenship, 1923-2019

"A Titan of Oak Island

"This dedication stands as a memorial to his abounding drive for answers and unwavering faith in God.

"Dedicated Husband & Father

"Fearless Soldier

"Preserver of History

"Tenacious Treasure Hunter

"Dan was an inspiration to all who called him a faithful friend"

The Lagina brothers explain that the monument on which the plaque is affixed is composed of rock from Oak Island and old drill pipes that Dan Blankenship used during his Oak Island treasure hunt. Rick and Marty honour the veteran treasure hunter in a eulogy, keeping their speeches intentionally brief, since Dan, in the words of his son, Dave, was a man of few words.

Analysis

Dr. Spooner's Third Analysis of the Swamp

In the previous episode, Dr. Ian Spooner extracted a stick wedged between the rocks which compose the Paved Area. In this episode, he had the stick carbon dated to about 1200 A.D., and took this as evidence that the Paved Area was artificially created at that time- a notion vaguely congruent with the Knights Templar theory and the Viking theory.

This is not the first theory that Dr. Spooner has developed regarding Oak Island's swamp. Back in Season 7, Episode 3, the geoscientist extracted core samples from the swamp's 'Ship Anomaly', from which he concluded that the triangle-shaped bog was formed sometime in the 1600s, and supported trees and other forms of terrestrial vegetation prior to its transformation into a wetland.

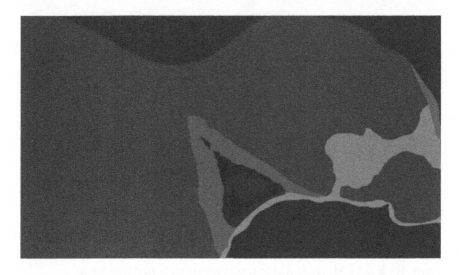

Back in Season 7, Episode 9, Dr. Spooner and his graduate students extracted sticks and other organic matter from the 'Eye of the Swamp'. The evidence gleaned from these samples, coupled with his discovery of unnaturally-interlayered organic matter and till in the swamp, led the geoscientist to conclude that the swamp first formed around 1220 A.D., and that the Eye of the Swamp was disturbed by man sometime between 1674 and 1700. He elaborated on this theory in Season 7, Episode 18, in which he suggested that the Eye of the Swamp constitutes the remains of a 300-year-old clay mine, and that the Paved Area constituted the roadway by which clay was transported from the mine onto ships.

Part III

Theories

The Knights Baronet Theory

———————⊷•⊶———————

In Season 6, Episode 20 of *The Curse of Oak Island*, researcher and author James McQuiston presented his own Oak Island theory in the War Room. McQuiston's theory revolves around the Knights Baronets of Nova Scotia, a chivalric order established by King James I of England as part of a scheme to populate the Acadian peninsula (French-controlled Nova Scotia) with Scottish settlers.

The Knights Baronet of Nova Scotia

The story of the Knights Baronet begins in the early 1600s, during the infancy of North American colonization. At that time, King James I of England (a.k.a. King James VI of Scotland) hoped to control a huge swath of North American territory stretching from his newly-established Colony of Virginia to his even younger Newfoundland Colony to the north. His designs were thwarted, however, by French explorers Samuel de Champlain and Pierre Dugua, Sieur de Mons, who had recently established a number of New French colonies in Acadia (the Canadian Maritimes and much of present-day Maine) and along the St. Lawrence River.

The oldest of these New French colonies was the settlement of Port-Royal, a village situated on the Bay of Fundy on the western coast of what is now Nova Scotia. Although King James had successfully commissioned Samuel Argall, the Admiral of the Virginia Colony, with razing the town to the ground in 1613, the French retained a considerable presence in Acadia. If James were to drive the French away from the colony, he would need to establish a colony of his own in the area.

In 1621, Sir William Alexander, one of James' Scottish courtiers, approached him with an interesting proposal intended to effect this end. Alexander suggested that the king finance a New Scottish colony in the heart of French Acadia by creating a new chivalric order and selling membership to Scottish aristocrats, using the funds raised to purchase outfits for prospective colonists. King James had tried a similar scheme in 1611 in order to populate Ireland with English settlers, with excellent results. The king agreed to the proposal, and on September 10, 1621, he appointed William Alexander the mayor of this vast new colony, which was to be called Nova Scotia, or "New Scotland". Several years later, on October 18, 1624, he announced his intention to form the Knights Baronets of Nova Scotia, through which he would finance this new colony.

King James I never lived to carry out his plan, dying of dysentery on March 27, 1625. His eldest living son and successor, King Charles I, promptly carried on where his father had left off, forming the Knights Baronets of Nova Scotia two months after James' death. Charles ultimately managed to sell 122 baronetcies to Scottish lairds and clan chiefs, which allowed William Alexander's son, also named William Alexander, to establish the colony of Charlesford in the ashes of the old Port-Royal.

The colony was short-lived. In the late 1620s, the English fought against the armies of French King Louis XIII in the Siege of La Rochelle, a conflict between Catholic France and a defending army of French Huguenots (Protestants). The Anglo-French War which revolved around this battle ended in 1629, and in 1632, the defeated Charles I signed a treaty returning all of New France (Charlesford included) to the French. The French-turned-English-turned-French settlement of Port-Royal, later called Annapolis Royal, would remain in French hands until 1710.

James McQuiston's Theory

Researcher James McQuiston, who appeared briefly in Season 6, Episode 20 of *The Curse of Oak Island*, outlines his fascinating Oak Island theory in three books:

- *Oak Island: Missing Links* (2016)
- *Oak Island 1632* (2017)
- *Oak Island Knights* (2018)

Drawing from a truly impressive collection of circumstantial evidence gleaned from a variety of 17th Century books, letters, and documents; genealogies; family traditions; folk legends; and an obscure Freemasonic tome called the *History of the Lodge of Edinburgh (Mary's Chapel) No. 1*, McQuiston formulated a chillingly plausible, evidence-rooted hypothesis regarding the contents of the Money Pit and the nature of its depositors. McQuiston's theory can be generally summarized thus:

Sir William Alexander, the high-ranking Scottish courtier who proposed the establishment of the Colony of Nova Scotia and the Knights Baronet to his king, James VI, was a man with royal ambitions. Inspired by Nicolas Durand de Villegaignon, a 16th Century French Protestant who attempted to establish a Huguenot colony in Brazil in the mid-1500s, Alexander hoped to found Nova Scotia, a Scottish kingdom in the New World over which he would reign as monarch.

In order to acquire the capital necessary to initiate the settlement of Nova Scotia, Alexander convinced King James VI, and later James' son, King Charles I, to establish the Knights Baronet of Nova Scotia, a chivalric order whose members would be granted baronetcies on the Acadian peninsula. In his book *Oak Island 1632*, McQuiston makes the case that a quarter of the Scottish lairds and clan chiefs who purchased membership in this Order were connected in some way, chiefly through blood ties and land holdings, with the bygone Knights Templar.

The Knights Baronet Theory

According to McQuiston's theory, the revenue acquired from the sales of the Nova Scotian baronetcies was not the only monetary source on which Alexander relied to finance his new kingdom. The Scottish courtier also depended on the financial support of one of his most loyal followers, a fellow Knight Baronet of Nova Scotia named Sir Alexander Strachan of Thornton.

In the early 1620s, Strachan had been engaged in an affair with Margaret Ogilvie, the second wife of George Keith, 5th Earl Marischal, who was one of the wealthiest and most powerful noblemen in Scotland at that time. In the autumn of 1622, while Keith lay on his deathbed in Dunnotrar Castle, Strachan and Ogilvie stripped Keith's mansion in Benholm, Scotland, of all the valuables contained therein. This enormous haul consisted of several thousand pounds of gold and silver coins, diamonds, pearls, precious stones, jewelry, gold buttons, and artwork. Although Strachan and Ogilvie were later indicted for this theft and required to relinquish a portion of their ill-gotten gains to Keith's son and successor, McQuiston maintains that Strachan brought the majority of this treasure with him across the Atlantic to Nova Scotia, hoping to safeguard it there until such a time as it could be used to finance Alexander's sovereign Kingdom of Nova Scotia.

McQuiston maintains that Sir William Alexander, while waiting for the British king to sanction his Nova Scotian enterprise, sailed to the Acadian peninsula with a corps of engineers and stone masons in 1622 and built a mansion for himself at the site of what is now New Ross, Nova Scotia, located on the Gold River about 28 kilometres (17 miles) northwest of Oak Island. McQuiston believes that the foundations of this ruined estate lie on property currently owned by Tim Loncarich and Alessandra Nadudvari, who appeared in Season 4, Episodes 1 and 2 of *The Curse of Oak Island*.

In 1625, King Charles I formed the Knights Baronet of Nova Scotia. In 1627, the latest of a long succession of Anglo-French Wars erupted in Europe, this conflict revolving around a Huguenot rebellion in the French city of La Rochelle. No longer restrained by the risk of offending the French, William Alexander the Younger, in 1628, led a company of seventy Scottish settlers across the Atlantic to establish the village of Charlesford in the ashes of Port-Royal, the old French colony situated on the southwestern coast of the Acadian peninsula.

The Scottish colonists were assisted in their endeavours by Claude de Saint-Etienne de la Tour, a French colonist and Acadian veteran who had helped maintain the old Port-Royal settlement prior to Samuel Argall's 1613 attack, and the father of the more famous Charles de Saint-Etienne de la Tour, the future Governor of Acadia and founder of the French fur trading post Fort La Tour (located at the site of present-day St. John, New Brunswick). Frustrated with France's apparent indifference towards the efforts of its Acadian settlers, Claude de la Tour decided to throw in his lot with the Scots, much to his son's disappointment.

In 1630, Claude de la Tour signed an agreement with William Alexander the Younger, which was incidentally witnessed by Alexander Strachan, in which he was granted possession of a region called 'Mirligaiche'- which McQuiston argues encompassed Mahone Bay, in which Oak Island is located- on the condition that he and the Acadians under his command "doth promise to be good and faithful vassals of the Sovereign lord the King of Scotland."

The Anglo-French War had come to an end in Europe the previous year, in the spring of 1629, with the signing of the Treaty of Susa. Unaware that the English and French had ceased hostilities, a Scottish adventurer named David Kirke had launched a three-ship assault on the French colony of Quebec in the summer of 1629, successfully convincing the colony's governor, Samuel de Champlain, to surrender the settlement. On account of this development, King Charles I of Great Britain and King Louis XIII of France were forced to come to a second agreement, this one pertaining to their New World holdings. The resultant Treaty of Saint-Germain-en-Laye, signed in 1632, returned all British settlements in Acadia and New France (Charlesford included) to the French.

In the spring of 1632, a company of French soldiers sailed to Charlesford to oversee the Scottish evacuation. According to

The Knights Baronet Theory

McQuiston's theory, the Scotsmen who subsequently left the settlement departed with their most valuable treasures, which included the ill-gotten loot acquired by Alexander Strachan; the Stone of Destiny, a stone historically used in Scottish coronation ceremonies (although the Stone of Destiny is supposed to currently reside in Edinburgh Castle, some suspect that the Edinburgh stone might be a fake, and that the true stone's whereabouts are unknown); and priceless Templar heirlooms brought to Nova Scotia by members of the Knights Baronet.

McQuiston contends that the Scottish settlers encountered a violent Atlantic storm on their return journey and were forced to seek refuge in Mahone Bay, a body of water belonging to their one-time ally, Claude de Saint-Etienne de la Tour. While waiting out the storm, the Scotsmen landed on Oak Island, an isle located near the mouth of the Gold River, the Gold being the waterway on which Sir William Alexander the Elder built his manor. On the orders of William Alexander the Younger, the Scotsmen dug the Money Pit and interred their treasures within it, hoping to retrieve them one day for the purpose of realizing their greatest ambition, the establishment of the Kingdom of Nova Scotia. The builders then filled in the Money Pit, sealing the shaft with nine equidistant platforms of oak logs, and placing the Stone of Destiny at the 90-foot level (McQuiston believes that the 90-foot stone might be the Stone of Destiny).

Following their Oak Island operation, the Scottish colonists sailed to the Old World. Unable to return to the New World as they had hoped on account of the English Civil Wars, McQuiston argues that some of these colonists later founded the very first Freemasonic lodges in Scotland and incorporated the story of the Money Pit, with its nine levels, into their secret rituals; over the years, a number of Oak Island theorists have pointed out a number of remarkable similarities between the legend of the Money Pit's discovery and the symbolism inherent in the Thirteenth Degree rituals of Scottish Rite Freemasonry. McQuiston goes on to make the case that the inordinate number of Freemasons who have taken an interest in the Oak Island mystery over the years stems from esoteric knowledge of the Money Pit's true backstory to which members of certain

Freemasonic lodges were privy, which was passed down from Freemason to Freemason throughout the generations.

Near the end of his book *Oak Island Knights*, McQuiston attempts to connect his theory with the William Phips theory put forth by engineers Graham Harris and Les MacPhie, contending that Phips was aware of the Oak Island treasure and attempted to retrieve it in the 1680s. One of the more striking pieces of evidence he cites in support of this sub-theory is that a chivalric medallion, which he argues belonged to Phips' treasure hunting sponsor, Christopher Monck, 2nd Duke of Albemarle, was discovered "several decades ago" in the dirt near Tim Loncarich and Alessandra Nadudvari's aforementioned New Ross property (allegedly the site of Sir William Alexander's bygone estate).

The Viking Theory

Over the years, a few theorists have attempted to connect the Oak Island mystery with the 10th Century Norse exploration of Canada's Atlantic Northeast, a shadowy element of North American history alluded to in medieval Scandinavian texts called the 'Icelandic Sagas', and affirmed by archaeological findings made on Newfoundland's Northern Peninsula.

The Norse Vikings

The Norse Vikings were a hardy sea-faring folk from Scandinavia who lived in small kingdoms during the Early Middle Ages. For most of the year, they lived as farmers and fishermen, scraping out as good a living as their harsh northern environment would allow. When summer came, wealthy farmers would leave their lands in the hands of their wives, recruit a company of loyal friends and kinsmen, and set sail in search of fortune and adventure.

From the late 700s until the mid-1000s, during what is known as the 'Viking Age', Norse raiders sailed up and down the coastlines and rivers of Europe, pillaging and plundering as they went. With lightning speed, they attacked villages, churches, and monasteries, retreating to their longships with any booty they could lay their hands on before their victims had a chance to organize any sort of resistance. For centuries, the sight of a Viking longship with a carved dragon's head on its prow and a row of shields lashed to its side struck terror into the hearts of peasants and clergymen from Moscow to Madrid.

Over time, the Vikings transitioned from reaving and pillaging to consolidating and colonizing. Many became settlers at the places they had once ravaged. For example, the enormous Norse raider named Rollo, whom some may recognize as a character from the History Channel series *Vikings*, became the first Duke of Normandy in the year 911; his great-great-great grandson, William the Conqueror, would go on to wrest England from control of the ruling Anglo-Saxon king at the Battle of Hastings (1066). Around the same time, Norse warlord Harald Fairhair united a cluster of petty Viking kingdoms, which had warred with each other for centuries, into a single Kingdom of Norway.

Many Viking chieftains who were unable to retain their power in this age of unification chose to sail west in search of new lands. In around 860 A.D., some of these political refugees discovered and settled Iceland. Less than a century later, their descendants would establish the Icelandic Commonwealth, which was governed in part by the Althing, the oldest parliament in the world.

Erik the Red and the Settlement of Greenland

In 960 A.D., a Norse Viking named Thorvald Asvaldsson fled from Norway to northwestern Iceland with his family, having been banished for committing manslaughter. His son, a red-bearded farmer called Erik the Red, was similarly banished from Iceland twenty two years later for a comparable crime. Accompanied by a handful of loyal friends and relatives, Erik the Red left his longhouse and headed out to sea, bound for a mysterious land to the west which had been spotted by Icelandic sailors blown off course.

The Viking Theory

Erik the Red and his crew spent three years exploring this new land, and discovered that it had areas which were suitable for farming. In 985, the red-bearded explorer returned to Iceland and regaled his fellow Vikings with tales of what he attractively dubbed *"Groenland"*, or "Greenland". Having convinced a number of Norsemen to help him settle this new territory, Erik the Red returned to Greenland that year and established a colony there, which was named Eriksfjord.

Erik the Red and his wife eventually had four children: a lucky son named Leif; a brave son named Thorvald; a selfless son named Thorstein; and a cunning daughter named Freydis. Their subsequent discovery of a mysterious land to the west became the stuff of legend. For generations, Scandinavians spoke of their New World adventures around smoky longhouse fires. Medieval storytellers eventually put these tales to parchment, writing what are known as the Icelandic Sagas.

The Viking Discovery of Canada

There are two sagas which detail the Viking discovery of the New World: *The Saga of Erik the Red* (written before 1265), and the older *Greenland Saga*, both of which were written several centuries after the events they purport to chronicle. The events outlined in the sagas are also referenced briefly in 11th Century German chronicler Adam of Bremen's book *Descriptio Insularum Aquilonis* (1075), a history of the northern world, as well as in 12th Century Icelandic historian Ari Thorgilsson's book *Islendingabok*, or "Book of the Icelanders".

The following are summaries of chapters of the Icelandic sagas which pertain to the Norse discovery of the Americas.

The Greenlander Saga

Bjarni Herjolfsson's Discovery

Around the time of Erik the Red's settlement of Greenland, a
Norseman named Bjarni Herjolfsson had a tradition of alternately
wintering in Norway, the Norse homeland, and in Iceland, where
his father, Herjolf, lived. One autumn, Bjarni sailed from Norway to
Iceland to discover that his father had emigrated to Erik the Red's
Greenlandic colony. Determined to winter with his father as was his
custom, he and his crew sailed west.

Bjarni and his men soon encountered storms which blew them off
course. When the fog cleared, the Norsemen found themselves
within sight of a strange wooded land. Ignoring the entreaties of his
curious crewmen, Bjarni refrained from embarking and sailed
north. He came within sight of two more strange lands, neither of
which he explored, before finally finding his way to Greenland.

The tale of Bjarni's discoveries became the talk of the colony, and
soon Leif Erikson, Erik the Red's eldest son, decided to lead an
expedition west in search of them. Although the elderly Erik the
Red initially agreed, with some reluctance, to accompany his son, an
omen convinced him to remain behind.

The Voyage of Leif Erikson

Leif Erikson and his crew sailed west and soon came to a barren, icy
land covered with flat stones. He called this place *Helluland,* or
"Flat-stone-land". Most historians believe that Helluland was likely
the eastern shores of Baffin Island, the largest island in Canada.

Finding Helluland to be of little interest, Leif and his crew
continued south. Eventually, they came to a rugged land of
evergreen woods and white shores. The Vikings called this
place *Markland,* or "Forestland". Most historians believe that
Markland is likely northern Labrador.

Leif and his crew continued south, sailing for two days with a wind that blew from the northeast, before coming to a temperate land carpeted with thick dewy grass. The Vikings felt that this would be a good place to spend the winter and set about building houses. That accomplished, Leif sent half his men out to explore this new land.

When one of Leif's friends, a German named Tyrker, failed to return, Leif led a search party to find him. The Norsemen eventually found Tyrker unharmed but babbling excitedly in German. When they finally managed to calm him down, Tyrker informed them, in Norse, that he had discovered grapevines not unlike those from his German homeland. Leif ordered his men to harvest the grapes, which were so plentiful that the Scandinavians were forced to store them in a small boat and tow it behind their main ship. Leif Erikson dubbed this new land *Vinland*, or "Wineland", on account of this pleasant discovery.

Today, there is some debate among historians over the location of Vinland. Many believe Vinland to be Newfoundland's Northern Peninsula, since archaeological evidence recovered there corresponds quite well with the sagas' descriptions of the colony that the Norse allegedly founded. Others, observing that wild grapes do not grow north of New Brunswick, maintain that Vinland must be located further south. Champions of the former theory counter this argument by suggesting that either Leif and his Vikings mistook gooseberries, which Newfoundland has in abundance, with grapes, or that Leif Erikkson invented the grape story out of whole cloth, giving the land he discovered an attractive name, like his father did upon discovering Greenland, in an attempt to attract colonists.

The Voyage of Thorvald Erikson

After spending a pleasant winter in Vinland, Leif Erikson and his crew returned to Greenland, their ships filled with grapes and timber. The tales they told of their adventures piqued the curiosity of their fellows, and soon Leif's brother, Thorvald, decided to see this New World for himself.

Setting sail with a crew of thirty men, Thorvald Erikson followed Leif's route west to Helluland, south down the coast of Markland, to Vinland. The Vikings found the derelict remains of Leif's camp and, Thorvald having leased these properties from his brother back in Greenland, spent the winter there.

In the spring, Thorvald and his men sailed west on an exploratory expedition. They found little sign of human presence and decided to return to Leif's camp to spend another winter.

The following summer, Thorvald and his crew made an exploratory expedition to the northeast. One day, after returning to their ship from an inland trek, the Vikings found three brown lumps on the sand not far from their vessel. They cautiously approached the objects and found that they were upside-down skin boats, beneath each of which slept three strange-looking men. Viking lore being littered with tales of goblins, dwarves, elves, and hostile spirits, Thorvald and his crew were anxious to learn whether the strange inhabitants of this foreign land were flesh-and-blood beings or supernatural entities. They began to murder the natives, and managed to kill eight of them; the last escaped in his boat.

Exhausted from the ordeal, Thorvald and his men lay down to sleep. They awakened just in time to see a large party of natives approaching them, brandishing bows and arrows. The Vikings formed a shield wall to defend themselves and allowed the natives, whom they called "*Skraelings*", to pelt them with projectiles. When the natives saw that their barrage had little effect on the Northmen, they retreated.

When Thorvald determined that none of his men had been wounded in the skirmish, he revealed that he had received a bone-shod arrow in his armpit, it having glanced off the side of the ship to circumvent his shield. Thorvald knew that he was mortally wounded and asked his men to bury him on a particular piece of land jutting into the sea, on which he had hoped to build a house. The Norsemen did as their captain requested and returned home to Greenland.

The Ghost of Thorstein Erikson

When Thorstein Erikson (Erik the Red's third son) heard of Thorvald's death, he determined to sail to Vinland to retrieve his brother's body. With 25 men and his wife, Gudrid, Thorstein appropriated his brother's ship and set sail for the New World.

After sailing all summer, Thorstein and his crew were unable to find Vinland. Eventually, they made landfall on a settlement on the western shores of Greenland, not far from where they had first embarked.

Winter was nearly upon them, and so Thorstein Erikson secured lodging for all his men. Without any money left for himself, he and Gudrid were forced to sleep on their ship. Fortunately, a local farmer named Thorstein the Black, who lived a lonely life and desired company, approached Thorstein Erikson and invited him and Gudrid to winter with him and his wife, Grimhild. The couple gratefully accepted his hospitality.

That winter, a sickness swept through the settlement and killed many of Thorstein Erikson's men. Thorstein Erikson himself eventually fell ill, along with his host's heavyset wife, Grimhild. Although both Thorstein and Grimhild had been healthy and robust, they, too, eventually succumbed to the malady.

Gudrid was deeply affected by her husband's passing and kept a gloomy vigil over her Thorstein's corpse, which her bereaved host had laid out on a bench inside his house. Thorstein the Black, taking pity on the grieving widow, picked her up in his arms and sat her down on his lap on a bench opposite Thorstein Erikson's body. The Norseman did his best to comfort his guest and promised to accompany her to her Eriksfjord, where Thorstein was to be buried.

No sooner had Gudrid thanked Thorstein the Black for his consolation than her late husband sat up on the bench. "Where is Gudrid?" the corpse asked. Astonished and terrified, neither the widow nor widower dared answer. The dead man repeated the question twice.

"Should I answer his questions or not?" Gudrid whispered to her host. Thorstein the Black shook his head.

The corpse remained seated and so, after transferring Gudrid to another chair further from the dead man, Thorstein the Black asked, "What wilt thou, Namesake?"

"I wish much to tell Gudrid her fortune," the corpse replied, "in order that she may be the better reconciled to my death, for I have now come to a good resting place." The dead man proceeded to inform Gudrid that she would marry an Icelander, and that she and her new husband would have many "powerful, distinguished, and excellent, sweet and well-favoured" descendants. She would move to Norway, then to Iceland, and would outlive her husband. She would travel the world, visit Rome, and live out the rest of her days as a nun in an Icelandic convent. When the prophecy was finished, Thorstein Erikson's corpse fell back onto the bench and lay still.

True to his word, Thorstein the Black took Gudrid to Eriksfjord. There, Thorstein Erikson's body was interred in the graveyard of the local church.

Thorfinn Karlsefni's Voyage

After Thorstein Erikson's ill-fated voyage, Greenlandic Vikings began discussing a potential future voyage to Vinland. Around that time, a Norwegian ship arrived in Greenland's western shore, captained by Thorfinn Karlsefni, a wealthy Icelander. Thorfinn was hosted by Leif Erikson, who introduced him to his sister-in-law, Gudrid. Thorfinn and Gudrid fell in love, and that winter they married, just as Thorstein Erikson had predicted.

When spring came, Thorfinn Karlsefni decided to lead an expedition to Vinland. Accompanied by sixty men, five women, and his wife, Gudrid, he sailed past Helluland and Markland to the Vinlandic houses that Leif Erikson had built. Having leased the houses from Leif, Thorfinn and his companions prepared for winter, butchering and processing the carcass of a beached whale that they found nearby.

The Viking Theory

That winter, Thorfinn Karlsefni and his Vikings wanted for nothing, finding plenty of timber, grapes, fish, and game. They also enjoyed fresh milk from a handful of cows that they had brought with them, which were protected against wild animals by a bull they had transported in the hold of their ship.

That summer, a band of Skraelings approached the pasture where the Norsemen kept their cattle. The bull began to bellow at the newcomers, and the natives, having never seen such an animal before, retreated in fear. The Skraelings then proceeded to Thorfinn's farm. Forewarned of their coming, the Vikings barricade themselves inside the farmhouse.

It soon became evident that the natives had come to trade, not to make war. The Vikings eventually emerged from the farmhouse and began to inspect the fine animal pelts the Skraelings had brought with them for barter. The natives indicated that they would like to exchange their pelts for the Vikings' swords and axes. Loathe to equip the Skraeling with steel weapons, however, Thorfinn instead had the women bring out milk and cheese. After sampling these exotic foods and finding them to their liking, the Skraelings happily exchanged their furs for dairy products and left contented.

Once the Skraelings were gone, Thorfinn had the Vikings build a palisade around his longhouse. While the work commenced, Gudrid gave birth to a boy, whom she and Thorfinn named Snorri. And thus Snorri Thorfinnson became the first white child to be born in the Americas.

That winter, the Vikings were visited again by a much larger force of Skraelings. Again, the natives appeared intent on trading, and threw bales of furs over the palisade. During the exchange, one of the natives reached for a Viking weapon. Startled, one of Thorfinn's men slew him. A panic ensued, and the natives retreated.

Thorfinn knew that the Skraelings would return to revenge their fallen comrade. Recalling the effect that the bull had made on them, he decided to unleash the animal in order to scare them off. When the natives arrived as anticipated, Thorfinn irritated the bull and allowed it to charge at unsuspecting natives. His plan worked, and the Skraelings retreated. He and his Norsemen killed many of the natives in the ensuing route.

The natives never returned to the Viking village that winter, and when spring came, Thorfinn and his company sailed back to Greenland with lumber, grapes, whale oil, and furs.

Freydis' Expedition

When the Norsemen of Greenland saw the rich haul that Thorfinn Karlsefni had brought from the New World, many began to consider making another expedition to Vinland. Two such men were brothers Helgi and Finnbogi- Icelanders who had arrived in Greenland that summer.

Another Northerner with her sights set on Vinland was Freydis, the only daughter of Erik the Red. That winter, Freydis payed a visited to Helgi and Finnbogi and suggested that they sail to Vinland together and split any profits they managed to acquire there. The brothers agreed to her proposal.

It was arranged that Freydis and the brothers would each bring thirty fighting men with them to the New World, in addition to their women, so that neither party would have an advantage over the other. Freydis duplicitously broke this agreement by hiding five additional men on her own ship. Helgi and Finnbogi were unaware of her deceit until they reached Vinland.

After a brief dispute, it was agreed that Freydis and her party would use the longhouses that Leif Erikson built, and that the brothers and their men would build their own dwelling.

No sooner had Helgi and Finnbogi constructed their longhouse than winter came. In order to pass the time, they invited Freydis' crew to play sports with them. Disputes between the players quickly sowed discord which resulted in both camps spending the rest of the winter alone, in their respective longhouses.

The Viking Theory

One morning, Freydis rose from her furs, slipped on
her *sark* and *smokkr* (shirt and skirt), and slipped out the door
without bothering to put on shoes or stockings. Wearing her
husband's cloak, she walked over to the brothers' longhouse, found
the door ajar, and stood in the threshold. Finnbogi, the only man
awake at that time, noticed Freydis in the doorway and asked what
she was doing there.

"I wish that thou wouldst get up and go out with me," she replied,
"for I will speak with thee." Finnbogi did as Freydis requested and
went outside to sit with her on a tree that the brothers had felled.

"How art thou satisfied here?" Freydis asked.

Finnbogi replied that he enjoyed Vinland and its abundance
resources, but admitted that he did not like the discord that had
sprung up between their two camps, and thought that there was no
reason for it. Freydis agreed before stating that the purpose of her
visit was to trade ships with the brothers, as theirs was bigger than
hers, and she wished to return to Greenland. Finnbogi agreed to her
proposal. With that, the two concluded their meeting.

Freydis returned to her longhouse and slipped into bed. Her frozen
feet awoke her husband, Thorvard, who asked why she was so cold
and wet.

With a bitter sob, Freydis falsely claimed that she had visited the
brothers in order to ask them about exchanging ships, only to be
beaten and used shamefully. "But thou, miserable man," she snarled
with reproach, "wilt surely neither avenge my disgrace nor thine
own." She then threatened to leave Thorvard once they arrived in
Greenland if he failed to avenge her.

Thorvard, none the wiser, threw off his furs in a rage. He roused his
kinsmen and led them to Helgi and Finnbogi's longhouse, where
the brothers and their men were asleep. Thorvard's Norsemen
bound each of their hapless countrymen and led them out of the
house, where Freydis had each of them executed.

At the end of the massacre, only five women remained from the brothers' camp, whom none of the men would consent to kill. "Give me an axe!" cried Freydis, seizing a weapon from one of her husband's men. The furious Norsewoman proceeded to hack each of her female compatriots to death.

When the slaughter was complete, Freydis rounded on her husband's crew and threatened to kill any of them who spoke of the bloodbath upon their return to Greenland. If asked what became of the brothers and their crew, they were to answer that they remained behind in Vinland.

When spring came, the Scandinavians loaded the brothers' ship with everything they had acquired that year and put to sea. The homeward voyage was an uneventful one, and the Vikings arrived at Eriksfjord in early summer.

In spite of Freydis' threat, word of the Vinland massacre began to circulate throughout the colony. Incensed, Leif Erikson captured three of Freydis' men and tortured them until they confessed the whole bloody business. Although Leif suggested that his sister deserved the same treatment, he decided to leave her be, believing that the curse that would hang over her posterity, which her wicked deeds had surely incurred, would be punishment enough.

The Saga of Erik the Red

The *Saga of Erik the Red* paints a very different picture of the Viking discovery of the Americas than that outlined in the *Greenland Saga*, although there is also much overlap between the two. Instead of Bjarni Herjolfsson, the *Saga of Erik the Red* contends that Leif Erikson was the first Norseman to see the shores of the New World.

When he was a young man, the saga goes, Leif left Greenland, the place of his birth, and travelled to Norway, his father's homeland.

There, he found his way into the service of Olaf Tryggvason, King of Norway.

Olaf converted Leif to Christianity and tasked him with bringing the Christian religion to Greenland. Leif obeyed and sailed west. During the voyage, "he was tossed about a long time out at sea, and lighted upon lands of which before he had no expectation. There were fields of wild wheat, and the vine-tree in full growth. There were also maple trees."

There, Leif rescued a party of shipwrecked Norseman and brought them back with him to Greenland and gave them food and lodging throughout the winter. "Thus," the saga goes, "did he show his great munificence and his graciousness when he brought Christianity to the land, and saved the shipwrecked crew. He was called Leif the Lucky."

Back in Greenland, Leif Erikson began to evangelize his fellow Norsemen. Many of the colonists, including Leif's mother, converted to Christianity. Leif's father, Erik the Red, was one of the few who refused to convert, staunchly adhering to the Norse paganism of his ancestors.

Erik the Red's Expedition

Although Erik the Red had little use for the new religion that his son brought to Greenland, he did take a keen interest in the bountiful land that Leif had discovered. He set out with twenty men to find it, but encountered a storm which blew his ship east nearly to Ireland.

Following that unsuccessful attempt, a much larger expedition was organized, consisting of many ships and 160 men. According to the saga:

"They were out at sea two half-days. Then they came to land, and rowed along it in boats, and explored it, and found there flat stones, many and so great that two men might well lie on them stretched on their backs with heel to heel. Polar foxes were there in abundance. This land they called 'Helluland'.

"Then they sailed with northerly winds two half-days, and there was then land before them, and on it a great forest and many wild beasts. An island lay to the southeast, and they found bears and called the island 'Bjarney' (Bear Island). The mainland, where the forest was, they called 'Markland' (Forest Land)."

Finally, the Viking explorers came to a pleasant cape where the coast was veined with creeks. As sailing was perilous along that stretch of coast, they sent two scouts to head south on foot to see what could be found. The men returned saying that there were two good lands further south. One was choked with wild grapes, while the other was rich with wild wheat.

The Vikings then sailed south down the coast and up a strait, at the mouth of which lay an island encircled by strong currents. According to the saga, "There were so many birds on [the island] that it was scarcely possible to put one's feet down for the eggs". The Norsemen continued up the firth, lowered their anchor, and prepared their camp.

After spending a hungry winter in the camp, near which there were mountains and large pastures, the expedition split up. One party attempted to return to Greenland but was blown off course; the Norsemen ended up in Ireland. The other group, led by Thorfinn Karlsefni, travelled south. After some time, they came to river which emptied into a lake, which, in turn, drained into the sea. The land near the river's mouth, which was dotted with large islands, was abundant in wild wheat, while its heights were choked with wild grapes. The river itself teemed with fish, and the woods were abundant with all variety of wild animals. Thorfinn and his company camped in the area for about half a month, spending their time hunting and fishing and playing games.

Encounters with the Skraelings

"Early one morning," the saga goes, "as they looked around, they beheld nine canoes made out of hides, and snout-like staves were being brandished from the boats, which made a noise like flails, and twisted round in the direction of the sun's motion."

The Viking Theory

Thorfinn and his companion, Snorri (his son's namesake), speculated as to the meaning of this strange activity. "It may be that it is a token of peace," Snorri suggested, before proposing that they approach the canoeists with a white shield- a Viking token of peace.

The Norsemen followed Snorri's suggestion and cautiously approached the shore with their white shield held high. The canoeists, in turn, began to paddle towards the shore. "They were short men," the saga goes, "ill-looking, with their hair in disorderly fashion on their heads. They were large-eyed and had broad cheeks. They stayed there a while in astonishment. Afterward, they rowed away to the south, off the headland".

The Northmen spent the winter near the mouth of the river, during which they saw neither snow nor any more of the mysterious natives, whom they called Skraelings.

"Now when spring began," the saga continues, "they beheld early one morning that a fleet of hide canoes was rowing from the south off the headland. There were so many that it was as if the sea were strewn with pieces of charcoal, and there was also the brandishing of staves as before from each boat. Then they held shields up, and a market was formed between them."

The natives proceeded to trade grey furs for red cloth. They also wished to purchase swords and lances, but Thorfinn and Snorri forbade their countrymen from selling the natives steel weapons. While the trading ensued, a bull that belonged to Thorfinn Karlsefni rushed out of the woods and bellowed loudly. The Skraelings became frightened and rowed south in their canoes.

Three weeks later, a large party of canoe-going Skraelings approached the Viking camp from the stream, brandishing spears and howling war cries. The Norsemen took red shields, a signal that they were ready for battle, and rushed to meet them. The Skraelings showered the Vikings with arrows and slung rocks. They also brought with them strange weapons which the saga describes thus:

"Karlsefni and Snorri saw the Skraelingjar were bringing up poles with a very large ball attached to each, comparable in size to a sheep's stomach, dark in color. These flew over Karlsefni's company towards the land, and when they came down they struck the ground with a hideous noise. This produced great terror in Karlsefni and his company, so that their only impulse was to retreat up the country along the river, because it seemed as if crowds of Skraelingjar were driving at them from all sides. And they did not stop until they came to some crags. There, they offered them stern resistance.

"Freydis came out and saw how they were retreating. She called out, 'Why do you run away from such worthless creatures, stout men that you are, when, as seems to me likely, you might slaughter them like so many cattle? Let me have a weapon. I think I could fight better than any of you.

"They gave no heed to what she said. Freydis tried to accompany them, but soon lagged behind because she was not well. She went after them into the wood and the Sraelingjar directed their pursuit after her. She came upon a dead man, Thorbrand, Snorri's son, with a flat stone fixed in his head. His sword lay beside him, so she took it up and prepared to defend herself.

"The Skraelingjar came upon her. She let down her sark and struck her breast with the naked sword. At this they were frightened, rushed off to their boats, and fled. Karlsefni and the rest came up to her and praised her zeal. Two of Karlsefni's men fell, and four of the Skraelingjar..."

Land of the One-Footers

Although the land was bountiful, the Vikings decided that the Skraeling were too numerous to allow for any permanent settlement and headed north. A hundred of them, Freydis and Bjarni included, decided to remain at the strait at which they had previously camped, while the remainder explored more of the region.

The Viking Theory

The saga then tells us that, while exploring a river north of Vinland, Thorfinn Karlsefni and his crew encountered a "One-Footer" (also known as a "monopod" or a "sciapod"), a mythological one-legged dwarf which hopped from place to place. The monster shot Thorvald Erikson in the lower abdomen with an arrow. The Viking pulled the projectile out of his gut and remarked that Vinland must be bountiful indeed, as he had grown such a belly that winter that the arrow had failed to harm him. The One-Footer then hopped away to the north.

After briefly visiting the land of the One-Footers, Thorfinn and his crew returned to the camp at the strait. That fall, Thorfinn and Gudrid had their first son, Snorri.

After spending three more years in the area, the Vikings sailed for home. On the way, they stopped in Markland, where they found a family of Skraelings. "One was a bearded man," the saga goes, "two were women, two children. Karlsefni's people caught the children, but the others escaped and sunk down into the earth. They took the children with them, and taught them their speech, and they were baptized."

The saga continues:

"The children called their mother Vaetilldi and their father Uvaegi. They said that kings ruled over the land of the Skraelingjar, one of whom was called Avalldamon, and the other Valldidida. They said that there were no houses, and the people lived in caves or holes. They said, moreover, that there was a land on the other side over against their land, and the people there were dressed in white garments, uttered loud cries, carried long poles, and wore fringes. This was supposed to be [White Man's Land]. Then came they to Greenland, and remained with Erik the Red during the winter."

The Discoveries at L'Anse Aux Meadows

In 1960, a 60-year-old Norwegian trapper named Helge Ingstad, along with his wife Anne Stine, set out to prove once and for all that the Viking sagas were true, and that the Norse really had explored and briefly colonized the Americas in the Middle Ages. Aided by a copy of the Skalholt map, a 16th Century Icelandic document which alleged to show the relative locations of Helluland, Markland, and Vinland, they began traveling around the rugged coast of Newfoundland, examining different areas and interviewing the locals.

"And people," said Helge in an interview in later life, "old fishermen, thought I was a little crazy asking about the settlement that was a thousand years old. But I kept on, and after many disappointments, late in the fall I came to the very northern part of Newfoundland, the very tip."

There, near the town of L'Anse aux Meadows, Helge and Anne met a grizzled old fisherman named George Decker.

"I asked him the old question," said Helge. "'Have you seen any old... ruins here?' And he was a very intelligent man. And he said, 'Yes, I have. Follow me.'"

Decker led the couple to an assortment of grassy mounds, which locals had long assumed were the remains of some old Beothuk or Mi'kmaq camp. Helge and Anne Ingstad proceeded to excavate the mounds. What they found changed North American history forever.

Helge and Anne unearthed a number of interesting artifacts beneath the mounds at L'Anse aux Meadows, including a soapstone spindle whorl, iron nails, and charcoal which they carbon dated to around 1000 A.D. The most interesting find, however, was a Viking brooch which proved almost without a doubt that the area was once a Norse settlement.

Today, archaeologists believe that the ruins at L'Anse aux Meadows once consisted of eight buildings, three of them longhouses capable of housing around eighty people. Near the residential halls was a smithy where nails were made.

Some believe that the Viking settlement at L'Anse aux Meadows is none other than Leif Erikson's Vinlandic colony. Others, noting that Newfoundland is devoid of wild grapes, believe Vinland to be further south, and suggest that the settlement at the tip of Newfoundland's Great Northern Peninsula served as a stopping point, perhaps being the burial place of Thorvald Erikson or one of the camps referred to in the sagas.

Although we may never know the true location of Vinland, we do know without a doubt that long before John Cabot, Christopher Columbus, or even Joao Vaz Corte-Real stepped foot on American shores, Canada was a colony of the Vikings.

The Oak Island Theory

There is little concrete evidence connecting the Viking voyages to the New World with the mystery of Oak Island. Among the few academics to suggest such a connection is Acadia University professor Dr. Doug Symons, who put forth his own theory in his May 2020 article *Evidence Supporting the Theory that Vikings Walked on Oak Island.*

Dr. Symons argues that the canopy oak trees which once grew on Oak Island, for which the island was named, are not oak trees at all, but rather butternut trees, pointing out that butternut trees currently grow on Clay Island, a spit of land located a mere 1.5 miles west of Oak Island. He cites this as potential evidence that Vikings visited Oak Island, since butternuts were among the artifacts discovered in

the Viking ruins of L'Anse aux Meadows, and are not native to the
island of Newfoundland.

Dr. Symons also suggests that the Paved Area in the Oak Island
swamp, which was uncovered throughout Season 7 throughout *The
Curse of Oak Island*, constitutes the remains of a dry dock on which
Viking mariners repaired their longships. He bases this theory on
the crushed stick discovered wedged between two of the Paved
Area's stones by Dr. Ian Spooner in Season 7, Episode 13, which
was later carbon dated to around 1200 A.D.- a date vaguely
consistent with that of the Viking voyages to the New World.
Symons posits that this stick might be one of many sticks comprising
a soft bed blanketing the hard stones onto which Norse explorers
dragged their boats prior to repairing them.

Another object suggestive of a Viking connection to Oak Island is
the Tory Martin stone, a rock inscribed with strange markings,
which gyrocope operator Tory Martin discovered in Season 6,
Episode 10 near the Old Well (the Old Well being an Oak Island
landmark located on Lot 16, which was first introduced to the show
by Fred Nolan back in Season 3, Episode 8). In Season 6, Episode
11, Rob Hyslop and Ryan Levangie of Azimuth Consulting Ltd.
conducted a LIDAR scan of the stone that Martin discovered in
order to better define the strange inscription it bore. Upon
examining the markings suggested by the LIDAR scan, Doug
Crowell suggested that the stone's inscription resembles Futhark, a
runic alphabet used by Dark Age Germanic Tribes, in which Proto-
Norse, the language spoken by the ancestors of the Vikings, was
sometimes written. In Season 6, Episode 12, the Fellowship of the
Dig showed the markings to runology expert Dr. Lilla Kopar, who
opined that they were probably not runes, but rather evoked the
"rhythm" of *textualis rotundra*, a particular type of Gothic script
used during the High Middle Ages, from the 12th to the 15th Century.

The Queen Scotia Theory

Some theorists believe that the Money Pit treasure was interred by Ancient Egyptian mariners. Foremost among these theorists today is Canadian-Austrian researcher Jack MacNab, who outlined his ideas in his 2020 book *Queen Scotia and the Egyptian Connection to Oak Island.*

MacNab believes that the Money Pit can trace its origins back to an ancient Irish-Scots legend which purports to explain the origins of the Scottish people and etymology of the word 'Scotland'- a legend with curious ties to Ancient Egypt and a mythological voyage into the Atlantic Ocean.

The Legend of Queen Scotia

According to Irish and Scottish mythology, around the time of the Hebrew Exodus, a Greek prince named Geytholos was exiled from his homeland by his father for his rebellious inclination, and sought asylum in Egypt. Geytholos found a place at the royal court at Memphis, and soon proved himself a worthy servant of the reigning Egyptian pharaoh, leading a successful military campaign against an invading Ethiopian army. As a reward for his loyalty, the pharaoh wed Geytholos to his daughter, who was named Scota.

Throughout the course of his service, Geytholos made several powerful enemies in the court of Memphis, most of whom who resented him for his foreign nature, his swift rise to power, and his uncommonly good standing with the pharaoh. When the Egyptian monarch drowned in the Red Sea during his pursuit of Moses and the Israelites, and the Kingdom of Egypt was subsequently thrown into turmoil, Geytholos' enemies seized power and banished the Grecian and his eighteen-year-old bride from Egypt.

Geytholos and Scota, along with other similarly-banished Egyptian nobles, wandered throughout the Mediterranean for years following their banishment, sailing west along the African coast. Eventually, they sailed through the Pillars of Hercules and up the Iberian coast to the northwestern corner of what is now Spain. They established a settlement there, in which Geytholos and Scota's two sons, Hyber and Hymec, were born.

During their time in Iberia, some of Geytholos' followers set sail in search of new lands. One of these explorers discovered a beautiful verdant island to the north- the land we know today as Ireland- and returned to the Iberian settlement to relay the good news to his Grecian leader.

Upon hearing tell of this attractive new land, Geytholos and Scota's son, Hyber, who possessed an adventurous spirit and a warlike disposition, decided to lead a raiding party there to see what plunder could be gotten. Accompanied by a party of loyal followers, Hyber sailed to Ireland and warred with its native inhabitants. After soundly defeating the island's natives and appropriating sufficient spoils of war to satisfy his inclinations, the Greco-Egyptian prince returned to the Iberian settlement.

Upon returning home, Hyber learned that his father, Geytholos, had been mortally wounded in a battle with local Iberians. With his dying breath, Geytholos implored both Hyber and Hymec to return to Ireland, seize it by conquest, and settle it. The brothers acceded to their father's last request and conquered Ireland. They named the new kingdom they established 'Scotia' in honour of their mother.

Hyber and Hymec's progeny became the Gaels. Centuries after the brothers' deaths, some of their descendants migrated across the North Channel and colonized the land which the Romans called Caledonia, which the Gaels named 'Scotland' after their ancient matriarch.

Queen Scotia's Voyage to Nova Scotia

Citing evidence put forth by native Nova Scotian John Bear MacNeil in his 2005 book *Basket Stories: A Mi'kmaq Heritage Book*, and in Egyptologist Lorraine Evans' book *Kingdom of the Ark* (2000), MacNab argues that the Egyptian Princess Scotia and her retinue sailed across the Atlantic Ocean to Cape Breton Island (a large island situated immediately north of the Nova Scotian Peninsula) sometime in the 14th Century B.C., after her sons' conquest of Ireland. That accomplished, Scotia and the Egyptian mariners under her command sailed south down the eastern coast of Nova Scotia to Oak Island. There, they constructed the Money Pit and buried the 90-foot stone, which MacNab suggests constitutes a slab of Egyptian porphyry inscribed with Libyco-Berber characters (the notions that the 90-foot stone was composed of Egyptian porphyry, and that the message inscribed on its surface was written in a North African script related to modern-day Tifinagh, have been put forth by other Oak Island theorists in the past). The stone, MacNab believes, served as a "time capsule" and a land claim designating the New World the territory of Scotia and her descendants.

MacNab bolsters the more general theory of pre-Columbian trans-Atlantic travel, upon which his Queen Scotia theory relies, by describing and displaying photographs of a number of mysterious stone structures which he personally discovered in the wilderness of Nova Scotia's eastern coast, some of which, he proposes, are ruins left behind by ancient trans-Atlantic mariners.

Index

———————•——◆——•———————

The bolded words in this index represent chapters, headings, and sub-headings. These various titles are designated by bolded numbers.

10-X (See 'Borehole 10-X')

1100 A.D.; 248

1179 A.D.; 146

1200 A.D.; 247-248, 250, 253, 282

13; **The Lucky Thirteen, 78**; 82, 261

1300s; 248

1490 A.D.; 158

1550 A.D.; 158

1575 A.D.; 52, 67

1600s; 38, 52, 54, 85, 112, 145, 157, 174-175, 248, 250, 254, 256,

1626 A.D.; 173, 175, 180, 203

1650 A.D.; 49, 142, 248,

1660 A.D.; 158

1674 A.D.; 145, 147, 254

1680 A.D.; 47, 127, 173, 175, 180, 262

1700s; 38, 51, 54-55, 81, 86, 90, 145, 147, 174 183, 192, 236, 242, 248, 254,

1735 A.D.; 47, 82, 193, 198

1745 A.D.; 86, 90, 162, 166

1746 A.D.; 81, 91

1750 A.D.; 49, 66, 128, 217,

Index

1760 A.D.; 48, 54, 164

1762 A.D.; 55

1765 A.D.; 55

1768 A.D.; 164

1770 A.D. 50, 53-55

1778 A.D.; 145

1784 A.D.; 82, 193, 198

1897 A.D.; 16, 74, 76-78, 83, 89, 203

1960s; 17, 20, 22, 33, 49, 79, 182, 280

1969 A.D.; 21, 31, 130, 133, 155, 158-159

1970 A.D.; 17, 53-54, 76

1971 A.D.; 17, 31, 39, 135-136

8A; 219-220, 225-231

90-Foot Stone; 15-16, 28, 54-55, 100-101, 105-106, 172, 174, 261, 285

Acadia University; 61, 64, 81, 144, 147, 232, 281

Acadian Theatre of the Nine Years' War; 175

Acorn; 233-235; **oak leaf and acorns, 239-240**

Aerhyve Aerial Technologies; 35

Alexander, Sir William; 187, 257-258, 260-262

All-Seeing Eye; 71, 143

Amundsen, Petter; 130, 202, 206, 208

Annapolis Royal; 168, 257; see 'Port Royal'

Anomalies by the Samuel Ball Foundation; 213

Anson, Admiral George; 128

Anson, Thomas; 128, 130

Antimony; 150, 153

Appeal to Heaven flag; 82

Arcadia; 110-113, 117-124, 126-130, 132, 134-138, 142-143

Axe; 49, 163; **rigging axe, 167-168**; 271, 274

Axe-hewn wood; 48, 156, 158-160, 185, 203, 218, 239

Bacon, Sir Francis; 202-203, 206, 208, 248, 250

Ball, Samuel; **The Mystery of Samuel Ball, 39-40; The Return of Samuel Ball's Family, 40-41**; 210-211, **Anomalies by the Samuel Ball Foundation, 213**; 244-246,

Ballad of Gilligan's Isle; 42

Barkhouse, Charles; 18, 22, 28, 34-35, 39-41, 49-50, 72-73, 79, 81, 96, 102-103, 107, 171, 183, 187, 196, 210, 215, 244-245, 248

Barlow, Scott; 93, 95-97, 115, 149, 156, 158, 161, 204, 232-234

Barnett & Associates; 39

Barrel bottom; 218, 222-224

Bay of Fundy; 256, 179

Begley, Jack; 18, 22, 26, 28-29, 36, 40, 46, 49, 82, 84, 97, 101, 114-115, 149, 155, 159, 163, 167, 171, 173, 180-183, 188-189, 195, 202, 206, 209, 212, 228, 236, 243, 245-246, 250

Berry, Evan; 38

Big Dig; 251-252

Blackmore, Valerie; 38-39

Blake, Matty; 25-27, 29, 31-32, 37, 40-42

Blankenship, Dan; 15, 17, **20-21**, 26, 28, **Dan's Reunion, 30-31**, 32, 34-35, 37, 39, 41, 46, 76, 100, 105, 158, 218-219, 252-253

Blankenship, Dave; 18, **21**, 26, 28-30, 32-33, 35, 44, 69, 84, 102, 115, 141, 150, 152, 207, 211, 218,

Blue clay; 11, 59, 76, 195, 209, 212-213

Bones; **The Bones Live Again, 38-39**; 48-50, 52, 180, 203, 217, 268

Bonny, Anne; 39

Booby trap; 16, 164, 189, 191, 228, **The Booby Trap Spike, 230**

Bookbindery; 15-16, 100-101, 106

Borehole 10-X; 17, 21, 28, 30-31, 37, **10-X Enhanced, 39**; 252

Borehole C1; 52, 209, 211, 214, 216-217, 220, 223-224

Index

Borehole F-14; 141

Borehole FG-12; 155-156, **160**, 173, 175, 180,

Borehole GAL1; 216

Borehole H8; 38, 52, 180, 217, 227, 230-231, 238-239, 247-248, 250

Borehole OC1; 209, 211, 214, 216-217, 220, 223-224

Borehole OITC-6; 78-79, 82, 89, 193, 196

Borehole S6; 48, 219, 227, 230

Boulder; 17, 36, 52, 71, 75, 154, 165, 172, 189, 191, 197, 200, 204, 208

Bourassa, Kelly; 51-54, 81-82, 201, 215, 244

Boyd, Anthony and Ivan; 40-41

Bracket; 181, **184**, 185, 190, 225, 244, 248

British; 22, 50, 55, 81, 91, 120, 128, 130, 164, 168, 259-260

Bronze; 217, 221

Bronze Age; 29

Brooch; 60, 81-82, 216, 248, 280

Brosseau, Dr. Christa; 72, 149-150, 153, 196-197, 199

Bump-out; 53, **98**, 102, 107, 115, 140, 144, 146, 148, 155, 159, 180

Busby, Jared; 207

Bushell, Thomas; 68

Button; 49-53, **the silver button, 54-55**; 215, 248, 259

Campbell, Pat; 117

Cape Breton Island; 32, 86, 91, 162, 177, 285,

Carbon Dating of the Wood from the Money Pit

Carbon dating; 38, 47, 65, 79, 82, 145-146, 158, 171, 173, **carbon dating of the wood from the Money Pit, 175**; 180, 198, 226, 245, 247, 253, 280, 282

Cave-In Pit; 16, 51, 61-62, **Cave-In Pit Anomaly, 66**; 77, 83-85, 88-89, 94, 150, 193-194, **Cave-In Pit Anomaly, 197-198**

Champlain, Samuel de; 112, 118, 122, 256

Chappell Shaft; 167, 236, 243-244

Chappell Vault; 231

Chappell, Mel; 14, 87, 91

Chappell, William; 14

Chappells Ltd.; 14, 98, 104,

Charles I, King of Britain; 257-260

Chateau de la Rochefoucauld; 29-30

Chester, Nova Scotia; 29

Chipp Reid's Theory; 90-91

Chisel; 54, Hand Point Chisel, 55; 84, 110, 163, 217, 220, 248

Choice Drilling; 51, 58-59, 63, 73, 78-79, 83, 100, 102, 104, 115, 140-141, 150, 155, 160, 171

Church, Benjamin; 173, 179,

Clay; 11, 58-59, 61, 63-64, 73, 76, 85, 128, 144, 150, 157, 166, 186, 189, 191-192, 195, 209, 212-213, 225, 254, 281

Clay mine theory; 209, 212-213, 254

Cloisonne; 60, 195

Coconut fibre; 16, 89, 188, 190-191, 233, 239, 243, 248

Cofferdam; 48, 53, 80, 98, 102, 107, 140, 144, 146, 148, 158-160, 201, 204

Coin; 49-50, 52, 55, 76, 81, 101, 248, 250, 259

Coir (see 'coconut fibre')

Composition of the Smith's Cove Flood Tunnel; 88

Concrete; 52, 157, 243, 251, 281

Copper; 49, 55, 81, 215, 217, 221

Core sample; 58-59, 61, 63-64, 69-70, 73-75; Upper-Beach Core Sample, 76; 78-79, 83-85, 88, 100, 102, 104, 115, 141, 144-147, 150-151, 155-156, 160, 172-173, 208, 253

Corjan Mol's Theory; 119-121

Creighton, Helen; 100, 106

Crib spike; 52-53, 94, 96, 102, 110, 155, 225-226, 229

Crossbow bolt; 52

Crowell, Doug; 61, 73, 81, 83-84, 87, 91, 93, 97-98, 100, 104-105, 114-115, 140, 146, 150, 156, 160, 162-165, 168, 170, 189, 203, 209-210, 216, 218-219, 223-224, 232, 234, 243, 247, 250, 282

Dam-it-Dams, 80

Dartmouth Heritage Museum, 100, 105-106, 172, 174

Dartmouth, Nova Scotia, 100, 105, 172

David Hanson's Theory; 67-68

Dean, Andrew and Matt; 41

Delway Enterprises; 194

Demont, Andrew; 32

Dendrochronology; 17-18, 48, 54, 82, 86, 90-91, 116, 157, 161-162; dendrochronological dating of the wharf, 166; 204, 206, 216, 237

DesBrisay, Mather Byles; 39

Divetech Ltd.; 239

Dorey, Gerald; 30-31

Dorian, hurricane (see 'Hurricane Dorian')

Dowsing; 17, 30-31

Dr. Spooner's Analysis; 74

Dr. Spooner's First Swamp Theory; 64-65

Dr. Spooner's Second Analysis of the Swamp; 147

Dr. Spooner's third analysis of the swamp; 253-254

Drayton, Gary; 18-18, 22, 27, 36, 47, 49-55; 60, 62, 66, 70-72, 75, 79, 81, 84, 94, 96, 101-102, 110, 114, 140, 144, 148-150, 153, 155, 157, 159, 163, 167-168, 171, 173-175, 181-186, 188, 190, 192, 194-198, 203, 207-209, 214-215, 220, 225-230, 236-237, 242, 244, 247, 250

Drilling Down (appendant series); 37

Drone; 35-36

Duc d'Anville Expedition; 81, 91, 176-177

Dynamite; 74, 76-77, 94

Eagle Canada; 47, 56, 66, 85, 89, 94, 97, 193, 231, 237

Egypt; 131, 283-285

Elizabeth I, Queen of England; 68

Enochean Chamber; 117

Erik the Red; **Erik the Red and the Settlement of Greenland; 264-265**; 266, 269, 272; **The Saga of Erik the Red, 274-275; Erik the Red's Expedition, 275-276**; 279

Evans stone; 82

Exploration Drilling in the Swamp; 63-64

Eye of the Swamp, 69; 71-72, **75**, 79, 143-145, 147, 166, 173, 183, 194-195, 197-198, 200, 207-209, 212, 225, 229, 232, 236, 250, 254

Eyland, Terry; 100-101, 105-105

FG-13 (drillhole); 150-151f

Flagstones; 11, 157

Follow-Up on the Stone at the Dartmouth Heritage Museum; 174

Fork tine; 228, **fork tine and the marlinespike, 229**

Fornetti, Peter; **22**, 28-29, 49, 72, 79, 84, 94, 100-101, 105, 140, 144, 148, 163, 167-168, 187, 201

Fort William Henry; 179

Fougere, Ruby; 165

Fouquet, Nicolas; 126-127

Freemasonry; 22-23, 54, 71, 143, 187, 258, 261-262

French; 29-30, 49, 60, 86, 90-91, 95, 110-112, 117-119, 121-123, 125-135, 137-138, 142, 162-164, 166, 168-169, 175, 177-179, 210, 248, 256-260

French Revolution; 30

Frick, John; 222

Frontenac, Governor Louis de Buade, Compte de; 178

Frost, John; 35-36

GAL1; 216

GPR (ground penetrating radar); 60-61, 66, 83, 85-86, 88, 114, **GPR Scan of the Oak Island Swamp, 117;** 187, 193, 198, 201, 210-211, 213, 225, 232, 245,

Gauthier, Alex; 85, 94, 97

Gerhardt, Billy; 18, **23**, 58, 79, 93, 95-96, 100, 103, 105, 107, 110, 140, 144, 152, 154, 156, 158, 165-166, 170-172, 174, 180, 182, 186, 188-189, 192, 194, 197, 201, 203-204, 209, 211, 225

Gilligan's Island; 42

Global GPR Services Inc.; 60

Gold; 52, 57, 112-113, 120, 216-217, 220, 248, 259, 261

Gold River; 113, 120, 259, 261

Graeser, Karl; 32

Graychick, Scott; 85

Great Excavations Inc.; 149, 152

Greece; 111-112, 118, 120, 123-124, 128, 130, 134, 136, 203, 205, 283

Greenlander Saga; 266-274

Grenadier's hat badge; 60

Guercino, Il; 110, 123-124

Guptill, Steve; 47-50, 60, 63, 70-71, 73, 75, 79-80, 94, 97-99, 109, 114, 117, 140, 144, 171, 182, 187, 207, 209, 219, 228, 236, 243, 250

H8 (borehole); 38, 52, 180, 217, 227, 230-231, 238-239, 247, 250

Hale, Derik; 245

Halifax Company; 15

Halifax, Nova Scotia; **14**, 72, 100-101, 106, 149, 158, 160, 162-163, 196, 199, 208, 212

Halpern, Zena; 146

Hamilton, Erwin; **15**, 37, 219,

Hand Point Chisel; 54, **55**, 110, 248

Hanson, David; 67-68

Harris, Graham; 176-177, 262

Harris, R.V.; 91

Havana, Cuba; 95

Hedden Shaft; 76, 214, 217, 241

Hedden, Gilbert; **14**, 76, 214, 216-217, 241

Henry IV, King of France; 118, 122

Henskee, Dan; 18, **22**, 44, 60, 66, 87, 91, 93, 103, 107, 150, 211, 243, 251

Highlands (Oak Island landmark); 94

Hiltz, Cyril; 32

Hinge; 53, 181, 228, 244

Hume, Ivor Noel; 53-54

Hurricane Dorian; 154, 157-158, **160**, 161

Hyslop, Rob; 282

Irving Equipment Ltd.; 53, 98, 107, 201, 204, 207, 216, 231

Isaac's Point; 49-52, 54-55, 110, 168, 215, 248

Italy; 127, 152-153, 222

James II, King of Britain; 177

James McQuiston's Theory, 258-262

Jardine, Mike; 53, 98, 102, 107, 204, 209, 247

Johnston, Don; 60-61, 66, 85-86, 114, 117, 187, 193, 198, 210-211, 213, 245

Kaizer, Leonard; 32

King Midas; 112-113, 119-120, 122, 124

Knights Baronet of Nova Scotia; 175, 186-187; **The Knights Baronet Theory, 256-262**

Knights Templar; 114, 121, 136-138, 146-147, **185**, 187, 203, 247, 250, 253, 258, 261

La Rochelle, France; 247, 259

Lagina, Alex; 18, **21-22**, 26, 28-29, 46, 51, 53-55, 59, 70-72, 75, 79, 81-82, 85-86, 94, 96-97, 102, 151, 157, 159, 165-166, 182, 187-188, 196-197, 201, 225-226, 228-229, 242, 245, 251, 257-262

Lamb, Lee; **20**, 33, 233, 235, 239

Laroque, Dr. Colin; 17-18, 48, 116, 162

Laser ablation; 150, 152-153, 195, 202, 205-206

Lead (metal); 60, 149-150, 152; **the lead tag, 153**; 155, 162-163, 195, 202-203; **mercury-tinged lead, 205-206,** 208, 248

Lead cross; 60, 149-150, 152, 195, 248

Lead tag; 152, **153**, 155

Leaf; 82, **231**, 233, 235; **the oak leaf and acorns, 239-240**

Leather; 15, 34-35, 226-227; **leather in the Money Pit, 230**

Legge, Carmen; 53-55, 62, 65-67, 94, 96, 110, 157, 159, 181, 183-184, 188-190, 225, 228-230, 236, 242, 248, 279

Leif Erikson; 265-268, 270, 272, 274-275, 281

Levangie, Ryan; 282

Limestone; 52, 62, 157, 165, 172, 239, 244

Lincoln, Henry; 120, 130, 133-138

Loncarich, Tim; 259, 262

Lot 2; 36

Lot 6; 101-102

Lot 8; 216, 248

Lot 11; 27, 96

Lot 16; 50, 282

Lot 17; 195

Lot 18; 202, 205, 208

Lot 21; 60, 66, 72, 81-82, 84, 187, 201, 203, 216, 248, 250

Lot 22; 55

Lot 25; 210-211, 213, 244-245; **the Lot 25 Tunnel, 245-246**

Lot 26; 52, 94, 110

Lot 27; 84, 163, 167

Lot 32; 94, 96

Louis XIII, King of France; 122, 125, 257, 260

Louis XIV, King of France; 126-127

Louisbourg; 86, 90-91, 162-166; **Louisbourg Connections, 168-169**; 170

Lucido, Vanessa; 186-187, 207, 209, 244, 247

Lunenburg, Nova Scotia; 39

L'Anse aux Meadows; **the discoveries at L'Anse aux Meadows, 280-281**; 282

MacInnes, Sarah; 163-165

MacNab, Jack; 283-285

MacPhie, Les; 176-177, 262

Mahone Bay; 10, 30, 54, 82, 113, 120, 197, 209, 260-261

Marie Antoinette, 30

Marlinespike; 228

Martin

, 165,
.6-218, 236

.ossian, Sonia; 29, 30

Maya blue; 212

McFarlane, Dr. Chris; 150, 152-153, 202-203, 205, 208

McGinnis, Daniel; 10, 40, 81, 84-86, 187, 201, 203

McLeod, Krista; 48

McMahon, Brennan; 51, 73

McQuiston, James; 186-187, 256, 258-262

Mega Bin; 56, 89

Mercury; 202-203; **Mercury-tinged lead, 205-206,** 208

Mercy Point; 65, 117, 196, 198

Metal Rods in Stumps in the Swamp; 198

Mexican; 28

Midas (see 'King Midas')

Middle East; 38-39

Mi'kmaq; 179, 280, 285

Mol, Corjan; 110-114; 117; **Corjan Mol's Theory, 119-121,** 136-137, 142

Monahan, Mike; 201

Monck, Christopher, 2nd Duke of Albemarle; 262

Money Pit; 11, 15-17, 40-41, 47-48, 50, 56, 58-59, 62, 66, 72-74, 76-77, 79, 81, 83-84, 87-89, 91-92, 94, 96-100, 102, 104-105, 115-116, 130, 139-141, 144, 150-151, 155-156, 160, 165, 168, 171-173, 175, 177, 182, 187-189, 191-193,

198, 203, 207, 209, 211, 214, 216, 218-220, 224-226, 228-229, **Leather in the Money Pit, 230**; 231, 233, 235, 237-238, 241, 243, 247-248, 250-251, 258, 261, 283, 285

Morash, Harvey; 30

Morford, Chris; 142-143

Mug & Anchor Pub; 54, 82, 197, 209

Mystery of Nicolas Poussin and Rennes-le-Chateau, 121-138

Nadudvari, Alessandra; 259, 262

Nail; 47, 52, 55, 101, 181, 183, 196-197, **nails from the Uplands Pit, 199**; 248, 280-281

Needle; 227-228, **the booby trap spike, 230**

New Brunswick; 117, 150, 176, 205, 260, 267

New Ross, Nova Scotia; 53, 71, 96, 143, 157, 188, 259, 262

New Structure at Smith's Cove, 107-108

Newfoundland; 177, 179, 256, 263, 267, 280-282,

Nichols, Jack; 80

Nine Years' War; **the Acadian Theatre of the Nine Years' War, 175-179**

Niven, Laird; 18, **23**, 36, 50, 52, 55, 60-61, 81-82, 85-86, 103, 107-108, 144, 146, 148, 166, 169, 172, 174, 180-182, 187-188, 200-201, 203, 210-211, 215, 219, 228, 244-245, 251, 257-258

Nolan, Fred; **Nolan's Cross, 17**; **The Nolan Family, 21**; **Saying Goodbye to Fred Nolan, 35**; 36, 47, 51, 56, 58, 61, 71, 79, 145, 156, 158-159, 196, 198, 234, 282

Nolan, Tom; **21**, 58, 79, 145, 149, 152, 170, 197

Nolan's Cross; **17**, 21, 61, 71, 75, 114, 120, 143, 165, 168, 197

Norse (see 'Viking')

Nova Scotia; 10, 21-23, 29, 39, 53-54, 71-72, 81, 90-91, 95-96, 100, 105-106, 111-113, 117, 120, 129, 143, 157, 172, 174, 186-188, 196-197, 203,

297

209, 211, 240, 256-259, 261, 285

OC1; 209, 211, 214, 216-217, 220, 223-224

OITC-6; 78-79, 82, 89, 193, 198

Oak Island Association; **14**, 87, 91, 218, 223

Oak Island Treasure Company; **14**, 17, 74, 76; **the Oak Island Treasure Company's Dynamiting Operation, 77**; 78, 83, 89

Oak leaf and acorns; 239-240

Oberg, Peter; 130

Onslow Company; **14**, 15-16, 59, 72, 98, 104

Origin of the Name 'Acadia'; 117-119

Pactolus River; 112-113, 119-120, 122, 124

Parchment; 132-134, 138, 180, 203, 230, 265

Paved Area (see 'Paved Wharf')

Paved Wharf; 72, 79, 152, 154, 156-158, 161, 165-166,

Paved Wharf Analysis, 159; 170-171, 200, 209-210, 225, 229, 245, 247, 250, 253-254, 282

Pentagram; 114, 120, 136, 143

Peters, Joe; 65

Phips, Sir William; 175-179, 262

Pickaxe; 62, 173, 183, 225, 236, 242

Pike Pole Point; 188, **190-191**, 248

Pilum; 52

Pirates; 11, 39

Plantagenet; 68

Port Royal; 177, 179, 256-257, 260

Poseidon; 30

Pottery; 203, 217, 236

Poussin, Nicolas; 110-114, 117, 119-120; the mystery of Nicolas Poussin and Rennes-le-Chateau, 121-138

Primitive Rebar; 157, **159**, 225, 229

Prohawk technology

Quarry hammer; 60-62, 66; (see 'Swage Blocks')

Quarrying; 36

Queen Anne's War; 91

Queen Scotia; **the Queen Scotia Theory, 283-285**

RF1; 235-236, 241-243, 247, 251

ROC Equipment; 185, 207, 216

ROV (remotely operated underwater vehicle); 239

Rackham, "Calico Jack"; 39

Rebar (see 'Primitive Rebar')

Reid, Chipp; 85-86; **Chipp Reid's Theory, 90-91**, 162

Rennes-le-Chateau; **the mystery of Nicolas Pouissin and Rennes-le-Chateau, 121-138**

Restall Tragedy; 20, 32-33

Restall family; **20**, 33, 234-235

Restall, Bobby; 15, 19, **20**, 32-33, 109, 182, 233-234

Restall, Richard "Ricky"; 15, **20**, 33-34, 49, 233-235, 239

Restall, Robert; **15, 20**, 33, 233, 239

Rideout, Kevin; 100-101, 105-106, 172, 174

Rigging Axe; 163, 167

Ring; 214-217, **the Ring in the Swamp, 220-222**

Roberts, Mike; 239

Robinson, Colton; 140, 172

Rochefoucauld; 29

Rod; **the rod in the stone, 36**

Rolfe, Joey; 239

Roman numerals; 17, 130, 148, 237, 241

Rome; 52, 112, 120, 122-123, 125-126, 221, 270, 285

Roosevelt, Franklin Delano; 37-38

Rosicrucians; 248, 250

Ross Farm Museum; 53, 96, 157, 183, 188, 228, 242

Saga of Erik the Red, 265, 274-279

Sampson, Tony; **23**, 42, 48-51, 65, 72, 114, 143, 152, 154, 156, 196, 198

Sauniere, Berenger; 131-134

Savelle, Matt; 117

Schiefelbein, Frank; 39

Scissors; 28

Scottish; 187, 256-261, 283

Scottish Rite Freemasonry; 261

Season 1; 26, 28, 37, 103, 107, 130, 202

Season 2; 29, 32, 55, 65, 117, 195

Season 3; 17, 28, 30, 37, 39, 159, 212, 221, 282

Season 4; 34-35, 38-39, 42, 47, 52, 65, 71, 80, 101, 128, 143, 146, 160, 195-196, 198, 210, 216, 259

Season 5; 29, 33, 38-39, 49, 52, 54-55, 92, 145, 149, 159-160, 168, 173, 180, 217, 250

Season 6; 15, 17-18, 36, 39, 41, 47-48, 52-54, 56, 60, 63, 81-82, 86, 89-90, 94, 100, 106, 109-110, 116, 150, 152, 155, 181-182, 186, 189, 193, 216, 219, 223, 227, 230, 238-239, 256, 258, 282

Seismic; 47, 50-51, 56, 58, 63, 72, 85, **upcoming seismic survey of the Eastern Drumlin, 89**; 94, 97, 193, 197-198, 231, 237-238

Septic Doctor, 245

Shaft 2; 98-100, 102, **104-105**, 115-116, 139-141, 150-151, 155-156, 160, 218

Shaft 5; 189, **the Uplands Structure: Shaft 5? 191**; 192, 201

Shaft 9; 87-88, **Shaft 9 and the Sluiceway, 91-92**; 93, 95-100, 104

Shakespeare, William; 68, 208

Shepherd's Monument; 128, 130

Shepherds of Arcadia; 110-113, 117, 119-120, 122, 127-128, 130, 132, 134-136

Ship Anomaly; 56-57, 58, 63, 71, 74, 79, 147, 185-186, 188, 190, 253

Shoes; Dan's Ancient Shoes, 34-35;

Shugborough Hall; 128

Silver; 49, 51-52, the silver button, 54-55; 95, 148-150, 215, 217, 221, 259

Skierka, John; 149, 152

Slipway; 18, 34, 48, 53-54, 79, 85, 90, 109-110, 141, 148, 152, 157, 162, 166, 180-181, 225, 229, 250

Sluiceway; 87-88; Shaft 9 and the Sluiceway, 91-92; 93, 95, 97

Smith, Danny; 207, 216, 226, 247

Smith, John; 10, 40, 187

Smith's Cove; 11, 16-18, 28-29, 32, 34, 47-48, 50-53, 60-62, 73-74, 76-80, 82-85, 88-91, 94, 98, 102-103, 107-110, 114, 116, 140, 144, 146, 148, 150-153, 155, 157-162, 166, 168, 170, 180-183, 188-189, 191-193, 197-198, 201, 204, 206, 210, 223, 225, 229, 233-234, 237, 239, 248

Smith's Cove flood tunnel; 16, 47, 60-62, 66, 74, 77-78, 83-84, composition of the Smith's Cove Flood Tunnel, 88-89; 91, 103, 108-109, 150-151, 161, 168, 170, 182, 189, 191-194, 197-198, 201, 206, 223

South Shore Cove; 16, 55, 71, 87, 91, 93, 97

South Shore Genealogical Society; 39

Spade; 183, 189

Spanish; 26-28, 47, 49, 52, 55, 91, 95-96, 175, 177, 179, 217, 220, 248

Spanish galleon; 47, 52, 55

Spanish maravedis; 49, 248

Spanish weapon; 96

Spear; 186, 277

Spike; 36-37, 47, 51-55, 94, 96, 102, 110, 155, 157, 159, 192, 196-197, 225-226, 228-229; the booby trap spike, 230;

Spooner, Dr. Ian; 61, Dr. Spooner's First Swamp Theory, 64-65; 69-70, Dr. Spooner's Analysis, 74; 75,

143, 145-146; **Dr. Spooner's Second Analysis of the Swamp, 147**; 166, 169-171, 173, 190, 197, 200, 207-209, 211-212, 226, 245, 247-248, 250, **Dr. Spooner's Third Analysis of the Swamp, 253-254**; 282

St. Mary's University; 72, 149, 196, 199, 208, 212

Staffordshire slipware; 55, 128

Stake in the Swamp; 36, 155, **158-159**; 185

Starburst; 49-50, 52, 215

Stone at the Dartmouth Heritage Museum; 105-106; follow-up on the stone at the Dartmouth Heritage Museum, 174

Stone compass; 29

Stone of Destiny; 261

Stone of Scone (see 'Stone of Destiny')

Strachan, Alexander; 259-261

Strap; 181, 183-184, 228

Sullivan, Randall; 39-40

Swage blocks; 62, **66**, 67, 72-73, 81, 84, 248, 250

Swamp; 11, 23, 27-28, 35-36, 41-42, 47-48, 50-52, 54, 56-59, 61; **exploration drilling in the swamp, 63-64**; Dr. Spooner's first swamp theory, **64-65**; 69-72, 74; **the Eye of the Swamp, 75**; 79-80, 89, 94, 114; **GPR Scan of the Oak Island Swamp, 117**; 120, 143-147, 149, 152, 154-157; **the stake in the swamp, 158-159**; 160-161, 164-166, 168-171, 173, 181, 183-186, 188-190, 194-197; **metal rods in stumps in the swamp, 198**; 200, 207-209, 211-212, 214, 217, **the ring in the swamp, 220-222**; 225-227, 229, 232, 236, 245, 247-248, 250, **Dr. Spooner's third analysis of the swamp, 253-254**; 282

Sweeny, Dana; 48

Sylva Sylvarum; 203

Taylor, Aaron; 208-209, 212

Teardrop; 231, 235, **237-239**, 243

Tedford, Mike; 140, 172

Tester, Craig; 18, 21, **22**, 26, 35, 46-48, 51, 59-62, 66, 73, 79, 82, 84-86, 94, 102-103,

116, 149, 156, 161, 171, 173, 180, 185, 193, 196, 203, 210, 216, 235-236, 242, 247, 250

Tester, Drake; **22**

The Hand Point Chisel; 54, 55, 110, 248

The Silver Button; 51, 54-55

Timeline; 247-250

Tobias, David; 15, 76

Tour, Charles de Saint-Etienne de la; 260

Tour, Claude de Saint-Etienne de la; 260-261

Triton Alliance; **15**, 17, 21, 30, 76, 87, 91

Troutman, Paul; 73-74, 78-79, 84, 204, 217

Truro Company; **14**, 16, 89, 183, 189, 191-192

Tunnel in the Uplands Pit; 206

Two islands; 36, 41, 66, 74

U-Shaped structure; 17, 48, 54, 79, 84-85, 89-91, 144, 146, 148, 182, 203, 206, 237, 241

University of New Brunswick; 150, 205

Upcoming Seismic Survey of the Eastern Drumlin; 89

Uplands; 182, 188-190, **the Uplands Structure: Shaft 5? 191**; 192, 194, 196-197, **nails from the Uplands pit, 199**; 201, 203-204; **the tunnel in the Uplands pit, 206**

Uplands Structure: Shaft 5? 191

Upper Beach Core Sample; 76-77

Valory, Ross; **Ross Valory's Journey, 37**

Vartolo, Pasquale; 37

Vaughan, Anthony; 10, 40

Verderame, Dr. Lori; 52

Vere, Edward de; 68

Verrazano, Giovanni da; 111, 118-119

Victorian; 51

Viking; 253; **the Viking Theory, 263-282**

Viking Discovery of Canada; 265

War Room; **18**, 35, 38, 40-41, 46, 48, 50, 62-63, 69, 71, 79, 82, 85, 95, 110, 112, 116, 139, 142, 145, 147, 149, 152, 161, 170, 173, 180, 186, 190, 193, 202, 204, 217, 231, 233-235, 247-248, 252, 256

War of Spanish Succession; 91, 179

Watson, Steve; 60-61, 66, 85-86, 114, 117, 187, 193, 198, 210-211, 213, 245

Western Shore, Nova Scotia; 10

Wharf; 51-52, 72, 79, 91, 140, **146**, 148, 150, 152-159, 161-162, 165, **dendrochronological dating of the wharf, 166**; 170-171, 200, 209-210, 225, 229, 247

White, Ed; 32-33

Wilson, Shawn; 71, 75, 149

Wolfville, Nova Scotia; 81

Women; 38-39

Wyndham Forensic Group; 38

Yang, Dr. Xiang; 72, 196, 199

An assortment of real Canadian mysteries published on
MysteriesOfCanada.com throughout the year 2019. Includes tales of
necromancy, cryptozoology, mad scientists, ghosts of Canada's grand
railway hotels, conspiracy theories, and miracles and mirages.
Available on Amazon.

Made in the USA
Monee, IL
25 August 2022

12478343R00177